Still Struggling for Equality

STILL STRUGGLING FOR EQUALITY

American Public Library Services with Minorities

Plummer Alston Jones Jr.

A Member of the Greenwood Publishing Group

Westport, Connecticut • London

Library of Congress Cataloging-in-Publication Data

Jones, Plummer Alston.
    Still struggling for equality : American public library services with minorities /
Plummer Alston Jones Jr.
        p. cm.
    Includes bibliographical references (p.) and index.
    ISBN 1–59158–243–1 (alk. paper)
    1. Libraries and minorities—United States—History—19th century. 2. Libraries and
minorities—United States—History—20th century. I. Title
    Z711.8.J67 2004
    027.473—dc22   2004048927

British Library Cataloguing in Publication Data is available.

Library of Congress Catalog Card Number: 2004048927
ISBN: 1–59158–243–1

First published in 2004

Libraries Unlimited, 88 Post Road West, Westport, CT 06881
A Member of the Greenwood Publishing Group, Inc.
www.lu.com

Printed in the United States of America

The paper used in this book complies with the
Permanent Paper Standard issued by the National
Information Standards Organization (Z39.48–1984).

10   9   8   7   6   5   4   3   2   1

In loving memory of my parents,
Plummer Alston Jones Sr. (1920–1987)
Elva Lucille (Pridgen Wright) Jones (1925–1972)

CONTENTS

ACKNOWLEDGMENTS

For moral support and encouragement, I will always be grateful to my colleagues in the Department of Librarianship, Educational Technology, and Distance Instruction of the College of Education at East Carolina University. For practical advice and assistance, I am indebted to my colleagues on the Reference and Interlibrary Loan staffs at the J. Y. Joyner Library at East Carolina University.

For professional support, I thank my colleagues in the American Library Association Library History Round Table and the Ethnic and Multicultural Information Exchange Round Table, the latter being the spiritual successor of the Committee on Work with the Foreign Born (1918–48).

For my family, friends, and students, I offer my thanks for your forbearance when I launch into a seemingly interminable discourse on my favorite subject—American public library services with minorities.

PREFACE

The United States has been shaped by many complex forces, the most powerful of which has been and continues to be immigration. Immigration is and always has been a morally complicated issue, a shifting mixture of good and bad. Along with the good of multiculturalism in the arts and education, and renewed energy, have been the bad of uncontrolled entry of undesirables, seemingly endless population growth, sometimes unfair competition in the American labor market, and social fragmentation.

Annual arrivals in the first three decades of the republic were estimated at less than 10,000 a year, well below 1 percent of the resident population in any given year. After 1820, Europe entered an astonishing century-and-a-half surge of population growth, generating a mass movement of peoples of which the settling of the British colonies was only the first ripple. During the nineteenth century and into the twentieth, Europeans driven by population pressures, starvation, and civil and religious unrest, some 50 to 60 million, came to colonize the temperate zones of North America, Argentina, Australia, and New Zealand.

The early immigrants from northern and western Europe beginning in the late eighteenth century, and those who emigrated later from southern and eastern Europe in the late nineteenth century, were for the most part rapidly absorbed into the mainstream of American society. Still, the melting pot of America did not produce a homogeneous population. Certain racial and ethnic groups, due to biological, cultural, and historical factors, remained unmelted, including blacks of African and Caribbean origins, Hispanics (from Spanish-speaking cultures in the Western Hemisphere) representing a mixture of racial and ethnic backgrounds, Asians and Pacific Islanders, and Native Americans (American Indians, Eskimos, and Aleuts).

Two centuries of slavery have made a profound impact upon black Americans and upon American society in general. In contrast to the millions of immigrants who left their homelands voluntarily to seek a better life in the New World, most black Americans arrived on these shores in chains during the triangular slave trade from England to Africa to America that began in 1619 in Jamestown, Virginia, approximately 12 years after the founding of this first permanent English settlement in the New World. Although the importation of slaves was outlawed in 1808, it has been estimated that 250,000 slaves were illegally imported between 1808 and 1860.[1]

American Indians have been treated not only as a minority but also as a foreign nation within the United States since the first European colonists arrived in the New World in 1607 and continuing until the first naturalization law was passed by the U.S. Congress in 1790. From 1607 to the Wounded Knee Massacre in 1890, there would be few years when whites and Indians were at peace. During this period the native peoples of the territories that were incorporated into the United States were decimated through military action and diseases, notably small pox, introduced by European settlers. The American Indian population decreased from an estimated 2 million at the time of European arrival to approximately two hundred thousand in 1900, an unparalleled devastation.[2]

Immigrants, African Americans, and Native Americans are not only numerical but also political minorities within American society. Minorities as such are subject to prejudice, discrimination, segregation, exploitations, persecution, and oppression. Just as racism was used to justify slavery and the slaughter of American Indians in the nineteenth century, it serves to reinforce and perpetuate social inequality in twentieth and twenty-first-century America. The effect of racism is to divide poor and working-class people of all races who have common economic interests, thereby keeping them passive and deprived. The eradication of racism could be expected to result not only in an end to racial injustice but in an improved equality of life for all exploited people.[3]

LEGAL AND JUDICIAL DECISIONS AFFECTING MINORITIES

When the first census of the United States was taken in 1790, there was a population of 3,227,000, most of whom were descendants of seventeenth- and eighteenth-century arrivals or recent immigrants themselves. Nearly 75 percent were of British origin, about 8 percent were of German origin, and the remaining residents were of Dutch, French, or Spanish origins, and of course, African origin—free blacks and black slaves. Less than 1 percent were American Indians.[4]

Naturalization Law of 1790

Although the 1790 naturalization law limited citizenship to free white persons, it was very liberal in requiring only two years of residency and the renunciation of former allegiances. In 1795, in response to fears about colonial foreign influence, Congress required five years of residency and a renunciation of titles of nobility as well as allegiances. In 1798, Congress, then under control of the Federalist Party, lengthened the period of residency to 14 years and pushed through the Alien Act, allowing the President to depart any alien considered to be a threat to the nation.

The Alien Act was allowed to expire when the Jeffersonian Democratic Republicans replaced the Federalists in power. In 1802, Congress reestablished the five-year provision of the 1795 act. In 1819, Congress passed a law requiring a manifest of all entering-ship passengers, including sex, occupation, age, and nation of origin.[5] Precise statistics on immigration are not available before 1820.

Northern and Western European Immigration

The wave of Catholic immigrants, both German and Irish, during the 1830s, 1840s, and into the 1850s, set off an anti-foreign reaction. The annual average immigration to the United States rose to 120,000 a year between 1820 and 1860. This surge in immigration is called by historian Otis L. Graham Jr., the first Great Wave.

Increasingly throughout the nineteenth century from 1820 onward, immigrants became the scapegoats to blame for the problems facing a rapidly changing society in the initial stages of urbanization and industrialization. Anti-Catholic groups grew, including such as the Order of the Star Spangled Banner and the American Party, its members soon called "know-nothings" for their habit of refusing comment on their plans to journalists and others.

The American Party's program included strong anti-slavery sentiment and political reforms such as child labor laws and ending imprisonment for debt. Historians have ignored these basic tenets of the American Party and have concentrated on their core belief, that the nation's great problem was Catholic political activity that had been made more potent every year by increasing German and Irish immigration. They focused on keeping Catholic immigrants already in the country from gaining political power. Lengthening naturalization requirements was their chief policy goal, and voting only for naturalized immigrants and citizens was another goal. In short, the American Party ended up advocating a provisional status for Catholic immigrants while failing to demand that the federal government gain control of immigration.[6]

Treaty of Guadalupe Hidalgo of 1848

The critical need for labor prevailed over such nativist sentiment in determining public laws concerning immigration, that is deciding who was to be admitted to the United States, and naturalization, that is deciding who was to be granted citizenship. By the time the first Anglo-American settlement was established in Texas in 1821, the territories of New Mexico and California, as well as Texas, were already populated by Mexicans. As successive waves of Anglos settled in Texas, they attempted to wrest control of the Mexican province, a provocation that led inexorably to the Mexican-American War and the eventual victory by the United States.

The Treaty of Guadalupe Hidalgo of 1848, concluding the Mexican-American War, ceded to the United States most of Mexico's former northern territory that once comprised all or parts of present-day California, New Mexico, Arizona, Nevada, Utah, and Colorado. Mexicans, who wished to remain in those territories ceded to the United States, became U.S. citizens by right of treaty. In practice, they were deprived of traditional property rights, reduced to a numerical minority by Anglo migration, and suffered discrimination in employment and at the hands of the law. Mexican Americans became like American Indians, a conquered indigenous people.[7]

Beginning of Immigration Restriction Efforts

The transcontinental railroad building boom opened up vast lands in the West to settlement. In 1862, Congress enacted the Homestead Act, which granted up to 160 acres of free land to settlers who would develop the land and remain on it for five years. Also in 1862, Congress granted naturalization to honorably discharged soldiers, an inducement to recruit aliens to serve in the Union Army during the Civil War.[8]

Thirteenth, Fourteenth, and Fifteenth Amendments to the Constitution

It was not until after the Civil War that the passage of the Thirteenth, Fourteenth, and Fifteenth Amendments to the U.S. Constitution, ratified in 1865, 1868, and 1870, respectively, freed the slaves, guaranteed the right of citizenship to all persons born in the United States regardless of race or national origin, and granted the right to vote to African Americans. In 1870, Congress enacted laws making naturalization easier for those who served in military or naval services or the merchant marine.

Even with these constitutional guarantees, most African Americans remained in the rural South as sharecroppers, who were economically exploited and socially oppressed to maintain segregation and their right to vote consistently denied. Blacks were denied the opportunity to learn to read and write, were kept ignorant of the workings of commerce, and were deprived of a normal family life, personal dignity, and security. Legal rights gained by the Thirteenth, Fourteenth, and Fifteenth Amendments existed primarily in theory for many years after their passage.[9]

U.S. Bureau of Indian Affairs

The colonization of North America had destroyed traditional ways of life, uprooting long-established societies and forcing whole peoples into political submission and economic dependence. By the 1870s, most American Indians had been installed on government-supported reservations under the custodianship of the U.S. Bureau of Indian Affairs (BIA). Over the next hundred years, federal policy fluctuated between support of the reservation system and "termination"—the cessation of federal responsibility, which represents the discontinuation of federal social services and the destruction of the remnants of their traditional way of life. Ironically, American Indians would not be served by public libraries until the late 1950s. Their library and information needs were served by the BIA or not at all.

Once established in the mid-nineteenth century, American public libraries became interested in serving the educational and recreational needs of citizens first and, later, residents. By 1875, 257 public libraries had been founded. The establishment of the American Library Association (ALA) in 1876 provided the national leadership for the further development of public libraries.

In the mid-nineteenth century, which saw the beginnings of the public library movement, most black Americans still had the legal status of chattels, and American Indians were widely considered vermin worthy only of extermination. Both Asian immigrants and Chicanos born in U.S. territory were objects of hostility and scorn. The democratic and humanitarian rhetoric upon which public libraries were founded was rarely extended to include these segments of the population.

Americanization efforts were directed almost entirely toward the assimilation of European immigrants, and few nineteenth-century libraries, even in the North, allowed unrestricted use by nonwhites. One exception was the Enoch Pratt Free Library, which from its founding in 1886 had a policy of full privileges for Baltimore's black readers. The general American climate was one of discrimination and neglect, which was to prevail for more than a century.[10]

NOTES

1. Maldwyn Allen Jones, *American Immigration,* 2nd ed. (Chicago: University of Chicago Press, 1992), 9–11; Otis L. Graham Jr., *Unguarded Gates: A History of America's Immigration Crisis* (Lanham, MD: Rowman & Littlefield Publishers, 2004), xi, 4–5; Norman Coombs, "Afro-Americans," in *Dictionary of American Immigration History,* ed. Francesco Cordasco (Metuchen, NJ: Scarecrow Press, 1990), 9–11; David J. Hellwig, "Afro-American Views of Immigrants, 1830–1930: A Historiographical-Bibliographical Essay," *Immigration History Newsletter* 13 (Nov. 1981): 1–5; Harlow G. Unger, ed., "African Americans," in *Encyclopedia of American Education,* 2nd ed. (New York: Facts on File, c2001, 1996), 39–42; Alton Hornsby, *Chronology of African–American History: Significant Events and People from 1619 to the Present* (Detroit: Gale Research, 1991), xx–xxiv; Robert M. Jiobu, *Ethnicity and Assimilation* (Albany: State University New York Press, 1988), 27–32; Marcia J. Nauratil, *Public Libraries and Nontraditional Clienteles: The Politics of Special Services* (Westport, CT: Greenwood Press, 1985), 100–102.

2. Unger, "American Indian," 64–67; Nauratil, *Public Libraries and Nontraditional Clienteles,* 102–4, 121–22.

3. Nauratil, *Public Libraries and Nontraditional Clienteles,* 99–100, 109.

4. Michael LeMay and Elliott Robert Barkan, eds., *U.S. Immigration and Naturalization Laws and Issues: A Documentary History* (Westport, CT: Greenwood Press, 1999), xxix; M. A. Jones, *American Immigration,* 27–29; Rudolph J. Vecoli, "Immigration," in *Oxford Companion to United States History,* ed. Paul S. Boyer and Melvyn Dubofsky (New York: Oxford University Press, 2001), 359.

5. U.S. Immigration and Naturalization Service, "Appendix 1: Immigration and Naturalization Legislation," in *Statistical Yearbook of the Immigration and Naturalization Service, 1997* (Washington, DC: U.S.G.P.O., 1999), A.1–1, A.1–2; LeMay and Barkan, *U.S. Immigration and Naturalization Laws and Issues,* 11–20; M. A. Jones, *American Immigration,* 57, 69–76; E. Willard Miller, and Ruby M.

Miller, *United States Immigration: A Reference Handbook* (Santa Barbara, CA: ABC-CLIO, 1996), 107–8; Philip Gleason, "American Identity and Americanization," in *Harvard Encyclopedia of American Ethnic Groups*, ed. Stephan Thernstrom, Ann Orlov, and Oscar Handlin (Cambridge: Belknap Press of Harvard University Press, 1980), 33–34; Reed Ueda, "Naturalization and Citizenship," in *Harvard Encyclopedia of American Ethnic Groups*, 736–37.

   6. M. A. Jones, *American Immigration*, 134–38; Graham, *Unguarded Gates*, 6, 31; LeMay and Barkan, *U.S. Immigration and Naturalization Laws and Issues*, 26–29; David Harry Bennett, "Nativist Movement," in *Oxford Companion to United States History*, 543; Vecoli, "Immigration," 359, 361; Gleason, "American Identity and Americanization," 35–38.

   7. LeMay and Barkan, *U.S. Immigration and Naturalization Laws and Issues*, 25–28; Carlos E. Cortes, "Mexicans," in *Dictionary of American Immigration History*, 509–10; Walter Fogel, "Twentieth-Century Migration to the United States," in *The Gateway: U.S. Immigration Issues and Policies*, ed. Barry R. Chiswick (Washington, DC: American Enterprise Institute for Public Policy Research, 1982), 193–94; Arnulfo D. Trejo, "Bicultural Americans with a Hispanic Tradition," *Wilson Library Bulletin* 44 (Mar. 1970): 717–20; Jiobu, *Ethnicity and Assimilation*, 20–27; Robert P. Haro, *Developing Library and Information Services for Americans of Hispanic Origin* (Metuchen, NJ: Scarecrow Press, 1981), 4–8; Nauratil, *Public Libraries and Nontraditional Clienteles*, 104–5; Patricia Beilke and Frank J. Sciara, *Selecting Materials for and about Hispanic and East Asian Children and Young People* (Hamden, CT: Library Professional Publications, 1986), 47–54, 77–83.

   8. LeMay and Barkan, *U.S. Immigration and Naturalization Laws and Issues*, 29–30; M. A. Jones, *American Immigration*, 147–49.

   9. LeMay and Barkan, *U.S. Immigration and Naturalization Laws and Issues*, 31–32; Hornsby, *Chronology of African–American History*, xxiv–xxvii; William S. Bernard, "Immigration: History of U.S. Policy," in *Harvard Encyclopedia of American Ethnic Groups*, 494–95; Ueda, "Naturalization and Citizenship," 739; Nauratil, *Public Libraries and Nontraditional Clienteles*, 100–101.

   10. Nauratil, *Public Libraries and Nontraditional Clienteles*, 109.

Chapter 1

PUBLIC LIBRARIES AND AMERICANIZATION, 1876 THROUGH THE 1940s

The Civil War and economic depressions of the 1870s brought a lull in immigration. In the 1880s, 5.2 million came, in the 1890s, 3.7 million. In the first decade of the twentieth century, 8.8 million came. The foreign born and their children comprised 34 percent of the total white population in 1880, rising to 40 percent by 1910. From 1880 to 1910 the American urban population tripled. By 1920, the nation's urban population was 41 percent foreign born. Since the South had never become a popular destination for immigrants, in most major northeastern cities the proportion was closer to two-thirds. Despite such overwhelming statistics, the regulation of immigration came slowly.

LEGAL AND JUDICIAL DECISIONS AFFECTING MINORITIES

In 1876, the same year as the founding of the American Library Association, the U.S. Supreme Court ruled that individual states could not regulate immigration. What regulation there had been was ineffectual inspection at seaports for obvious physical or mental disease. New York City charity officials were alarmed at the prospect of losing the fees collected from ship owners and urged the government to take over immigration control and exclude immigrants unable to support themselves. The immigration law of 1882 named the secretary of the treasury as the responsible executive. The law barred criminals, lunatics, idiots, and those likely to become a public charge, extending colonial and state traditions. This was not a firm federal grip on immigration. Inspection at the docks was still left to the states, and the law was not intended to restrict immigration. Those few who were excluded had always been excluded. There were no criteria for selecting from the many applicants those whom America would permit to enter.

In the 1880s, Europeans began to arrive in renewed numbers due to industrialization and farm mechanization, which moved south and east in Europe. Over the next 50 years nearly 30 million Europeans migrated to the United States. These were the New Immigrants from new places—Italy, Russia, Poland, Serbia, Croatia, Bulgaria, Hungary, Armenia, Greece, and Portugal. Two million of the world's 7.5 million Jews relocated to America out of central and eastern Europe in these years. Simultaneously, the Chinese and Japanese were coming to the West Coast, especially to California.[1]

Chinese Exclusion Act of 1882

In China, the T'ai-P'ing Rebellion (1851–64), economic depression, and recurrent threat of famine made life precarious for millions of Chinese, while at the same time news of the California gold rush presented America as a land of promise. The years from 1849 to 1882 were the period of heaviest Chinese immigration—most came to the United States as contract laborers or so-called coolies under a debt obligation. The physical characteristics of the Chinese, strange language and customs, and a concentration in urban Chinatowns made them objects of hostility, suspicion, and often violence.

The swelling anti-Chinese sentiment, particularly virulent during the U.S. depression of the 1870s, resulted in Congress passing the Chinese Exclusion Act of 1882, the first restrictionist U.S. immigration law. The Chinese Exclusion Act suspended immigration of Chinese laborers to the United States for 10 years. Although the law permitted Chinese laborers already in the United States to remain in the country after a temporary absence, it provided for the deportation of Chinese illegally in the United States and barred Chinese from naturalization. Chinese other than laborers, including teachers, students, merchants, and government officials, could and did legally travel to the United States; however, Chinese were declared ineligible for citizenship though their American-born children were citizens. With the cessation of Chinese immigration, American agriculturists turned to Japan as a source of cheap labor.[2]

General Allotment Act of 1887

Also in the 1880s, Congress faced the stark reality of tens of thousands of American Indians living on large tracts of highly coveted land. With advice from the religious communities that had been involved with the conversion of the Indians to Christianity, Congress formulated more coercive strategies to drive American Indians from their native lands.

In contrast with the official policy of "separation," which had been applied toward Indians before 1887, the new official policy was the assimilation or, as it was often phrased, the "civilization of the Indians." The General Allotment Act, or Dawes Act of 1887, intending to make Indians into white men, assigned a title to 160 acres to each family head, just as the Homestead Act of 1862 had done for thousands of white settlers. Congressional intent behind the 1887 act was to make American Indians hardworking, economically self-sufficient persons by granting them responsibility for land. Other Americans would profit also, since after all Indian family heads had been assigned land, the U.S. government could distribute the surplus to non-Indians, who were more than ready to settle on it. Members of the terminated tribes found survival difficult in the often hostile larger American society.[3]

Southern and Eastern European Immigration

By 1890, immigrants from southern and eastern Europe, as well as China and Japan, were beginning to outnumber the immigrants from northern and western Europe, who had constituted the majority of the U.S. populace in 1790, a century earlier. From laws banning the Chinese to those excluding other Asians, and finally to the imposition of literacy tests, U.S. immigration and naturalization laws had become restrictionist and racist. Bars were put in place to keep out the mentally ill, convicts, those suffering from contagious diseases, those liable to become public charges, and those of Asian origins.

Canadian Migration

A large though indeterminate number of migrants had come overland to the United States from Canada, both from the Maritime Provinces and Quebec, since before the Civil War. For a generation after the Civil War, emigration to the United States took place on such a scale as to threaten Canada with depopulation. In the last three decades of the nineteenth century, while many farmers in the Midwest and plains states migrated to areas of the Southwest, the Great Basin states of the West, and sections of the Great Lakes states to improve their economic status; other Midwest and plains states farmers chose migration to the vast, unexploited Canadian prairie region.[4]

Contract Labor Law

The Contract Labor Law, or Foran Act, named for its Congressional sponsor, was passed in February 1885 to make it unlawful to import aliens into the United States under contract for the performance of labor or services of any kind. Exceptions were for aliens temporarily in the United States engaging other foreigners as secretaries, servants, or domestics; actors, artists, lecturers, and domestic servants; and skilled aliens working in industries not yet established in the United States.[5]

The Immigration Act of March 1891, the first comprehensive law for federal control of immigration, established the Bureau of Immigration under the U.S. Department of the Treasury to administer all immigration laws, with the exception of the Chinese Exclusion Act of 1882. It allowed the secretary of the treasury to prescribe rules for inspection along the borders of Canada, British Columbia, and Mexico so as not to obstruct or unnecessarily delay or impede passengers in ordinary travel between these countries and the United States, and it called for the deportation of any alien who entered the United States unlawfully. By 1893, both houses of Congress for the first time had standing committees on immigration.[6]

Plessy v. Ferguson

In 1896, the U.S. Supreme Court decided the case of *Plessy v. Ferguson* by establishing the legal principle of "separate-but-equal" and giving a constitutional basis to legal segregation based on race, the so-called Jim Crow laws. This doctrine was very important in restricting the rights of all citizens of color in the United States, including African Americans, Asians, Hispanics, and American Indians, by allowing state governments to pass laws segregating them from white schools and places of accommodation.

Restrictive immigration laws and the need for factory labor during World War I and afterward encouraged the migration of African Americans from the rural South to the urban centers of the North. This trend continued into the postwar period. Had black Americans been invited to testify before governmental bodies in these years, their representatives would have added their appeals for stemming the tide of foreign labor as Tuskegee Institute's Booker T. Washington had done in his Atlanta Exposition address in 1895. Blacks often suffered from competition for jobs and housing from the Irish, Croats, Serbs, Slovenes, Bulgarians, and Italians after 1900 in the steel-industry towns of Pennsylvania.[7]

In Re Rodriguez and *Wong Kim Ark v. United States*

In 1897, a federal district court in west Texas rendered its decision in *In Re Rodriguez,* affirming the citizenship rights of Mexicans in the United States on the basis of the Treaty of Guadalupe Hidalgo of 1868, signed at the close of the Mexican-American War. In 1898, the U.S. Supreme Court ruled in *Wong Kim Ark v. United States* that a native-born person of Asian descent was a citizen of the United States despite the fact that his or her parents may have been resident aliens ineligible for naturalization.[8]

Spanish-American War

In 1898, at the close of the Spanish-American War, the United States assumed control over Guam, Puerto Rico, the Philippines, and Cuba, and also annexed Hawaii as a territory. In 1900 citizenship status was granted to Hawaiians, exempting them from some of the steps required in the naturalization process. Puerto Ricans, who were granted U.S. citizenship in 1917, immigrated to the continental United States for much the same reason as European immigrants. Since then, Puerto Ricans have immigrated in large numbers, trading conditions of poverty for a chance at economic mobility.

Literacy Act

The Dillingham Commission suggested a literacy test as a screening device for potential immigrants. An immigrant would have had to be able to read several sentences of the Constitution in any language of his or her choice. The immigrant's family members were exempt. This principle of selection meant choosing future Americans for their promise as individuals rather than by any group affiliation.

The first literacy bill was enacted in 1896 by both houses but vetoed by President Grover Cleveland. In February 1903, Congress passed legislation to prohibit entry to and naturalization of anarchists. In March 1903, following the assassination of President William McKinley by an American-born anarchist Leon Czolgosz, Congress passed an immigration act that barred the immigration of anarchists, believing in the overthrow of the U.S. government by force or violence.[9]

The Naturalization Act of June 1906 included both a literacy test for admission and an English language test for naturalization. Nativist groups were joined by labor unions in advocating this new requirement. Although business leaders opposed the new law because of their advocacy for new and cheaper labor sources, the ability to speak the English language was accepted as a requirement for citizenship.[10]

Gentleman's Agreement with Japan and the Dillingham Commission

In 1907, President Theodore Roosevelt issued the executive order for the Gentleman's Agreement with Japan, by which Japan would voluntarily restrict the immigration of laborers from Japan and Korea. Ironically, picture brides were permitted to immigrate.

Dillingham Commission of 1909

The 1907 agreement with Japan also included the creation of the U.S. Joint Commission on Immigration, later known as the Dillingham Commission, to make an investigation of the immigration system. Begun in 1909, the Dillingham Commission, named after its chair, Senator William P. Dillingham, recommended in its 1911 report a literacy test and further restrictions on immigration, particularly of southern and eastern Europeans and Asians.

The Dillingham Commission focused on European immigration. The commission suggested methods of selecting immigrants, including a literacy test and a ban on unskilled workers entering the United States without their families. The commission also suggested another method for consideration: the limitation of the number of each nationality arriving each year to a certain percentage of the average of that nationality arriving during a given period of years.

The Dillingham Commission's recommendations did not address Mexican immigration. Until the Mexican Revolution in 1911, most Mexican Americans were born in the United States. After this date, first to escape political upheaval and later in search of employment opportunities, increasing numbers of Mexicans immigrated to the United States. Mexican immigration was encouraged by the federal government, especially during and following World War I, to ameliorate labor shortages.[11]

Immigration Act of 1917 and Literacy Law for Immigrants

Congress passed a literacy law in 1913, but it was vetoed by President William Howard Taft. In 1915, after it was passed once again, President

Woodrow Wilson vetoed it. Following the entry of the United States into World War I in February 1917, Congress enacted another literacy bill and overrode yet another veto.

Incorporating the findings and suggestions of the 1907 U.S. Joint Commission on Immigration, the 1917 act excluded illiterate aliens. The 1917 act singled out Mexicans for exemption from the literacy test requirement for the duration of World War I in recognition of their importance as a back-door source of cheap and plentiful labor.

The Immigration Act of 1917 law also codified a list of aliens to be excluded and banned all immigrant laborers, but not all applicants, from a so-called Asiatic Barred Zone. For the duration of World War I, immigration to the United States was interrupted but only temporarily.[12]

Americanization Movement Before and After World War I

There was no federal Americanization legislation, but at least three federal agencies conducted aggressive campaigns. The U.S. Bureau of Naturalization developed its own textbook for use in the public schools, an action the Bureau of Education regarded as an entrenchment upon its turf. Both agencies lobbied local superintendents of schools to adopt their particular curricular materials and tried to win the support of employers' associations, but neither agency acknowledged the right of the other to play a role in the movement. The wartime Committee on Public Information, in keeping with its mandate to promote patriotism as well as to disseminate information, had commandeered the editorial pages of the foreign-language press during World War I and thereafter.

Active as local, state, and federal agencies were, the greatest impetus behind the Americanization movement came from the more than 100 private organizations, each of which created its own Americanization programs. These ranged from Henry Ford's on-the-job English and citizenship classes for his alien employees to the sympathetic celebrations of ethnic heritages sponsored by the International Institutes of the Young Women's Christian Association.[13]

Puerto Ricans Granted U.S. Citizenship

In March 1917, Congress granted citizenship to Puerto Ricans. In July of that same year, the U.S. Department of State and U.S. Department of Labor issued a joint order requiring passports and certain other information from all aliens seeking to enter the United States during World War I. The act also required the issuing of visas from an American consular officer in the country of origin rather than allowing a person to enter the United States and then seek permission to enter after having already arrived at the U.S. shores or ports of entry.[14]

In May 1918, Congress amended the naturalization laws to apply special privileges to Filipinos, seamen serving in the U.S. merchant marine or on U.S. fishing vessels, persons whose naturalization process was interrupted by the war, or other persons serving in the U.S. armed forces. In August 1918, Congress granted the president powers to exclude the entrance or departure of aliens during a time of war.[15]

Red Scare

In October 1919, during a period later to be known as the Red Scare that followed in the wake of World War I, Congress passed a law equating membership in Communist organizations as grounds for exclusion and deportation. In the course of the Palmer Raids of 1919–20, named for Attorney General A. Mitchell Palmer, thousands of alien radicals were seized and hundreds were deported, many of them being shipped to Russia in December 1919 in an army transport nicknamed the Soviet Ark.[16]

As the Communist-inspired hysteria of the Red Scare decreased in the early 1920s, nativists turned their attention from immigrants already in the United States to restricting the entry of further immigrants. The publication of the results of the U.S. Army's wartime psychological tests on soldiers had helped to strengthen the case for immigration restriction. The fact that soldiers from southern and eastern Europe had markedly lower IQ scores than those from northern and western Europe and those born in the United States was viewed as proof of Anglo-Saxon intellectual superiority.[17]

Native Americans Granted Citizenship in 1919 and 1924

In 1919, Congress enacted a law granting honorably discharged Native Americans citizenship for their services during World War I. In 1924, all American Indians who had not previously accepted allotments of land from the U.S. government under the General Allotment Act of 1887 were granted U.S. citizenship.[18]

Quota Law of 1921

In fiscal year 1920–21, 800,000 immigrants entered American ports, only 1,500 of them rejected by the literacy test. In May 1921, the Quota Law, the first quantitative immigration law, was passed by Congress and signed into law by President Warren G. Harding. It limited the number of aliens of any nationality entering the United States to 3 percent of the foreign-born persons of that nationality who resided in the United Sates in 1910.

This rationale harked back to the Dillingham Commission's suggestion and was predicted to produce totals of 200,000 for northern and western Europe and 155,000 for southern and eastern, cutting immigration to approximately 360,000 quota immigrants. A. Philip Randolph, an African American leader, expressed his approval of further reducing immigration, since the decline of European migration, coupled with the increased labor demands brought on by World War I, had opened the doors of Pennsylvania's steel mills to incoming African Americans, particularly from the South.

The 1921 act exempted from this limitation aliens who had resided continuously for at least one year immediately preceding their application in one of the independent countries of the Western Hemisphere. Nonimmigrant aliens, including government officials and their households, aliens in transit through the United States, temporary visitors for business and pleasure, and aliens whose immigration was regulated by treaties, were exempted. The Act of May 11, 1922, extended the Quota Law for two years with amendments that changed the residency requirement from one year to five years in a Western Hemisphere country.

Total immigration to the United States did decline under the 1921 and 1922 acts. European immigration slumped from over 800,000 in 1921, 310,000 in 1922, 523,000 in 1924, and 707,000 in 1924, to less than 150,000 by the end of the decade. Much of the increase in immigration came from Mexico, Canada, and other nonquota countries.

Ironically, throughout the 1920s when the United States decided to limit immigration, the other four major immigrant-receiving countries, Canada, Argentina, Brazil, and Australia, were taking similar measures. All five countries, Anglo-Saxon and Latino alike, opted for selection systems designed in different ways to replicate the nation's historical structure of nationalities.[19]

Ozawa v. U.S. and *U.S. v. Bhagat Singh Thind*

In 1922, the U.S. Supreme Court in *Ozawa v. United States* upheld the constitutionality of restricting Japanese aliens from becoming naturalized citizens on the grounds that they were not Caucasian. In 1923, the U.S. Supreme Court ruled in *United States v. Bhagat Singh Thind* that white persons meant those persons who appeared and would commonly be viewed as white. Thus, East Asian Indians, although Caucasian, were not considered white and were therefore ineligible for naturalization. Ironically, these points had earlier been declared moot with the passage of the Fourteenth Amendment earlier in 1868.[20]

Immigration Act of 1924

The Immigration Act of May 1924, the first permanent limitation on immigration, established the national origins quota system based on two provisions. The first, in effect until the end of June 1927, set the annual quota of any quota nationality at 2 percent of the number of foreign-born persons of such nationality resident in the continental United States in 1890, for a total aggregate quota of 164,667. The second, in effect from the first of July 1927 (later postponed to the first of July 1929) to the end of December 1952, used the national origins quota system, which required that the annual quota for any country or nationality would have the same relation to 150,000 as the subtotal of inhabitants of a particular national origin in the continental United States in 1920 had to the total number of inhabitants.[21]

The provisions of the 1924 act, also known as the National Origins Act, established consular control of immigration by mandating that no alien would be permitted entrance to the United States without an immigration visa issued by an American consular officer abroad. The U.S. Department of State and the U.S. Immigration and Naturalization Service would share control of immigration. It introduced the provision that as a rule, no alien ineligible to become a citizen would be admitted to the United States as an immigrant, a provision aimed primarily at Japanese aliens and others Asians. A preference quota status was established for unmarried children under 21; parents, spouses of U.S. citizens aged 21 and over; and quota immigrants aged 21 and over who were skilled in agriculture, together with their wives and dependent children under age 16. Nonquota status was accorded to wives and unmarried children under the age of 18 of U.S. citizens, and natives of Western Hemisphere countries, with their families.[22]

Asian Immigration Limited

The anti-Japanese movement culminated in the Immigration Act of 1924, which ended all Asian immigration except for that of Filipinos, who as U.S. nationals were unaffected. In fact, from 1924 to 1952, few Asians other than Filipinos immigrated to the United States. Active recruitment of Filipino agricultural laborers followed the exclusion of other Asian immigrants, for both Hawaiian sugar plantations and California farms. Filipino workers generally found themselves at the bottom of the wage scale and victims of continuing discrimination. The Tydings-McDuffie Act of 1934 limited Filipino immigration to an annual quota of 50, and further legislation the next year provided for repatriation of Filipinos at federal expense. Few took advantage of this dubious offer.[23]

U.S. Border Patrol

In 1925, Congress created the U.S. Border Patrol to halt illegal immigration along the over 5,000 miles of border with Canada and Mexico. An estimated 500,000 had entered the United States illegally during the 1920s alone from the borderlands region, which extends nearly 2,000 miles across the American states of Texas, New Mexico, Arizona, and California, and the Mexican states of Nuevo Leon, Coahuila, Tamaulipas, Chihuahua, Sonora, and Baja California Norte.[24]

Permanent National-Origins Quotas Established in 1929

Recorded immigration to the United States averaged 305,000 per year from 1925 to 1929 under the interim quotas. In 1929, President Herbert Hoover proclaimed new and permanent quotas based on the national-origins system, with the total to be admitted from the Eastern Hemisphere limited to just over 150,000. During the 1930s, immigration dropped sharply to an average of 53,000 a year.

The quota system, coupled with the economic impact of the Great Depression of the 1930s, reduced overall immigration, although there continued to be no restrictions placed on the open immigration from the Western Hemisphere. Nevertheless, between 1932 and 1944, one-quarter of a million refugees from Europe entered the United States, 100,000 of them Jews. During the Depression, Congress turned its energies toward clarifying the status of immigrants already in the United States and Native Americans.[25]

Naturalization Law Reforms and Indian Reorganization Act

In 1934, Congress amended the naturalization law to clarify the citizenship status of children of U.S. citizens who were born outside the United States, the status of such children upon the naturalization of their parents, and the status of women who were citizens and married to foreigners. Also in 1934, Congress passed the Indian Reorganization Act that established modern tribal governments. In 1935, Congress allowed for the naturalization of alien veterans, including veterans of Allied armies, and granted the right of citizenship to Asian veterans of World War I.[26]

Alien Registration Act of 1940 and Public Safety Act of 1941

In the 1940s, immigration averaged about 100,000 a year but with an upward trend after World War II. It was estimated that, subtracting emigration, only 1.7 million people migrated to the United States during this period, the equivalent of two years' arrivals prior to implementation of restriction measures of the 1920s.

In June 1940, Congress passed the Alien Registration Act, which required the registration of all aliens and fingerprinting of those over 14 years of age. The Public Safety Act of June 1941 directed a consular officer to refuse a visa to any alien seeking to enter the United States for the purpose of engaging in activities that would endanger the safety of the United States.[27]

European Aliens During World War II

When the United States entered World War II, there was the expected fear that aliens from other countries would not be loyal to their adopted nation. Of the almost 1 million enemy aliens in the United States in 1941, in addition to millions of naturalized citizens who had been born in enemy territories, almost all were unwavering in their American allegiance.

Immigrants of Italian descent, many of whom had been subjected to discrimination and violence during World War I, faced less harassment during World War II. Out of nearly 700,000 Italian enemy aliens, only 4,000 were apprehended by the Federal Bureau of Investigation (FBI), and of those, only about 200 were interned. By the fall of 1942, they were no longer classified as enemy aliens.

Of the 300,000 enemy aliens from Germany, only a few hundred were interned, despite the fact that this was the second time within 25 years that the United States had been at war with Germany and that most Americans regarded Germany as the major enemy. The rest suffered no serious discrimination and were freely accepted both in war industries and in the armed services.[28]

Internment of Japanese Americans During World War II

In early 1942, after the Japanese attack on Pearl Harbor, Hawaii, on December 7, 1941, President Franklin Delano Roosevelt issued Executive Order 9066, which led to the evacuation, relocation, and internment of Japanese and Japanese Americans in relocation camps. In 1943 the U.S. Supreme Court ruled in *Hirabayashi v. United States* that the executive orders establishing curfew and evacuation programs were constitutionally based as military necessities covered by the War Powers Act of 1918.[29]

Ban on Chinese Immigration Lifted in 1943

During World War II, in response to the U.S. wartime alliance with China, Congress repealed the 60-year ban on Chinese immigration in December 1943 and allowed for their naturalization, and China was granted an immigration quota of 105. In 1949 the pro-Western government of China fell to revolutionary forces and 1,600 Chinese students and professors already in the United States were given visas.[30]

Korematsu v. United States

In 1944, the U.S. Supreme Court decided in *Korematsu v. United States* the constitutionality of interning Japanese American citizens. That same year, in a rare reversal of opinion, the U.S. Supreme Court ruled paradoxically that their internment was an unconstitutional violation of the habeas corpus rights of American citizens, including some 70,000 native-born citizens of Japanese ancestry, the Nisei or second-generation Japanese Americans.[31]

War Brides Act of 1945

At the end of World War II, President Harry Truman issued a directive that resulted in the admission of some 40,000 war refugees. In 1945, Congress enacted the War Brides Act that allowed 120,000 alien wives, husbands, and children of members of the armed forces to immigrate to the United States outside of the quota system.[32]

Ban on Filipino and East Asian Indian Immigration Lifted in 1946

On July 2, 1946, Congress passed legislation granting Asian Indians and Filipinos admission to the United States as quota immigrants and eligibility for naturalization. The Japanese were at this point the only Asians barred from becoming naturalized citizens of the United States. Two days later, on the fourth day of July, the Republic of the Philippines was established with independent rule and the U.S. Congress granted the Philippines an immigration quota of 100.[33]

Displaced Persons Act of 1948

A serious international refugee question emerged as the war ended. Millions of Europeans displaced by wartime forced-labor assignments or living inside the war-expanded boundaries of a Russian Communist empire faced the choice of submission, rebellion, or flight. Official estimates ran from 8 million to 20 million displaced persons in Europe in 1945, with 1.8 million living in Allied camps.

Truman ordered that refugees be given priority within quotas in 1945 and pressed Congress to pass the first refugee policy measure in U.S. history, the Displaced Persons Act in 1948, which had been advocated by such groups as the American Jewish Committee, supported by the American Federation of Labor (AFL), but opposed by the American Legion. The act permitted the admission of more than 450,000, or 40 percent of the 1 million Europeans who were relocated to 113 countries by charging their entry against their homelands' future quotas. Most of them would have been ineligible under the laws of the 1920s.

Federal funds were appropriated for refugee relocation within the United States and disbursed to religious and civic voluntary agencies, which were becoming an increasingly potent lobby for expanded refugee programs. These displaced-persons measures of the 1940s and 1950s had the effect of building a refugee resettlement industry around the federal funds appropriated for this purpose.[34]

Mexican Bracero and Western Hemisphere Labor Programs

Throughout the 1920s, an estimated 500,000 Mexicans crossed the border into the United States to work in the expanding irrigation-driven agricultural economies from Texas to California as well as the industries of the Midwest. Mobilization for World War II, especially the draft, produced a domestic agricultural labor shortage, particularly in the Southwest, as well as an industrial labor shortage. In February 1944, Congress passed legislation allowing the importation of temporary agricultural and industrial laborers from throughout the Western Hemisphere for employment in agriculture and industries essential to the war efforts. Agreements were subsequently made with British Honduras, Jamaica, Barbados, and the British West Indies to supply workers throughout the war.[35]

After World War II, southwestern growers told Congress that there remained a dearth of American labor to perform seasonal farm labor at cheap wages. In October 1949, Congress enacted the Agricultural Act of 1949, which codified prior laws and provisions for temporary agriculture workers and formally established the Mexican Bracero Program as well as permitted the legal immigration of temporary agricultural workers from throughout the Western Hemisphere.[36]

LIBRARY SERVICES WITH MINORITIES

Andrew Carnegie and the Development of Public Libraries

By 1890, only 7 of America's 16 largest cities had municipally supported central libraries. The philanthropy of Andrew Carnegie, a Scottish immigrant, would soon increase that number. Carnegie's gifts accounted for more than 1,400 library buildings. This building boom spurred many communities that had avoided applying to Carnegie initially to provide libraries on their own at a later date. Libraries increased in the last decades of the nineteenth century, but major growth continued after the Carnegie period. While there was regional variation as to number and quality of libraries, no state was without public library service by the 1920s. By 1926 there were 5,954 public libraries serving 57 percent of the American population. By the mid-1930s, there were 6,235 libraries serving 63 percent of the population.[37]

Beginnings of Library Service with Immigrants

Following the lead of the Boston Public Library, public libraries in large cities established branch libraries in the 1880s and 1890s. Branch libraries were the result of the spread of urban areas, particularly as housing patterns became differentiated along economic and ethnic lines. Branch libraries were established to take some of the pressure for providing popular materials off the main or central headquarters library; to make library services available in sections whose inhabitants were not heavy users of the central library; to place library services closer to residents, who could not afford public transportation to the central library; and to provide services to special population groups, notably non-English-speaking immigrants, but also, to a lesser extent in the North, African Americans.

Public libraries also experimented with other patterns of distribution of materials. Home libraries, which were small, personalized collections selected for individuals, clubs, and societies with limited geographical access to libraries, were distributed. Delivery stations or deposit collections were placed in factories, department stores, and other business establishments. Traveling libraries, modeled after the well-developed systems operated by state library commissions in the scarcely populated areas of the Midwest as early as 1902, were adapted to serve the needs of fluid urban immigrant communities.

Throughout the last decades of the nineteenth century and into the early twentieth century, public libraries amassed foreign-language collections that reflected the particular needs of the ethnic and national groups represented in their respective communities. Libraries compiled and published statistics on acquisitions, cataloging, circulation, and other aspects of foreign-language collection use and maintenance.

Although foreign-language books were imported directly from Europe, more often they were acquired through vendors and dealers in the major centers of domestic and international trade. Acquisitions librarians in large urban public libraries often went on buying trips abroad to purchase books not only for their own respective libraries, but also in cooperation with other public libraries collecting in the same languages, and to familiarize themselves with the cultural and educational opportunities as well as the book trades of the homelands of their immigrant patrons.[38]

ALA Committee on Work with the Foreign Born Established in 1918

When World War I began in Europe, Americanization or assimilation activities in public libraries were intensified in response to reports that one-quarter of the entire male population old enough to vote had been born abroad and fewer than half of them had become citizens. Armed forces personnel responsible for training foreign-born citizens for participation in American military units had discovered that many immigrant citizens could neither speak nor understand English well enough to respond to instructions or orders.

In 1918, the ALA established the Committee on Work with the Foreign Born (CWFB) to address the needs of immigrants for library services to help them learn to speak English and to prepare them for citizenship. Early leaders included John Foster Carr, the first chair, a publisher of immigrant guides; Eleanor (Edwards) Ledbetter, Broadway Branch librarian of the Cleveland Public Library; and Jane Maud Campbell, first supervisor of work with the foreign born of the Massachusetts Free Public Library Commission.

The ALA CWFB was from the very beginning a clearinghouse for Americanization information. Through correspondence, publications, and their personal examples, committee members lent advice on the selection and acquisition of foreign-language books and on publicizing the library's resources for the immigrant community.[39]

Americanization Movement and Public Libraries After World War I

After World War I, librarians began the laborious process of replenishing their foreign-language collections, which had suffered due to wartime interruptions of the international book trade, wear and tear on the few titles available, and, in some cases, removal and destruction of censored titles. Increasingly, there was a demand for books in both foreign languages and easy English about the history, customs, laws, industry, economics, agriculture, and customs of the United States. The availability of books in all the foreign languages spoken by the immigrant communities was limited.

The Americanization of the immigrant remained a patriotic duty as it had been during World War I, absorbing the energies of thousands of libraries, schools, churches, fraternal orders, patriotic societies, and civic and business organizations. The Americanization movement reached its height around 1921, when more than 30 states and hundreds of cities had adopted Americanization measures. Some of this legislation simply provided for the establishment of night classes in the public schools where immigrants could study English and civics. Other measures were more punitive, including banning the use of foreign languages in public settings or prohibiting immigrants, who had not been naturalized, from holding particular jobs.[40]

Adult Education Movement in Public Libraries

Throughout the 1920s, librarians began to view the Americanization process increasingly as an integral part of the newly identified adult education movement, which was attuned not only to the needs of illiterate foreign-born immigrants but also to the needs of illiterate American-born adults, including African Americans and whites from the Appalachians and rural South. The once distinctly separate goals of American public libraries—to educate the general populace and to Americanize immigrants—were merging. Many public libraries saw as their collective mission to build a literate citizenry composed of both foreign- and native-born Americans who were imbued with a spirit of tolerance and internationalism.

The ALA's study on adult education activities in American public libraries and its survey of American public libraries, both funded and supported by the Carnegie Corporation, documented a wide array of library resources and services for the Americanization of immigrants but also the beginnings of adult education for illiterate whites and blacks. In July 1924, the ALA, with funding from the Carnegie Corporation, appointed the Commission on the Library and Adult Education that was composed of seven librarians representing public, school, and academic libraries. The commission's 1926 report, *Libraries and Adult Education,* described the nature and extent of library educational work with adult immigrants and concluded that there was no distinct difference between adult education and adult immigrant education. Adult education and democratization had replaced Americanization as the goals of the public library toward adult citizens and immigrants alike.

In 1927, based on the responses of approximately 1,200 American public libraries, the 4-volume *Survey of Libraries in the United States* presented a detailed summary of general library resources and services offered in libraries throughout the nation, as well as specific resources and services offered for immigrant clienteles. The section of the survey directly related to public library work with immigrants was based on the responses received from fewer than 40 libraries.

The section of book selection included statistics of the book stock of 28 public libraries in 33 foreign languages. The 28 cities represented all of the major census divisions of the country but primarily cities in the Northeast and Midwest. The 33 languages presented, with the exception of extremely limited Japanese holdings in public libraries in Los Angeles and Portland (OR), could all be classified as Indo-European. Among the most progressive programs in 1927 included those in Cleveland, Detroit, Gary (IN), Grand Rapids (MI), Indianapolis, Minneapolis, New Bedford (MA), New York, and St. Louis.

Four years later in 1931, using the statistics in the 1927 ALA study, William Madison Randall, a professor at the Graduate Library School of the University of Chicago, discovered that the ratio of foreign-language books provided by public libraries to the foreign-born population was consistently lower than the ratio of English-language books provided by public libraries to the native-born population.[41]

Beginnings of Library Service with African Americans

In the South, no public library service was available to blacks prior to the Civil War. In the decade 1900 to 1910, a number of southern public libraries extended service to blacks, typically through restricted privileges at the main library or by establishing separate facilities. Negro libraries were provided in Charlotte, Galveston, Houston, Louisville, Memphis, and Savannah. Segregation in library facilities was in keeping with the separate but equal doctrine established in 1896 by the U.S. Supreme Court in *Plessy v. Ferguson*. The majority of southern blacks lacked access to any library service in the years leading up to World War I.

The 1920s were a period of general library development in the South as elsewhere in the country, and some southern states and regional library associations included service to blacks in their programs of expansion. In 1922, the Work with Negroes Round Table was established with the ALA. While it survived only two years and had little lasting impact, the Round Table generated a survey of public libraries concerning service to blacks. Replies from 98 libraries revealed a general lack of interest. Only one of the libraries employed a black librarian, and black representation on library boards was found to be token at best, even in the North.

Two other notable developments of the 1920s were the active role played by the Harlem branch of the New York Public Library in the Harlem Renaissance and the founding in 1925 of the Hampton Institute Library School in Virginia, the first school for blacks to award degrees in library science. During the Great Depression of the 1930s, President Franklin Delano Roosevelt's Works Progress Administration brought library service to thousands of African Americans for the first time. While such efforts often had the effect of stimulating interest in and the desire for libraries in previously unserved communities, they were inadequate in themselves to compensate for decades of neglect.[42]

At the 1936 ALA annual conference in Richmond, Virginia, the segregation laws were so strict that black librarians could not sit with friends in restaurants, meeting rooms, or any other public places. They could not attend many of the section or roundtable meetings, particularly those where meals were being served. Special living accommodations had been provided for black members on previous occasions, but their attendance at meetings had never before been restricted. Letters of protest led the ALA Council to adopt a policy, which became official on December 28, 1937, that in all facilities assigned to the ALA for use in connection with its conference or otherwise under its control, all members shall be admitted upon terms of full equality.

In 1938, only 99 of 744 library service units in the 13 southern states (excluding those of the WPA) provided service to blacks. By the early 1940s the number of libraries providing such service had increased to 121, but 75 percent of southern African Americans still lacked any public library service. Eliza Atkins Gleason, the first African American to receive a doctorate degree in librarianship, suggested that the library needs of blacks might be more satisfactorily met, especially in the South, through contractual arrangements with black college libraries rather than by appeal to white-controlled public libraries.

Southern librarians, bound by the Jim Crow laws of their states, requested the ALA Council to reconsider the new policy. A special Committee on Racial Discrimination was named to study the issue, with Ernestine Rose, librarian of the 135th Street Branch of the New York Public Library, as chair. In May 1940, the committee made its report at the ALA annual conference in Cincinnati. The committee stood behind the 1937 policy and ruled that ALA officials were directed to exert every reasonable effort to implement it. The ALA Council accepted the committee's report, but few ALA leaders spoke out against segregation in libraries.

In 1941, Eliza Atkins Gleason's study of public library service to African Americans showed that only four states offered integrated services to black and white users. As a result of such discrimination, African Americans in the South formed their own state associations and professional groups. The North Carolina Negro Library Association became the first black library association admitted as an ALA chapter in 1943.

In 1948, Emily Miller Danton conducted a survey that revealed that while segregation was the standard practice, many librarians, who were required to enforce segregation laws in their libraries, had doubts about the value of doing so. Danton documented that as late as fiscal year 1947, 17 states, Alabama, Arkansas, Delaware, Florida, Georgia, Kentucky, Louisiana, Maryland, Mississippi, Missouri, North Carolina, Oklahoma, South Carolina, Tennessee, Texas, Virginia, and West Virginia, as well as the District of Columbia, had laws that segregated blacks and whites in all public facilities, including schools and libraries. Only 12 states had laws banning segregation.[43]

Library Service with Interned Japanese in World War II

The Publicity Committee of the ALA Section for Library Work with Children sponsored a symposium that addressed the issue of library service to Japanese Americans on the Pacific Coast during wartime. Zada Taylor, children's librarian of the Los Angeles Public Library, shared her experiences in Los Angeles as well as responses from children's librarians in Fresno, Pasadena, San Diego, and San Francisco. Taylor also shared reactions from Japanese American students, American citizens by right of being born in the United States, about their evacuations to and experiences at the Manzanar internment camp in eastern California near Death Valley. Responses from the children's librarians ranged from sympathy for the internees and questioning the need for such drastic measures, to total agreement with the decision to isolate the Japanese immigrant community for the sake of its and national security.[44]

The treatment of the Japanese was a matter of concern mainly in California and in the Midwest where the internment camps were located. Clara Estelle Breed, librarian at the San Diego Public Library, and Anne Carroll Moore, newly retired children's librarian from the New York Public Library who was in California at the time teaching children's librarianship courses at the University of California at Berkeley, wrote about the situation for *Library Journal* and *Horn Book*, respectively.[45]

Library of Congress and Acquisition of Foreign-Language Materials

In early 1943, the Library of Congress established the Cooperative Acquisitions Project for Wartime Publications to set up mechanisms for the acquisition of publications from Portugal, Spain, Italy, France, and Algeria. In 1948, the Farmington Plan, established by former Librarian of Congress, Archibald MacLeish, was the largest acquisitions program ever implemented. Although its original focus was collecting publications from Europe, it added Mexico from 1948 onward, and three other Latin American countries soon thereafter.[46]

Americanization Efforts Subsumed by the Adult Education Movement

After World War II, the ALA Committee on Work with the Foreign Born began to address the needs of Filipino and Mexican immigrants as well as European refugees and displaced persons. A fundamental transformation had occurred. The movement to Americanize the immigrant community, which had been subsumed initially by the adult education movement, was overshadowed by the movement to empower citizens and aliens alike to become full participants in the dynamics of a pluralistic society.

The ALA CWFB had witnessed these changes and tried to adapt to them. As early as 1928, there had been a move to upgrade from committee to section status within the ALA, but it was deferred while the ALA executive staff considered, but never decided upon, the feasibility of creating at ALA headquarters a department for work with the foreign born. By 1935, ALA CWFB members began to question the appropriateness of the phrase "work with the foreign born," since the majority of their work was for the benefit of American-born children of foreign descent and very rarely for the foreign born themselves. Consequently, there was a second call to upgrade from committee to section status and to consider a name change to the ALA Section for Interracial Service, although neither came to pass.

The fact that the ALA CWFB met jointly with the ALA Adult Education Round Table in 1941 was a further indication of the relatedness and overlapping of purpose of the organizations. In 1945, there was serious consideration given to a change in name to the ALA Committee on Intercultural Relations in the United States. Three years later in 1948, the ALA CWFB disbanded. It was succeeded in 1949 by the ALA Committee on Intercultural Action. Much of the enthusiasm for library service to immigrants specifically was absorbed in the provision of literary services for minorities generally. As early as 1946, the Adult Education Section was established within the ALA Public Library Division.[47]

The 1950s witnessed the further restriction of immigration from Asia and Africa, the integration of libraries and other public service institutions to serve African Americans, and the beginnings of public library services with American Indians.

NOTES

1. Otis L. Graham Jr., *Unguarded Gates: A History of America's Immigration Crisis* (Lanham, MD: Rowman & Littlefield Publishers, 2004), 6, 9, 15, 17.

2. Michael LeMay and Elliott Robert Barkan, eds., *U.S. Immigration and Naturalization Laws and Issues: A Documentary History* (Westport, CT: Greenwood Press, 1999), 49–56, 72–76, 88–89; U.S. Immigration and Naturalization Service, "Appendix 1: Immigration and Naturalization Legislation," in *Statistical Yearbook of the Immigration and Naturalization Service, 1997* (Washington, DC: U.S. G.P.O., 1999), A.1–3 ; Maldwyn Allen Jones, *American Immigration*, 2nd ed. (Chicago: University of Chicago Press, 1992), 175, 213–14, 226, 231; Sucheng Chan, "Chinese," in *Dictionary of American Immigration History*, ed. Francesco Cordasco (Metuchen, NJ: Scarecrow Press, 1990), 125–26; Robert M. Jiobu, *Ethnicity and Assimilation* (Albany: State University New York Press, 1988), 32–40; Marcia J. Nauratil, *Public Libraries and Nontraditional Clienteles: The Politics of Special Services* (Westport, CT: Greenwood Press, 1985); Patricia Beilke and Frank J. Sciara, *Selecting Materials for and about Hispanic and East Asian Children and Young People* (Hamden, CT: Library Professional Publications, 1986), 64–67; Rudolf J. Vecoli, "Immigration," in *Oxford Companion to United States History*, ed. Paul S. Boyer and Melvyn Dubofsky (New York: Oxford University Press, 2001), 361–62; William S. Bernard, "Immigration: History of U.S. Policy," in *Harvard Encyclopedia of American Ethnic Groups*, ed. Stephan Thernstrom, Ann Orlov, and Oscar Handlin (Cambridge: Belknap Press of Harvard University Press, 1980), 490; Reed Ueda, "Naturalization and Citizenship," 740; Graham, *Unguarded Gates,* 11.

3. Harlow G. Unger, ed., "American Indian," in *Encyclopedia of American Education,* 2nd ed. (New York: Facts on File, c2001, 1996), 64–67; Nauratil, *Public Libraries and Nontraditional Clienteles,* 102–4, 121–22.

4. M.A. Jones, *American Immigration,* 97–98; Francesco Cordasco, "Canada, Immigration Policy and the American Farmer," in *Dictionary of American Immigration History,* 103; Vecoli, "Immigration," 362.

5. U.S. Immigration and Naturalization Service, "Appendix 1: Immigration and Naturalization Legislation," A.1–3; LeMay and Barkan, *U.S. Immigration and Naturalization Laws and Issues,* 56–57, 59–64; M.A. Jones, *American Immigration,* 163.

6. LeMay and Barkan, *U.S. Immigration and Naturalization Laws and Issues,* 66–70; M.A. Jones, *American Immigration,* 225; David M. Reimers, "Immigration Legislation," in *Dictionary of American Immigration History,* 384; Graham, *Unguarded Gates,* 16.

7. LeMay and Barkan, *U.S. Immigration and Naturalization Laws and Issues,* 76–79; Charlene Cain, "Public Library Service to Minorities," in *Adult Services: An Enduring Focus for Public Libraries,* ed. Kathleen M. Heim and Danny P. Wallace (Chicago: ALA, 1990), 215; Nauratil, *Public Libraries and Nontraditional*

Clienteles, 110; Thomas C. Holt, "Afro-Americans," in *Harvard Encyclopedia of American Ethnic Groups,* 13; Graham, *Unguarded Gates,* 16, 19.

8. LeMay and Barkan, *U.S. Immigration and Naturalization Laws and Issues,* 79–84; Alton Hornsby, *Chronology of African–American History: Significant Events and People from 1619 to the Present* (Detroit: Gale Research, 1991), xxxii–xxxiv; Ueda, "Naturalization and Citizenship," 741.

9. LeMay and Barkan, *U.S. Immigration and Naturalization Laws and Issues,* 89–93; M.A. Jones, *American Immigration,* 222–25; Graham, *Unguarded Gates,* 41–42.

10. U.S. Immigration and Naturalization Service, "Appendix 1: Immigration and Naturalization Legislation," A.1–4; LeMay and Barkan, *U.S. Immigration and Naturalization Laws and Issues,* 93–97; Ueda, "Naturalization and Citizenship," 740.

11. U.S. Immigration and Naturalization Service, "Appendix 1: Immigration and Naturalization Legislation," A.1–4, A.1–5; LeMay and Barkan, *U.S. Immigration and Naturalization Laws and Issues,* 97–101, 103–6; M.A. Jones, *American Immigration,* 152–57, 227; David Nelson Alloway, "Gentlemen's [i.e., Gentleman's] Agreement," in *Dictionary of American Immigration History,* 240; Beilke and Sciara, *Selecting Materials for and about Hispanic and East Asian Children and Young People,* 67–71; Jiobu, *Ethnicity and Assimilation,* 41–49; Yuji Ichioka, "Recent Japanese Scholarship on the Origins and Causes of Japanese Immigration," *Immigration History Newsletter* 15 (Nov. 1983): 2–7; Nauratil, *Public Libraries and Nontraditional Clienteles,* 104; Graham, *Unguarded Gates,* 40.

12. U.S. Immigration and Naturalization Service, "Appendix 1: Immigration and Naturalization Legislation," A.1–5; LeMay and Barkan, *U.S. Immigration and Naturalization Laws and Issues,* 106–12; M.A. Jones, *American Immigration,* 231, 240; Kitty Calavita, "Immigrants and Labor," in *Dictionary of American Immigration History,* 362–63; E. Willard Miller and Ruby M. Miller, *United States Immigration: A Reference Handbook* (Santa Barbara, CA: ABC-CLIO, 1996), 90–91; Bernard, "Immigration: History of U.S. Policy," 492; Graham, *Unguarded Gates,* 42.

13. M.A. Jones, *American Immigration,* 233–34; John F. McClymer, "Americanization Movement," in *Dictionary of American Immigration History,* 23–28; Nicholas V. Montalto, "International Institute Movement," in *Dictionary of American Immigration History,* 408–12; Plummer Alston Jones Jr., *Immigrants, Libraries, and the American Experience* (Westport, CT: Greenwood Press, 1999), 10–12; Plummer Alston Jones Jr., "The ALA Committee on Work with the Foreign Born and the Movement to Americanize the Immigrant," in *Libraries to the People: Histories of Outreach,* ed. Robert S. Freeman and David M. Hovde, with a foreword by Kathleen de la Pena McCook (Jefferson, NC: McFarland, 2003), 97–98; Unger, "Americanization," 70; Cheryl Metoyer-Duran, *Gatekeepers in Ethnolinguistic Communities* (Norwood, NJ: Ablex Publishing, 1993), 2–3; Deanna B. Marcum and Elizabeth W. Stone, "Literacy: The Library Legacy," *American Libraries* 22

(Mar. 1991): 202–5; Ruth Jacobs Wertheimer and Kathleen M. Foy, "Children of Immigrants and Multiethnic Heritage: Australia, Canada, the United Kingdom, and the United States," *Library Trends* 29 (Fall 1980): 348–49; Donnarae MacCann, "Libraries for Immigrants and 'Minorities': A Study in Contrasts," in *Social Responsibility in Librarianship: Essays on Equality,* ed. Donnarae MacCann (Jefferson, NC: McFarland, 1989), 97–116; Philip Gleason, "American Identity and Americanization," in *Harvard Encyclopedia of American Ethnic Groups,* 39–47; Ueda, "Naturalization and Citizenship," 743–45.

14. LeMay and Barkan, *U.S. Immigration and Naturalization Laws and Issues,* 112–15; Beilke and Sciara, *Selecting Materials for and about Hispanic and East Asian Children and Young People,* 54, 57.

15. LeMay and Barkan, *U.S. Immigration and Naturalization Laws and Issues,* 116–21; Marion T. Bennett, *American Immigration Policies: A History* (Washington, DC: Public Affairs Press, 1963), 76–79; Nauratil, *Public Libraries and Nontraditional Clienteles,* 107.

16. LeMay and Barkan, *U.S. Immigration and Naturalization Laws and Issues,* 127; M. A. Jones, *American Immigration,* 234–35.

17. Gleason, "American Identity and Americanization," 42–43.

18. Unger, "American Indian," 64–67; Nauratil, *Public Libraries and Nontraditional Clienteles,* 102–4, 121–22.

19. U.S. Immigration and Naturalization Service, "Appendix 1: Immigration and Naturalization Legislation," A.1–5, A.1–6; LeMay and Barkan, *U.S. Immigration and Naturalization Laws and Issues,* 133–35; M. A. Jones, *American Immigration,* 237–41, 244–47; Bernard, "Immigration: History of U.S. Policy," 492–93; Graham, *Unguarded Gates,* 44, 46–47, 57, 60.

20. LeMay and Barkan, *U.S. Immigration and Naturalization Laws and Issues,* 136–40; Chan, "Japanese," in *Dictionary of American Immigration History,* 439; Raymond B. Williams, "Asian Indians," in *Dictionary of American Immigration History,* 45; Ueda, "Naturalization and Citizenship," 741.

21. U.S. Immigration and Naturalization Service, "Appendix 1: Immigration and Naturalization Legislation," A.1–6, A.1–7; LeMay and Barkan, *U.S. Immigration and Naturalization Laws and Issues,* 144–51; M. A. Jones, *American Immigration,* 237, 249; Miller and Miller, *United States Immigration: A Reference Handbook,* 91–92; Bernard, "Immigration: History of U.S. Policy," 493.

22. LeMay and Barkan, *U.S. Immigration and Naturalization Laws and Issues,* 151; Unger, "American Indian," 67; Theodore W. Taylor, *The Bureau of Indian Affairs,* foreword by Phillip Martin (Boulder, CO: Westview Press, 1984), 19–20; Delores J. Huff, *To Live Heroically: Institutional Racism and American Indian Education* (Albany: State University of New York, 1997), 5; Ueda, "Naturalization and Citizenship," 743.

23. Plummer Alston Jones Jr., *Immigrants, Libraries, and the American Experience* (Westport, CT: Greenwood Press, 1999), 23–25; Wertheimer and Foy, "Children of Immigrants and Multiethnic Heritage: Australia, Canada, the United

Kingdom, and the United States," 339, 348–49; Arthur P. Young, "Aftermath of a Crusade: World War I and the Enlarged Program of the American Library Association," *Library Quarterly* 50 (Apr. 1980): 191–207; Nauratil, *Public Libraries and Nontraditional Clienteles,* 107.

24. U.S. Immigration and Naturalization Service, "Appendix 1: Immigration and Naturalization Legislation," A.1–7; LeMay and Barkan, *U.S. Immigration and Naturalization Laws and Issues,* 151–52; Robert A. Seal, "Mexican and U.S. Library Relations," in *Advances in Librarianship,* ed. Irene Godden, vol. 20 (New York: Academic Press, 1996), 98–99; Theresa Salazar and Maria Segura Hoopes, "U.S./Mexican Borderlands Acquisition: Defining and Pursuing the Materials," in *Multicultural Acquisitions,* ed. Karen Parrish and Bill Katz (New York: Haworth Press, 1993), 233–34; David M. Reimers, "Recent Immigration Policy: An Analysis," in *The Gateway: U.S. Immigration Issues and Policies,* ed. Barry R. Chiswick (Washington, DC: American Enterprise Institute for Public Policy Research, 1982), 13.

25. U.S. Immigration and Naturalization Service, "Appendix 1: Immigration and Naturalization Legislation," A.1–7; LeMay and Barkan, *U.S. Immigration and Naturalization Laws and Issues,* 163–65; Graham, *Unguarded Gates,* 58, 73.

26. LeMay and Barkan, *U.S. Immigration and Naturalization Laws and Issues,* 170–73.

27. U.S. Immigration and Naturalization Service, "Appendix 1: Immigration and Naturalization Legislation," A.1–8; LeMay and Barkan, *U.S. Immigration and Naturalization Laws and Issues,* 175–84; Ueda, "Naturalization and Citizenship," 745–46; Graham, *Unguarded Gates,* 58.

28. M.A. Jones, *American Immigration,* 207–11; Ueda, "Naturalization and Citizenship," 745–46.

29. LeMay and Barkan, *U.S. Immigration and Naturalization Laws and Issues,* 184–87, 191–96; Beilke and Sciara, *Selecting Materials for and about Hispanic and East Asian Children and Young People,* 69–70; David Nelson Alloway, "Relocation Centers," in *Dictionary of American Immigration History,* 621–22.

30. U.S. Immigration and Naturalization Service, "Appendix 1: Immigration and Naturalization Legislation," A.1–9; LeMay and Barkan, *U.S. Immigration and Naturalization Laws and Issues,* 196–97; David Nelson Alloway, "Act to Repeal the Chinese Exclusion Acts, to Establish Quotas, and for Other Purposes," in *Dictionary of American Immigration History,* 5; Jiobu, *Ethnicity and Assimilation,* 37; Edward Prince Hutchinson, *Legislative History of American Immigration Policy, 1798–1965* (Philadelphia: Published for the Balch Institute for Ethnic Studies, by the University of Pennsylvania Press, 1981), 264–65; Graham, *Unguarded Gates,* 72, 75, 77–78.

31. U.S. Immigration and Naturalization Service, "Appendix 1: Immigration and Naturalization Legislation," A.1–9; LeMay and Barkan, *U.S. Immigration and Naturalization Laws and Issues,* 198–203.

32. U.S. Immigration and Naturalization Service, "Appendix 1: Immigration and Naturalization Legislation," A.1–9; LeMay and Barkan, *U.S. Immigration and Naturalization Laws and Issues,* 206–7; M.A. Jones, *American Immigration,* 244.

33. U.S. Immigration and Naturalization Service, "Appendix 1: Immigration and Naturalization Legislation," A.1–10; M.A. Jones, *American Immigration,* 247–48; Williams, "Asian Indians," 45; Chan, "Filipinos," in *Dictionary of American Immigration History,* 218–19; R.N. Sharma, "Library Services to Indian-Americans in the United States," *MultiCultural Review* 3 (Mar. 1994): 44–51; Gail Singleton Taylor, Jvotsna Sreenivasan, and Arun N. Toke, "Children's Books on India and the Indian-American Experience," *MultiCultural Review* 7 (Dec. 1998): 39–50; Frank Alan Bruno and Patricia F. Beilke, "Filipinos and Filipino Americans: Helping K-8 School Librarians and Educators Understand Their History, Culture, and Literature," *MultiCultural Review* 9 (June 2000): 30–37, 53–54; Hornsby, *Chronology of African–American History),* xxxiv; Hutchinson, *Legislative History of American Immigration Policy, 1798–1965,* 274–75; Nauratil, *Public Libraries and Nontraditional Clienteles,* 107; Beilke and Sciara, *Selecting Materials for and about Hispanic and East Asian Children and Young People,* 71–74; Graham, *Unguarded Gates,* 77–78.

34. LeMay and Barkan, *U.S. Immigration and Naturalization Laws and Issues,* 170–71; U.S. Immigration and Naturalization Service, "Appendix 1: Immigration and Naturalization Legislation," A.1–10; M.A. Jones, *American Immigration,* 244–45; David Nelson Alloway, "Displaced Persons Act of 1948," in *Dictionary of American Immigration History,"* 175–76; Miller and Miller, *United States Immigration: A Reference Handbook,* 109–10; Robert A. Divine, *American Immigration Policy, 1924–1952* (New Haven: Yale University Press, 1957), 110–45; Hutchinson, *Legislative History of American Immigration Policy, 1798–1965,* 280–82, 291–92; Reimers, "Recent Immigration Policy: An Analysis," 14–24; Bernard, "Immigration: History of U.S. Policy," 494; Graham, *Unguarded Gates,* 74–75.

35. U.S. Immigration and Naturalization Service, "Appendix 1: Immigration and Naturalization Legislation," A.1–9; LeMay and Barkan, *U.S. Immigration and Naturalization Laws and Issues,* 197–98; M.A. Jones, *American Immigration,* 259–61; Graham, *Unguarded Gates,* 72, 75, 77–78.

36. LeMay and Barkan, *U.S. Immigration and Naturalization Laws and Issues,* 116–21, 216–18; M.A. Jones, *American Immigration,* 250, 264; Francesco Cordasco, "Bracero Program," in *Dictionary of American Immigration History,* 89–92; Bennett, *American Immigration Policies,* 80; Robert P. Haro, *Developing Library and Information Services for Americans of Hispanic Origin* (Metuchen, NJ: Scarecrow Press, 1981), 4–8; Walter Fogel, "Twentieth-Century Migration to the United States," in *The Gateway: U.S. Immigration Issues and Policies,* 194–97; Beilke and Sciara, *Selecting Materials for and about Hispanic and East Asian Children and Young People,* 47–54.

37. Charles A. Seavey, "Public Libraries," in *Encyclopedia of Library History*, ed. Wayne Wiegand and Donald G. Davis Jr. (New York: Garland Publishing, 1994), 521.

38. P. A. Jones Jr., *Immigrants, Libraries, and the American Experience*, 12–21; Frank B. Sessa, "Public Libraries, International: History of the Public Library," in *Encyclopedia of Library and Information Science*, ed. Allen Kent, Harold Lancour, and Jay E. Daily, vol. 24 (New York: Marcel Dekker, 1976), 285; Seavey, "Public Libraries," 518–28.

39. P. A. Jones Jr., "The ALA Committee on Work with the Foreign Born and the Movement to Americanize the Immigrant," 96–110.

40. M. A. Jones, *American Immigration*, 233–34; McClymer, "Americanization Movement," 23–28; Montalto, "International Institute Movement," 408–12; P. A. Jones Jr., *Immigrants, Libraries, and the American Experience*, 10–12; P. A. Jones Jr., "The ALA Committee on Work with the Foreign Born and the Movement to Americanize the Immigrant," 98–100; Unger, "Americanization," 70; Metoyer-Duran, *Gatekeepers in Ethnolinguistic Communities*, 2–3; Marcum and Stone, "Literacy: The Library Legacy," 202–5; Wertheimer and Foy, "Children of Immigrants and Multiethnic Heritage: Australia, Canada, the United Kingdom, and the United States," 348–49; MacCann, "Libraries for Immigrants and 'Minorities': A Study in Contrasts," 97–116; Gleason, "American Identity and Americanization," 39–47; Ueda, "Naturalization and Citizenship," 743–45.

41. P. A. Jones Jr., *Libraries, Immigrants, and the American Experience* (Westport, CT: Greenwood Press, 1999), 105–7; Gillian D. Leonard, "Multiculturalism and Library Services," in *Multicultural Acquisitions*, 3–19; Cain, "Public Library Service to Minorities," 216–18; Kathleen M. Heim, "Adult Services: An Enduring Focus," in *Adult Services*, 12–13; Connie Van Fleet, "Lifelong Learning Theory and the Provision of Adult Services," in *Adult Services*, 169.

42. P. A. Jones Jr., *Libraries, Immigrants, and the American Experience*, 118–19; P. A. Jones Jr., "The ALA Committee on Work with the Foreign Born and the Movement to Americanize the Immigrant," 104; Nauratil, *Public Libraries and Nontraditional Clienteles*, 110–11.

43. Doris Hargrett Clack, "Segregation and the Library," in *Encyclopedia of Library and Information Science*, ed. Allen Kent, Harold Lancour, and Jay E. Daily, vol. 27 (New York: Marcel Dekker, 1979), 184–204; John C. Colson, "The United States: An Historical Critique," in *Library Services to the Disadvantaged*, ed. William Martin (Hamden, CT: Linnet Books, 1975), 68–69; Nauratil, *Public Libraries and Nontraditional Clienteles*, 112.

44. M. A. Jones, *American Immigration*, 259–62; P. A. Jones Jr., *Libraries, Immigrants, and the American Experience*, 121; Zada Taylor, "War Children on the Pacific: A Symposium Article," *Library Journal* 67 (15 June 1942): 558–62; P. A. Jones Jr., "The ALA Committee on Work with the Foreign Born and the Movement to Americanize the Immigrant," 104–5.

45. Kathy Brady, "Letters from Home: Love and Friendship in Times of War: With Books and Moral Support, a Children's Librarian [Clara Estelle Breed] Helped Young Japanese Americans Endure Internment during World War II," *American Libraries* 33 (May 2002): 73–74.

46. Robert B. Downs, "The Significance of Foreign Materials for U.S. Collections: Problems of Acquisitions," in *Acquisition of Foreign Materials for U.S. Libraries,* ed. Theodore Samore (Metuchen, NJ: Scarecrow Press, 1982), 2–11; Philip J. McNiff, "Cooperation in the Acquisition of Foreign Materials," in *Acquisition of Foreign Materials for U.S. Libraries,* 12–13.

47. P.A. Jones Jr., *Libraries, Immigrants, and the American Experience,* 118, 122; P.A. Jones Jr., "The ALA Committee on Work with the Foreign Born and the Movement to Americanize the Immigrant," 105–6; Marcum and Stone, "Literacy: The Library Legacy," 202–5; Stephen Stern, "Ethnic Libraries and Librarianship in the United States: Models and Prospects," in *Advances in Librarianship,* ed. Irene P. Godden, vol. 15 (New York: Academic Press, 1991), 83–86; Heim, "Adult Services: An Enduring Focus," 12–13.

Chapter 2

PUBLIC LIBRARIES AND THE BEGINNING OF FEDERAL FUNDING IN THE 1950s

During the decade of the 1950s, the population of the United States was approximately 150 million, with approximately 90 percent white and 10 percent black. Statistics on Native American peoples, Asians and Pacific Islanders, and residents of Hispanic origins were not collected by the U.S. government. The term Hispanic was used to characterize Spanish-speaking persons of different racial origins.[1]

LEGAL AND JUDICIAL DECISIONS AFFECTING MINORITIES

Postwar World War II Migration from Rural to Urban Areas

Between 1950 and 1960, there were massive movements from rural and small town areas to metropolitan areas, from core cities to suburbs, and from the South and Midwest to Florida, the Southwest, and the Pacific Coast. The net migration out of the Dakotas, Virginia, West Virginia, the Carolinas, Georgia, Tennessee, Kentucky, Alabama, Mississippi, Arkansas, Louisiana, Oklahoma, Texas, Montana, Wyoming, New Mexico, Alaska, and Hawaii was more than 1.5 million, making a significant impact on schools, libraries, and similar public services in areas where the migrants eventually settled.

Labor shortages and government-subsidized training programs during World War II had provided African Americans and immigrants, and to a lesser extent American Indians, with an entrée to a range of semiskilled industrial jobs. A considerable part of the migration consisted of unskilled and semiliterate agricultural laborers, mostly African American, Puerto Rican, or Mexican, who had been displaced by the introduction of new farm machinery and chemical weedkillers and pesticides. Hundreds of thousands were driven from the farms to become ill-adapted residents of the ghettos in large northern core cities, where they were set apart by race and ethnicity.[2]

By the mid-1950s, due primarily to a shift in industrial growth from the central city to the suburbs, there was a dearth of well-paid jobs in urban areas. For African Americans especially, the reduction of employment opportunities and the consignment of minority groups to poverty and ghettoization, coupled with the rising expectations engendered by the civil rights movement, led to violent protest and increased dependence on illegal activities for income.[3]

The admission of refugees, displaced persons, war brides and husbands, and fiancé(e)s under special legislative acts, as well as the admission of millions of nonquota immigrants or immigrants counted outside the established legal limits from the Western Hemisphere, gradually eroded the impact of the Immigration Act of 1924. By 1950, it was clear that the original purpose of the 1924 act—to limit immigration into the United States to persons from countries other than those of northern and western Europe—had not been successful. In the aftermath of Hitler's atrocities toward Jews, Gypsies, and other religious and political minorities in Europe during World War II, the scientific and political communities of the United States no longer argued the superiority or inferiority of any particular national, ethnic, or racial group.[4]

Many American Indians migrated to the cities during and after World War II in response to increased employment opportunities. Economists have agreed that urban Indians were better off in nearly every way than the majority who remained on reservations. Urban Indians are better educated, have significantly lower unemployment wages, two-thirds higher family income, and fewer dependent children than residents of reservations. Indians on reservations suffer the worst economic deprivation of any American minority. The physical and social conditions of reservation life have led to a high incidence of self-destructive behavior among American Indians, including suicide, violent crime, and alcoholism.[5]

Guamanians Become U.S. Citizens

In August 1950, Congress declared Guamanians to be citizens of the United States and eliminated immigration restrictions on them. Guam had been ceded to the United States by Spain at the end of the Spanish-American War of 1898. That same month, on August 19, 1950, Congress passed a law making spouses and minor children of alien members of the American armed forces, regardless of race or ethnicity, eligible for immigration and nonquota status, if their marriages occurred before March 19, 1952.[6]

In September 1950, Congress passed the Internal Security Act to strengthen national internal security by increasing the grounds for exclusion and deportation of alleged alien subversives and to add communists to the classes of persons considered to be risks to internal security. The act required all resident aliens to report to the Immigration and Naturalization Service (INS) their addresses annually within 10 days of the first day of January and gave the U.S. Attorney General authority to supervise deportable aliens pending their deportation.[7]

Mexican Bracero Program

In July 1951, Congress further amended the Agricultural Act of 1949, which served as the basic framework under which the Mexican Bracero Program would operate until 1962. The need of Southwestern farmers for cheap Mexican labor was satisfied by the fact that Mexicans, as citizens of the Western Hemisphere, were eligible for immigration into the United States and exempt from legally established quotas of the National Origins Act of 1924.

The 1951 law stipulated that the U.S. government would establish and operate reception centers at or near the Mexican border; provide transportation, subsistence, and medical care from the Mexican recruiting centers to the U.S. reception centers; and guarantee the compliance of employers relating to transportation and wages. U.S. employers were required to pay the prevailing wages in the area, guarantee the workers employment for three-fourths of the contract period, and provide workers with free housing and adequate meals at a reasonable cost.[8]

McCarran-Walter Act of 1952

Special problems of dealing with refugees, the human hardship caused by the inflexibility of the quota system established by the Immigration Act of 1924, and the growing hysteria and fear of communism associated with the cold war, all pointed to the need for a major revision of U.S. immigration policy. The passage of the McCarran-Walter Act of June 1952, named for its Congressional sponsors, was later known as the Immigration and Nationality Act (INA).

The 1952 act made all races eligible for naturalization and eliminated gender discrimination with respect to immigration. By repealing the racial ban on citizenship, the act made thousands of elderly Japanese (the Issei or first generation) eligible for citizenship, most of whom had been interned in 1 of the 10 concentration camps for Japanese Americans during World War II. It introduced a system of selected immigration based on occupational needs and family unification by fixing quota preferences to skilled aliens, whose services were urgently needed in the United States, and relatives of U.S. citizens and residents.

The 1952 act revised, but did not eliminate, the national-origins quota formula. The annual quota for a geographical area was set at one-sixth of 1 percent of the number of inhabitants in the continental United States in 1920 whose ancestry or national origin was attributable to that area. All countries were allowed a minimum quota of 100, with a ceiling of 2,000 for countries in the so-called Asia-Pacific Triangle, which defined a section of the world that included the Asian continent and almost the entire Pacific Ocean. At the time the act was passed, there were 20 independent nations within this triangle, each given a special quota of 100 per year.

While in all cases quotas were charged to the country of birth, the Asia-Pacific Triangle provision stipulated that persons of half or more Asian ancestry were to be charged to that Asian country's quota. As such, a person born in Colombia of Japanese ancestry would not enter under the quota of Colombia, a Western Hemisphere country that had no quota, but as part of the much smaller quota allocated to Japan. The intent of the law was clearly directed at the hundreds of thousands of persons of Asian backgrounds living in Latin America and Canada, who would otherwise have been eligible to come in as nonquota immigrants from the Western Hemisphere.

The 1952 act limited the quota of colonies and dependent areas to approximately 100, sharply reducing immigration from the West Indies. While defenders of the bill claimed all colonies were subject to the same restriction, critics noted that West Indian blacks were most affected by the change. Previously allowed to use the unfilled portion of the large British quota, each Caribbean colony of the United Kingdom was given a quota of 100 immigrants. This policy, aimed at reducing the number of immigrants from the Caribbean to the United States, had the effect of shifting Caribbean immigration to the British industrial centers.[9]

Procedurally, the 1952 act reinforced the annual alien address-reporting system put in place by the 1950 Internal Security Act and established a central index of all resident aliens for use by U.S. security and enforcement agencies. Most significantly, the 1952 act did not impose a quota for Western Hemisphere countries. It ignored the Mexican Bracero Program that permitted the immigration of thousands of Mexicans to work as agricultural laborers in the Southwest and thus exacerbated the problem of illegal immigration. As a result, in 1955, Congress extended the program to June 30, 1959.[10]

President Truman vetoed the bill. Although he agreed that immigration laws were in need of revision and approved of the elimination of racial barriers, he opposed the continuation of the national-origins quota system, which had discriminated against the countries of southern and eastern Europe. He noted that it had been increasingly necessary to pass special legislation to admit many of these southeastern Europeans, notably those who were refugees from totalitarian regimes. He objected also to the unfair racial provision regarding quotas for the Asia-Pacific Triangle. Truman had previously objected to the provisions in the 1950 Internal Security Act that allowed the revocation of naturalization and deportation of persons suspected to be subversives, arguing that the provision gave too much power to the attorney general. Congress overrode Truman's veto by a vote of 278 to 113 in the House and 57 to 26 in the Senate.[11]

U.S. Commission on Immigration and Naturalization of 1952

Immediately following the passage of the 1952 act, President Truman appointed a special Commission on Immigration and Naturalization. In January 1953, the commission released its report, *Whom Shall We Welcome*. The commissioners concurred with President Truman that the national origins system had failed in its avowed purpose as a selection system by being arbitrary, discriminatory, and not based on facts and national needs. The commission recommended that the 1952 act be reconsidered and revised from beginning to end. Specifically, the commissioners proposed abolishing the national origins system and increasing annual immigration to 250,000 with an added annual 100,000 political-asylum seekers for three years, chosen on the basis of asylum, family reunification, and occupational or skills needs in the United States.[12]

By the time the refugee program of the Displaced Persons Acts of 1948 and 1950 terminated in June 1952, the great majority of those uprooted by World War II had been resettled. Their occupational backgrounds as either unskilled or semiskilled workers meant that ignorance of English was usually not a hindrance to immediate employment. In most cases, displaced persons from World War II met with more tolerance than the prewar refugees.

Puerto Rican Immigration

In 1952, Puerto Rico became a commonwealth, thus affording it some governmental autonomy while maintaining ties with the United States. Although there was a good deal of shuttling back and forth between Puerto Rico and New York City communities in East Harlem, South Bronx, and Brooklyn, by 1957 there were more than 550,000 Puerto Ricans living there and perhaps 175,000 more were scattered between Chicago, Philadelphia, and a number of smaller industrial centers in the Northeast. As a result of half a century of American political control over Puerto Rico, and having been exposed since birth to American food, clothes, appliances, and ideas, they were already semi-Americanized.[13]

Korean War

In January 1953, with the outbreak of the Korean War, President Truman, as one of the last acts of his presidency, issued a proclamation establishing emergency powers to control persons leaving or entering the United States. In August 1953, early in the presidency of Dwight D. Eisenhower, Congress passed the Refugee Relief Act that authorized the issuance of special nonquota visas allowing 214,000 refugees to become permanent residents of the United States during a 41-month period. The group contained large numbers of German ethnic refugees, as well as Poles, Italians, Greeks, and some Arabs and Asians. These immigrants were required to obtain U.S. citizen sponsors who would assure them of jobs and housing, unless their sponsors were close relatives.[14]

Brown v. Board of Education of Topeka, Kansas

The landmark 1954 U.S. Supreme Court decision in *Brown v. Board of Education of Topeka, Kansas* declared segregation of the races illegal and opened the door for similar lawsuits by other minority groups. The decision further forced the passage of state and federal laws banning segregation and discrimination in housing, education, work, and every other area of American life. The U.S. Supreme Court ruled that separate facilities, including schools and libraries, were no longer deemed equal. Toward the end of the 1950s, the human rights concerns addressed in the 1954 decision had broadened to embrace not only racial equality but also the rights of ethnic linguistic groups.[15]

In the summer of 1954, the INS's Operation Wetback forced the repatriation of approximately 1 million Mexicans from the United States. In addition to the 4.5 million workers who had been contracted under the provisions of the Mexican Bracero Program, there were just as many, if not more, illegal workers, or wetbacks, that had crossed the border in search of work.[16]

In November 1954, Ellis Island, the gateway to America since 1892, closed along with five other seaport processing and detention centers at Boston, Seattle, San Francisco, San Pedro, and Honolulu. Ellis Island, situated in the shadow of the Statue of Liberty, had served for 62 years as the chief immigration station and port of entry to more than 20 million immigrants.[17]

Hungarian Parolees

At the end of 1956, President Eisenhower called upon Congress to allow the immigration of some of the 200,000 Hungarian refugees of the failed Hungarian Revolution against the Soviets. Using the parole authority granted him by the 1952 act, President Eisenhower admitted approximately 38,000 Hungarians. Of these, approximately 5,000 were granted visas under the Refugee Relief Act of 1953, due to expire at the end of 1956. Another 12,000 entered as parolees, to be questioned and examined later, and the rest were admitted under the quota system.

The Hungarian refugees were airlifted to Camp Kilmer, New Jersey, where a reception center had been prepared, and from there they were dispersed throughout the country with the help of voluntary agencies, which met the cost of their resettlement and assisted them in finding sponsors, jobs, and housing. In July 1958, Congress granted permanent-resident status to Hungarian parolees who had resided in the United States for at least two years.[18]

Library Services Act (LSA) of 1956

Starting with the end of World War II, 10 years of national effort on the part of librarians, trustees, and interested citizens went into the promotion of federal legislation to fund public libraries. In 1950, Congress passed the Financial Assistance for Local Educational Agencies Affected by Federal Activities Act, which provided funds for the construction and operation of schools in areas receiving federal aid. Also in 1950, a similar Public Library Service Demonstration bill was introduced. Although the bill passed in the Senate, it was defeated in the House by a vote of 161 to 164. In 1951, lobbying for federal funding for libraries continued, and the LSA was introduced. After an uphill fight, the bill finally passed both houses of Congress and was signed into law on July 19, 1956, by President Eisenhower.[19]

Refugee-Escapee Act of 1957

In July 1957, Congress enacted legislation to permit the enlistment of aliens into the U.S. Army. Just a few months later, a series of acts was passed to ameliorate the plight of refugees already in the United States. The Refugee-Escapee Act of September 1957 addressed the problem caused by charging the admission of refugees to national quotas by removing the mortgaging of immigrant quotas imposed under the Displaced Persons Act of 1948 and subsequent acts. The 1957 act facilitated the reunification of families for spouses, children, stepchildren, illegitimate children, and adopted children. In September 1959, Congress passed legislation to provide for the entry of fiancé(e)s and relatives of alien residents and citizens of the United States.[20]

National Defense Education Act of 1958

The National Defense Education Act of 1958, which provided funds to state and local school systems for strengthening instruction in science, mathematics, and modern foreign languages, followed in the wake of the launching of the first Sputnik in 1957 by the Soviet Union. The act generated support for a broadening of the high school curriculum and the improvement of school libraries.[21]

In 1959, Alaska and Hawaii became the 49th and 50th states of the United States. Alaskan residents included significant populations of Inuits (Eskimos). Hawaii, which had been a U.S. territory from 1900 to 1959, had from 1864 onward attracted European and Asian immigrants to labor in its burgeoning sugar industry.[22]

Cuban Refugees

In the early 1950s, militant anti-Batista Cuban exiles had been active in New York and Miami, where a concentrated area of Cuban settlement had begun to take shape in the neighborhood already being called Little Havana. Beginning on New Year's morning of 1959, when General Fulgencio Batista fled the island and the revolutionary government of Fidel Castro took over the reins of Cuba, the first exiles were hundreds of Batista's close collaborators, who feared reprisals from the regime that had ousted them. Soon after, they were joined in the United States by a massive exodus that originated with Cuba's business establishment and professional class but quickly included early defectors from Castro's own ranks, as well.

Because of political circumstances, the émigrés were mostly destitute upon arrival, but many were familiar with the United States, already having often visited for business or pleasure prior to the revolution. President Eisenhower again used his parole authority to admit the Cuban refugees. Ultimately, some 800,000 Cuban refugees entered the United States. Eisenhower also used his parole authority to admit Chinese arriving from Hong Kong in the late 1950s.[23]

LIBRARY SERVICES WITH MINORITIES

Development of Public Library Systems

In the post–World War II era, the economic boom, the ready availability of inexpensive automobiles, and the development of tract-housing suburbs led to the decline of inner cities and the subsequent decline of old central libraries. In this climate, branch libraries in suburban areas often became the primary source of service for the citizens of metropolitan areas, while the central library accounted for an increasingly lower portion of usage.

Public library systems developed along two distinctive lines as part of a national trend toward larger service units, including (1) a federated system in which individual libraries retained their identity, autonomy, and governing boards, or (2) a consolidated system in which the individual libraries merged into a single administrative unit. Library systems transcended the political boundaries that normally set limits to location and administration of branches and created new political districts by encompassing several counties or otherwise separate political units within a single system.[24]

Public Library Inquiry

The ALA requested the Social Science Research Council to study and assess the public library's actual and potential contributions to American society. The resulting Public Library Inquiry was sponsored by the Carnegie Corporation, an advocate of public libraries dating back to the Carnegie library building grants in the early twentieth century. Political scientist Robert D. Leigh headed the inquiry and recruited a staff of 24 research associates and assistants from the fields of the social sciences to produce a six-volume published report and several unpublished reports based on statistical analysis of questionnaires, interviews, and field visits to a sample of 60 public libraries.

With regard to adult education, the Public Library Inquiry found that the public library had not become a major center of formally organized adult education under its own initiative. There was also the disappointing conclusion that, for many people, public libraries had little significance as sources of information. The Public Library Inquiry pointed out that even though book circulation and reading were climbing in the late 1940s, public libraries failed to serve some 75–85 percent of the population in their communities.

That being the case, libraries were encouraged to emphasize service to the few who actually used their services, rather than seek to serve all members of the community. Persuaded that they were serving the community's leadership, albeit a small segment of the community's population, librarians lived complacently with that concept until the urban turnaround of the 1960s, when the creation of African American ghettos and the white flight to the suburbs eliminated traditional clienteles. The Public Library Inquiry has no references to library work with immigrants.[25]

Puerto Ricans

A regional library system was initiated in 1952 for the New York Public Library to serve the boroughs of Staten Island, The Bronx, and Manhattan, where thousands of immigrants from across the globe, including many Puerto Ricans, had settled. The three library centers were St. George in Staten Island in 1952, Fordham in the Bronx in 1954, and Donnell Library Center in Manhattan in 1955. Each center provided extensive reference, advisory, and lending services, and bookmobile service was provided on a regularly scheduled basis in areas of The Bronx and Staten Island that were remote from a branch library. The Donnell Foreign Language Library at the Donnell Library Center developed a major circulating collection representing the literature of more than 80 languages, as well as substantial numbers of foreign reference books and periodicals.[26]

In 1952, a Senior Citizens Center was established at the Flatbush Branch of the Brooklyn Public Library (BPL), but senior citizens came from all over the borough to the daily programs. Many of them were foreign-born immigrants who, even though they had lived in this country for many years, still had difficulty in reading and writing English. In 1953, the Know Your Fellow Americans: The Puerto Ricans program was part of the BPL adult education series. More than 750 people attended the first program, which was held in the Ingersoll Branch, due to the cooperation of the leading citizens from the Puerto Rican community, intensive staff planning, and publicity in libraries, neighborhood agencies, and Spanish-language newspapers.[27]

African Americans

In 1953, Lucretia Parker conducted a study that revealed conditions were improving for African Americans, and at that time 39 cities in 11 states were offering integrated services. Another study was conducted in 1953 by the Southern Regional Education Board that revealed that 88 cities provided fully desegregated service to blacks. Eli M. Obler conducted a survey of other national professional organizations to determine the extent to which they exerted leadership against segregation. Although he found that the ALA compared favorably, he criticized the ALA for not exercising leadership in solving this national problem.[28]

Following the *Brown v. Board of Education* decision, Florence Bell's survey on services to African Americans, *Library Service in Thirteen Southern States, 1954–1962,* confirmed that integrated library service had grown in the South for the 13 states that provided it. This represented a modest improvement over the situation described in Eliza Atkins Gleason's 1941 study, which showed that only four states provided such service from main libraries, the majority of services being offered by so-called colored branches.[29]

The nascent civil rights movement in the 1950s obtained some improvements in library services with African Americans. In 1952, the Louisville Free Public Library became the first public library in the South to open its doors to blacks.[30]

Adult Education in Public Libraries

Public libraries in the 1950s were involved in providing adult education programs, including not only English and citizenship classes for adult immigrants, but also reading and literacy classes for disadvantaged white and African American adults, particularly poor Southerners who had migrated to Northern cities during the Great Depression of the 1930s. In 1954, ALA published Helen Lyman Smith's survey, *Adult Education Activities in Public Libraries*, which showed that librarians were no longer dwelling exclusively upon the foreign born in discussions of service to ethnic groups and were concerned with a wider range of adult education concerns. She documented that only 153 libraries out of a total of 1,692 offered services to the foreign born. She concluded that by the 1950s, democracy for all U.S. citizens and residents had replaced Americanization for immigrants as the societal context for public library service to adults.[31]

In 1955, the Brooklyn Public Library cooperated with the New York City Health Department to carry on a pilot program in the branches in three low-income neighborhoods that featured physicians, nurses, and nutritionists as speakers. In 1956 alone, 55 programs were held in 13 branches, with an average attendance of 35 at each program. The programs, held in a Spanish-speaking area and presented mostly in Spanish, attracted so many people that they had to be moved to a local school to accommodate the audience.

Also in 1955, the Brooklyn Public Library's Reading Improvement Program was initiated in collaboration with Brooklyn College as a free, eight-week experimental research program to improve the reading ability of adults. This program met its goals, and a manual was developed to assist librarians in carrying on the program. In 1958, the BPL received a grant from the Carnegie Corporation to continue the program.[32]

LSA Funding and Projects

The LSA, the first major federal legislation passed for the support of public libraries, was signed into law in June 1956 to provide for the extension and improvement of rural public library services in the 50 states and Puerto Rico. In August 1956, Guam was added to the list of eligible areas. The act called for state control of funds, with states being required to submit plans to the U.S. Office of Education for approval. The legislation specified $7.5 million dollars per year, but only $2 million dollars were appropriated in fiscal year 1957, $5 million in fiscal year 1958, $6 million in fiscal year 1959, and the full amount in fiscal year 1960. The LSA provided federal grants to aid states in serving the estimated 27 million rural residents without access to local public library services, and the five and a half million others to whom services were inadequate.

Many public library systems in the United States trace their origins to LSA funding. Money was made available for outreach programs to rural communities of under 10,000 inhabitants, where disadvantaged populations of poor and often illiterate African Americans and whites lived. Federal funds were channeled through state library agencies, which were also strengthened by the infusion of federal funds for planning and implementation of statewide library programs.[33]

ALA and Minorities

In 1956, the ALA Public Libraries Division's Coordinating Committee on the Revision of Public Library Standards produced *Public Library Service: A Guide to Evaluation with Minimum Standards*. These guidelines recommended that if libraries worked together, sharing their services and materials, they could meet the full needs of their users. The implication was that without joint action, libraries would not be able to meet the needs of their evolving constituencies, including immigrants, African Americans, American Indians, and other minority and ethnic groups. Although the ALA had taken an official stand against holding segregated conferences 20 years earlier, the 1956 ALA Conference at Miami Beach was considered the first completely desegregated association meeting to be held in the South.[34]

The ALA Committee on Intercultural Action, the successor of the ALA Committee on Work with the Foreign Born (1918–48), existed from fiscal year 1949 through fiscal year 1957, when its duties and responsibilities were dispersed throughout already-existing ALA divisions. Its activities were never reported. By 1957, the Adult Services Division was established as an ALA division to serve the information and recreation needs of adults, whether in the majority or the minority.[35]

American Indians

Before the 1950s, library service to American Indians consisted of bookmobiles in rural areas and access to the often irrelevant collections of local public libraries in the cities. After the passage of the Library Services Act of 1956, the State Library of New Mexico used federal funds to begin service to the Navajo and Pueblo Indian reservations in northwestern New Mexico.

Using a state-owned bookmobile that made the difficult trips along the desert trails and isolated roads of the upper Rio Grande region, the library staff stopped at villages and trading posts and left book collection deposits at 14 stations. Books supplied for the Navajos and Pueblos had to be in Spanish or English, since Navajo and Pueblo are spoken, not written, languages. In 1958, using LSA funds, the Colorado River Tribal Council of Parker, Arizona, established a library on its reservation, a national first for Native Americans.[36]

Seminar on the Acquisition of Latin American Library Materials (SALALM)

In 1959, the Latin American Cooperative Acquisitions Project (LACAP) of the Library of Congress, an undertaking involving some 40 research libraries, including the New York Public Library, was developed by a commercial library firm, Stechert-Hafner, in cooperation with the SALALM. SALALM's first meeting had been held June 14–15, 1956, at the University of Florida under the leadership of Marietta Daniels (later, Shepard) of the Organization of American States (OAS). Daniels met with a group of 26 librarians to discuss problems pertaining to the acquisition of library materials from Latin America and the Caribbean area.[37]

The 1960s witnessed the passage of civil rights, voting rights, and education and library legislation that ameliorated the plight of disadvantaged citizens. The imposition of barriers for immigrants from the Eastern Hemisphere ushered in an era of preferential treatment for immigrants from the Western Hemisphere.

NOTES

1. U.S. Census Bureau, "No. 10: Resident Population—Selected Characteristics, 1950 to 2000, and Projections, 2025 and 2050," in *Statistical Abstract of the United States: 2001*, 121st ed. (Washington, DC: U.S. G.P.O., 2001), 13.

2. Dan Lacy, "Social Change and the Library: 1945–1980," in *Libraries at Large: Tradition, Innovation, and the National Interest*, ed. Douglas M. Knight and E. Shepley Nourse (New York: R.R. Bowker, 1969), 4–5; Connie Van Fleet and Douglas Raber, "The Public Library as a Social/Cultural Institution: Alternative

Perspectives and Changing Contexts," in *Adult Services: An Enduring Focus for Public Libraries*, ed. Kathleen M. Heim and Danny P. Wallace (Chicago: ALA, 1990), 470–71; Marcia J. Nauratil, *Public Libraries and Nontraditional Clienteles: The Politics of Special Services* (Westport, CT: Greenwood Press, 1985), 101; Rudolph J. Vecoli, "Immigration," in *Oxford Companion to United States History*, ed. Paul S. Boyer and Melvyn Dubofsky (New York: Oxford University Press, 2001), 363; Thomas C. Holt, "Afro-Americans," in *Harvard Encyclopedia of American Ethnic Groups*, ed. Stephan Thernstrom, Ann Orlov, and Oscar Handlin (Cambridge: Belknap Press of Harvard University Press, 1980), 15.

3. Nauratil, *Public Libraries and Nontraditional Clienteles*, 101.

4. Robert A. Divine, *American Immigration Policy, 1924–1952* (New Haven: Yale University Press, 1957), 146–63.

5. Nauratil, *Public Libraries and Nontraditional Clienteles*, 103.

6. U.S. Immigration and Naturalization Service, "Appendix 1: Immigration and Naturalization Legislation," *Statistical Yearbook of the Immigration and Naturalization Service, 1997*, (Washington, DC: U.S. G.P.O., 1999), A.1–10; David Nelson Alloway, "Guamanians," in *Dictionary of American Immigration History*, ed. Francesco Cordasco (Metuchen, NJ: Scarecrow Press, 1990), 265–66; Michael LeMay and Elliott Robert Barkan, ed., *U.S. Immigration and Naturalization Laws and Issues: A Documentary History* (Westport, CT: Greenwood Press, 1999), 116–21; Marion T. Bennett, *American Immigration Policies: A History* (Washington, DC: Public Affairs Press, 1963), 81.

7. U.S. Immigration and Naturalization Service, "Appendix 1: Immigration and Naturalization Legislation," A.1–10, A.1–11; LeMay and Barkan, *U.S. Immigration and Naturalization Laws and Issues*, 116–21; Bennett, *American Immigration Policies*, 81.

8. U.S. Immigration and Naturalization Service, "Appendix 1: Immigration and Naturalization Legislation," A.1–11; Francesco Cordasco, "Bracero Program," in *Dictionary of American Immigration History*, 90–91; Maldwyn Allen Jones, *American Immigration*, 2nd ed. (Chicago: University of Chicago Press, 1992), 264; Robert M. Jiobu, *Ethnicity and Assimilation* (Albany: State University of New York Press, 1988), 22–24; LeMay and Barkan, *U.S. Immigration and Naturalization Laws and Issues*, 116–21; Bennett, *American Immigration Policies*, 82–83.

9. U.S. Immigration and Naturalization Service, "Appendix 1: Immigration and Naturalization Legislation," A.1–12; LeMay and Barkan, *U.S. Immigration and Naturalization Laws and Issues*, 220–25; M.A. Jones, *American Immigration*, 251–55; Nauratil, *Public Libraries and Nontraditional Clienteles*, 107; Thomas J. Archdeacon, *Becoming American: An Ethnic History* (New York: Free Press, 1983), 207; Mary Elizabeth Brown, "Patrick Anthony McCarran (1876–1954): Cold War Immigration," in *Shapers of the Great Debate on Immigration: A Biographical Dictionary* (Westport, CT: Greenwood Press, 1999), 191–204; E. Willard Miller, and Ruby M. Miller, *United States Immigration: A Reference Handbook* (Santa Barbara,

CA: ABC-CLIO, 1996), 92–95, 110–11; LeMay and Barkan, *U.S. Immigration and Naturalization Laws and Issues,* 116–21; Bennett, *American Immigration Policies,* 133–52; Divine, *American Immigration Policy, 1924–1952,* 164–91; Edward Prince Hutchinson, *Legislative History of American Immigration Policy, 1798–1965* (Philadelphia: Published for the Balch Institute for Ethnic Studies, by the University of Pennsylvania Press, 1981), 307–10; David M. Reimers, "Recent Immigration Policy: An Analysis," in *The Gateway: U.S. Immigration Issues and Policies,* ed. Barry R. Chiswick (Washington, DC: American Enterprise Institute for Public Policy Research, 1982), 24–28; Reed Ueda, "Naturalization and Citizenship," in *Harvard Encyclopedia of American Ethnic Groups,* 746–47.

    10. M.A. Jones, *American Immigration,* 249–51; Hutchinson, *Legislative History of American Immigration Policy, 1798–1965,* 313.

    11. U.S. Immigration and Naturalization Service, "Appendix 1: Immigration and Naturalization Legislation," A.1–10, A.1–11; LeMay and Barkan, *U.S. Immigration and Naturalization Laws and Issues,* 116–21, 225–31; M.A. Jones, *American Immigration,* 246, 253, 277; Bennett, *American Immigration Policies,* 153–69.

    12. LeMay and Barkan, *U.S. Immigration and Naturalization Laws and Issues,* 233–36; Hutchinson, *Legislative History of American Immigration Policy, 1798–1965,* 314–16; Reimers, "Recent Immigration Policy: An Analysis," 28–31; Otis L. Graham Jr., *Unguarded Gates: A History of America's Immigration Crisis* (Lanham, MD: Rowman & Littlefield Publishers, 2004), 80–81.

    13. Francesco Cordasco, "Puerto Ricans," in *Dictionary of American Immigration History,* 603–4; M.A. Jones, *American Immigration,* 252–55; Nauratil, *Public Libraries and Nontraditional Clienteles,* 105; Arnulfo D. Trejo, "Bicultural Americans with a Hispanic Tradition," *Wilson Library Bulletin* 44 (Mar. 1970): 720–22; Robert P. Haro, *Developing Library and Information Services for Americans of Hispanic Origin* (Metuchen, NJ: Scarecrow Press, 1981), 9–12; Patricia Beilke and Frank J. Sciara, *Selecting Materials for and about Hispanic and East Asian Children and Young People* (Hamden, CT: Library Professional Publications, 1986), 54–58.

    14. U.S. Immigration and Naturalization Service, "Appendix 1: Immigration and Naturalization Legislation," A.1–12; David W. Haines, "Refugees," in *Dictionary of American Immigration History,* 611–12; Sucheng Chan, "Koreans," in *Dictionary of American Immigration History,* 472; LeMay and Barkan, *U.S. Immigration and Naturalization Laws and Issues,* 116–21, 236–39; Miller and Miller, *United States Immigration: A Reference Handbook,* 111–12; Bennett, *American Immigration Policies,* 194–97; Reimers, "Recent Immigration Policy: An Analysis," 31–32.

    15. Charlene Cain, "Public Library Service to Minorities," in *Adult Services* 215–17; Holt, "Afro-Americans," in *Harvard Encyclopedia of American Ethnic Groups,* 18.

16. Francesco Cordasco, "Operation Wetback," in *Dictionary of American Immigration History,* 570–71; Walter Fogel, "Twentieth-Century Migration to the United States," in *The Gateway: U.S. Immigration Issues and Policies,* 197–200.

17. August C. Bolino, "Ellis Island," in *Dictionary of American Immigration History,* 195–97; LeMay and Barkan, *U.S. Immigration and Naturalization Laws and Issues,* 241–42; M.A. Jones, *American Immigration,* 264; Bernard, "Immigration: History of U.S. Policy," in *Harvard Encyclopedia of American Ethnic Groups,* 491.

18. U.S. Immigration and Naturalization Service, "Appendix 1: Immigration and Naturalization Legislation," A.1–12; August J. Molnar, "Hungarians," in *Dictionary of American Immigration History,* 309–10; David M. Reimers, "Immigration Legislation," in *Dictionary of American Immigration History,* 385; LeMay and Barkan, *U.S. Immigration and Naturalization Laws and Issues,* 242–48; M.A. Jones, *American Immigration,* 246; Archdeacon, *Becoming American: An Ethnic History,* 209; LeMay and Barkan, *U.S. Immigration and Naturalization Laws and Issues,* 116–21; Bennett, *American Immigration Policies,* 204–6.

19. Edward G. Holley and Robert F. Schremser, *The Library Services and Construction Act: An Historical Overview from the Viewpoint of Major Participants* (Greenwich, CT: JAI Press, 1983), 147–48, 151; R. Kathleen Molz, *The Federal Roles in Support of Public Library Services: An Overview,* prepared for the Federal Roles in Support of Public Library Services Project (Chicago: American Library Association, 1990), 9; Connie Van Fleet, "Lifelong Learning Theory and the Provision of Adult Services," in *Adult Services* 178; Van Fleet and Raber, "The Public Library as a Social/Cultural Institution: Alternative Perspectives and Changing Contexts," 456–500; Gillian D. Leonard, "Multiculturalism and Library Services," in *Multicultural Acquisitions,* ed. Karen Parrish and Bill Katz (New York: Haworth Press, 1993), 6; Lowell A. Martin, *Enrichment: A History of the Public Library in the United States in the Twentieth Century* (Lanham, MD: Scarecrow Press, 1998), 140–45; Dennis Thomison, *A History of the American Library Association, 1876–1972* (Chicago: ALA, 1978), 192–93; Gerald R. Shields, "Federal Legislation and Libraries," in *Libraries in the Political Process,* ed. E.J. Josey (Phoenix: Oryx Press, 1980), 5–6; Alex Ladenson, *Library Law and Legislation in the United States* (Metuchen, NJ: Scarecrow Press, 1982), 124–29; Germaine Krettek, "Library Legislation, Federal," in *Encyclopedia of Library and Information Science,* ed. Allen Kent, Harold Lancour, and Jay E. Daily, vol. 15 (New York: Marcel Dekker, 1975), 337–54.

20. U.S. Immigration and Naturalization Service, "Appendix 1: Immigration and Naturalization Legislation," A.1–13; Haines, "Refugees," 612; M.A. Jones, *American Immigration,* 278.

21. Bruce Wetterau, "Education," in *The New York Public Library Book of Chronologies* (New York: Stonesong Press of Prentice Hall Press, 1990), 341.

22. Helen G. Chapin, "Hawaiians," in *Dictionary of American Immigration History,* 285–86; M.A. Jones, *American Immigration,* 175, 247.

23. Raymond A. Mohl, "Cubans," in *Dictionary of American Immigration History*, 153–54; Sucheng Chan, "Chinese," in *Dictionary of American Immigration History*, 127; Reimers, "Immigration Legislation," 385; Nauratil, *Public Libraries and Nontraditional Clienteles*, 105; Beilke and Sciara, *Selecting Materials for and about Hispanic and East Asian Children and Young People*, 58–61; LeMay and Barkan, *U.S. Immigration and Naturalization Laws and Issues*, 116–21; Bennett, *American Immigration Policies*, 234–35; Cain, "Public Library Service to Minorities," 218; Tony A. Harvell, "Miami and the Cuban Revolution: Ties Across the Straits of Florida," in *SALALM and the Area Studies Community: Papers of the Thirty-Seventh Annual Meeting of the Seminar on the Acquisition of Latin American Library Materials, Nettie Lee Benson Latin American Collection, University of Texas at Austin, Austin, Texas, May 30–June 4, 1992*, ed. David Block ([Albuquerque]: SALALM Secretariat, General Library, University of New Mexico, 1992), 28–40.

24. Martin, *Enrichment: A History of the Public Library in the United States in the Twentieth Century*, 145–55; Charlotte J. Hubach, "New York's Ottendorfer Branch Library," *Stechert-Hafner Book News* 8 (May 1954): 101–3; Frank B. Sessa, "Public Libraries, International: History of the Public Library," in *Encyclopedia of Library and Information Science*, vol. 24 (New York: Marcel Dekker, 1976), 285; Stephen Stern, "Ethnic Libraries and Librarianship in the United States: Models and Prospects," in *Advances in Librarianship*, ed. Irene P. Godden, vol. 15 (New York: Academic Press, 1991), 86–87.

25. Richard Vasquez, "Libraries Lure Barrio Youth," *California Librarian* 31 (July 1970): 200–3; Nauratil, *Public Libraries and Nontraditional Clienteles*, 107; Martin, *Enrichment: A History of the Public Library in the United States in the Twentieth Century*, 101–114; Haynes McMullen, "Services to Ethnic Minorities Other than Afro-Americans and American Indians," in *A Century of Service: Librarianship in the United States and Canada*, ed. Sidney L. Jackson, Eleanor B. Herling, and E. J. Josey (Chicago: ALA, 1976), 58; Edwin Castagna, "A Troubled Mixture: Our Attitudes Toward the Unserved as Librarians in a Professional Capacity," in *Library Service to the Unserved: Papers Presented at a Library Conference Held at the University of Wisconsin–Milwaukee, School of Library and Information Science, November 16–18, 1967*, ed. Laurence L. Sherrill, Library and Information Science Studies, no. 2 (New York: R. R. Bowker, 1970), 15–24; John H. Rebenack, "Public Libraries, International: Contemporary Libraries in the United States," in *Encyclopedia of Library and Information Science*, vol. 24: 291–92; Kathleen M. Heim, "Adult Services: An Enduring Focus," in *Adult Services*, 15; Van Fleet, "Lifelong Learning Theory and the Provision of Adult Services," 176; Margaret E. Monroe, "Reader Services to the Disadvantaged in Inner Cities," in *Advances in Librarianship*, vol. 2: 253–54.

26. John Mackenzie Cory, "The New York Public Library," in *Encyclopedia of Library and Information Science*, vol. 19 (New York: Marcel Dekker, 1976), 378–80; Margaret E. Monroe, "The Cultural Role of the Public Library," in *Advances in Librarianship*, vol. 11: 27–31.

27. Eleanor Frances Brown, *Library Service to the Disadvantaged* (Metuchen, NJ: Scarecrow Press, 1971), 403; Eleanor T. Smith, "Public Library Service to the Economically and Culturally Deprived: A Profile of the Brooklyn Public Library," in *The Library Reaches Out: Reports on Library Service and Community Relations by Some Leading American Librarians,* comp. and ed. Kate Coplan and Edwin Castagna (Dobbs Ferry, NY: Oceana Publications, 1965), 227–29, 234–35.

28. A.P. Marshall, "Service to Afro-Americans," in *A Century of Service: Librarianship in the United States and Canada,* 62–78.

29. Bernice Lloyd Bell, "Public Library Integration in Thirteen Southern States," *Library Journal* 88 (15 Dec. 1963): 4713–15; Eliza Atkins Gleason, *The Southern Negro and the Public Library: A Study of the Government and Administration of Public Library Services to Negroes in the South,* with a foreword by Louis R. Wilson (Chicago: University of Chicago Press, 1941); Cain, "Public Library Service to Minorities," 217.

30. Nauratil, *Public Libraries and Nontraditional Clienteles,* 112.

31. Helen Lyman Smith, *Adult Education Activities in Public Libraries: A Report of the ALA Survey of Adult Education Activities in Public Libraries and State Library Extension Agencies of the United States* (Chicago: ALA, 1954); Margaret E. Monroe, "The Adult and the Public Library," *Minnesota Libraries* 21 (Sept. 1965): 191–97; Heim, "Adult Services: An Enduring Focus," 11–16; Cain, "Public Library Service to Minorities," 212–17; Harlow G. Unger, ed., "Adult Basic Education (ABE)," in *Encyclopedia of American Education* (New York: Facts on File, c2001, 1996), 30; Unger, "Adult Education," in *Encyclopedia of American Education,* 30–32.

32. Brown, *Library Service to the Disadvantaged,* 452–53; Fern Long, "New Citizens in the Library," *ALA Bulletin* 51 (Jan. 1957): 27–28; Smith, "Public Library Service to the Economically and Culturally Deprived: A Profile of the Brooklyn Public Library," 229–30, 233–34.

33. Holley and Schremser, *The Library Services and Construction Act: An Historical Overview from the Viewpoint of Major Participants,* 147–48, 151; Molz, *The Federal Roles in Support of Public Library Services: An Overview,* 9; Van Fleet, "Lifelong Learning Theory and the Provision of Adult Services," 178; Van Fleet and Raber, "The Public Library as a Social/Cultural Institution: Alternative Perspectives and Changing Contexts," 456–500; Leonard, "Multiculturalism and Library Services," 6; Martin, *Enrichment: A History of the Public Library in the United States in the Twentieth Century,* 140–45; Thomison, *A History of the American Library Association, 1876–1972,* 192–93; Shields, "Federal Legislation and Libraries," 5–6; Ladenson, *Library Law and Legislation in the United States,* 124–29; Krettek, "Library Legislation, Federal," 337–54.

34. Sessa, "Public Libraries, International: History of the Public Library," 285–86; Cain, "Public Library Service to Minorities," 217; Nauratil, *Public Libraries and Nontraditional Clienteles,* 112.

35. Plummer Alston Jones Jr., *Libraries, Immigrants, and the American Experience* (Westport, CT: Greenwood Press, 1999), 186–87; Heim, "Adult Services: An Enduring Focus," 16–17.

36. Janet N. Naumer, "Library Services to American Indians," in *Library and Information Services for Special Groups*, ed. Joshua I. Smith (New York: Pub. in cooperation with the American Society for Information Science and the ERIC Clearinghouse on Library and Information Sciences, by Science Associates/ International, 1974), 46; Brown, *Library Service to the Disadvantaged*, 417–21; Rebenack, "Public Libraries, International: Contemporary Libraries in the United States," 308–9; Nauratil, *Public Libraries and Nontraditional Clienteles*, 112; John C. Colson, "The United States: An Historical Critique," in *Library Services to the Disadvantaged*, ed. William Martin (Hamden, CT: Linnet Books, 1975), 71; William H. Farrington, "Statewide Outreach: Desert Booktrails to the Indians," *Wilson Library Bulletin* 43 (May 1969): 864–71.

37. M.A. Jones, *American Immigration*, 280–82; Robert Downs, "Significance of Foreign Materials for U.S. Collections," in *Acquisition of Foreign Materials for U.S. Libraries*, ed. Theodore Samore (Metuchen, NJ: Scarecrow Press, 1973), 4–5; Philip J. McNiff, "Cooperation in the Acquisition of Foreign Materials," in *Acquisition of Foreign Materials for U.S. Libraries*, ed. Theodore Samore (Metuchen, NJ: Scarecrow Press, 1973), 15; Donald F. Wisdom, "The First Two Decades of SALALM: A Personal Account," in *SALALM and the Area Studies Community: Papers of the Thirty-Seventh Annual Meeting of the Seminar on the Acquisition of Latin American Library Materials, Nettie Lee Benson Latin American Collection, University of Texas at Austin, Austin, Texas, May 30-June 4, 1992*, 118–52; Salvador Guerena and Edward Erazo, "Latinos and Librarianship," *Library Trends* 49 (Summer 2000): 157; Marietta Daniels Shepard, "Reading Resources and Project LEER," *Wilson Library Bulletin* 44 (Mar. 1970): 747; Margaret E. Monroe, "The Cultural Role of the Public Library," 17; Suzanne Hodgman, "SALALM Membership, 1956–1990: A Brief Overview," in *Latin American Studies into the Twenty-First Century: New Focus, New Formats, New Challenges: Papers of the Thirty-Sixth Annual Meeting of the Seminar on the Acquisition of Latin American Library Materials, University of California, San Diego, and San Diego State University, San Diego, California, June 1–6, 1991*, 215–23, ed. Deborah L. Jakubs ([Albuquerque]: SALALM Secretariat, General Library, University of New Mexico, 1993).

Chapter 3

PUBLIC LIBRARIES AND CIVIL RIGHTS IN THE 1960s

By the 1960s, the U.S. population was approximately 178 million, with approximately 89 percent white and 11 percent black. In 1960, more than 77 million Americans, or more than two-fifths of the nation, lived in poverty or deprivation. About 40 percent of American adults had only eight years of education or less. Racial statistics on Native American peoples, Asian and Pacific Islanders, and residents of Hispanic origins were not collected by the federal government.[1]

Considerable gains were made by black Americans during the 1960s. The median income of black families more than doubled during this decade and political and social recognition far exceeded that of a generation earlier. A strong sense of pride in African American culture emerged.

Asian Americans were often subjects of a positive but slightly condescending stereotyping, according to which they were perceived as being highly independent, holding education in reverence, and having considerable entrepreneurial abilities. This stereotype did not take into consideration the significant differences among the Asian groups. The Japanese had a somewhat lower poverty rate than whites, but the Filipino rate was substantially higher. A large proportion of the Southeast Asian boat people had arrived here destitute. Chinese, Japanese, and Filipino Americans all had a higher proportion of college graduates than did the white population, but Asian Americans also had a higher proportion of people with no formal education at all. The fact that many Asian Americans were highly educated had not resulted in much employment advantage.

In the 1960s, a Second Great Wave, the successor to Otis L. Graham's Great Wave, was generated by global population growth, lowered transportation costs, and a widespread awareness of the wealth gap between developed and underdeveloped nations. Reforms of American immigration law and policy during the 1960s were intended to bring improvements in the form of opening equal access to all nationalities. However, the reforms brought surprising effects: a threefold expansion of legal immigrants, augmented by burgeoning numbers of illegal immigrants, and a radical shift in the source countries of American immigration.[2]

LEGAL AND JUDICIAL DECISIONS AFFECTING MINORITIES

Fair Share Refugee Act of 1960

In July 1960, Congress passed the Fair Share Refugee Act, also known as the World Refugee Year Law, to assist in the resettlement of refugees from communist countries, mostly Cubans, who had been paroled by the president and the attorney general, and of refugees and displaced persons from World War II, who were still in United Nations refugee camps. The 1960 act did not alter the national-origins quota system but weakened it by erasing mortgages on future quotas and by giving favored treatment to refugees largely because of the cold war anticommunist atmosphere. The federal government's Cuban Refugee Program (CRP), which handled the processing and resettlement of the Cuban exiles in Miami and their redistribution throughout the United States, soon discovered that a large portion of Cubans who resettled elsewhere eventually returned to Miami.

Public Law 480 for Acquisition of Foreign-Language Materials

In 1961, Congress passed Public Law 480, a natural outgrowth of the Library of Congress's Farmington Plan established in 1948 for acquisition of foreign library materials. The Public Law 480 program authorized the expenditure of blocked currencies for the acquisition of multiple copies of publications in certain countries where surplus funds had accumulated, including, at that time, Ceylon, India, Indonesia, Israel, Nepal, Pakistan, the United Arab Republic, and Yugoslavia. SALALM was incorporated in 1968 when A. Curtis Wilgus of the Library of Congress was elected its first president.

In September 1961, Congress liberalized the quota provisions of the 1952 act by eliminating the ceiling of 2,000 on the aggregate quota for the Asia-Pacific Triangle and insured a minimum quota of 100 for newly independent nations. The election of John Fitzgerald Kennedy, a second-generation Irish Catholic, eased the way for an attack on the national origins quota system. The growing agitation of the civil rights movement marked a changing national attitude toward equality for all races that undercut the discriminatory policy embodied by the INA of 1952.[3]

Migration and Refugee Assistance Act of 1962

In October 1962, Congress passed the Migration and Refugee Assistance Act to grant visas outside the quotas to aliens eligible as brothers, sisters, and children of citizens and those with special occupational skills. Passed in part as a response to the Cuban refugee problem, the 1962 act also strengthened the role of the executive branch in the planning and implementation of immigration policy and authorized loans and grants for the education and training of refugees.[4]

President Kennedy's budget request for 1963 had specified improvement of community library services for people of all ages and concluded that all public libraries, urban and rural, should be eligible for federal assistance, including construction funds. After the assassination of President Kennedy in November 22, 1963, President Lyndon Baines Johnson followed suit in his January 1964 State of the Union address by asking for funds to build more schools, libraries, and hospitals.

LSA to Library Services and Construction Act (LSCA)

After being extended for five years in August 1960, the LSA of 1956 was funded at the full level of $7.5 million in each of fiscal years 1961 through 1964. In September 1962, Samoa was added to the list of areas eligible for LSA funds.

The legislative transformation of the LSA of 1956 into the LSCA was a component of President Johnson's Great Society program. After an uphill battle and heated debate, the act was signed into law by President Johnson February 4, 1964, after a vote of 89 to 7 in the Senate and 254 to 107 in the House. Initially, LSCA had two titles. Title I (Public Library Services) represented the expansion of the rural-based LSA of 1956 to urban areas, with increased funding for salaries and wages, training funds for new librarians, books and other library materials, library equipment, and general operating expenses. Title I was funded at $25 million in each of fiscal years 1965 and 1966 and $35 million in each of fiscal years 1967 through 1970. Title II (Library Construction) made federal grants available for building libraries, just when Carnegie library buildings were beginning to fall into disuse. Title II received no appropriation in fiscal year 1964, and in subsequent years its funding was uneven. In each of fiscal years 1965 and 1966, Title II received appropriations of $30 million; in fiscal year 1967, $40 million; and in fiscal year 1968, approximately $34 million. In fiscal year 1969, Title II appropriation sunk to approximately $24 million and in fiscal year 1970 plummeted to just under $10 million.

Amendments to the LSCA were passed by the Congress in July 1966, just when the concept of library systems was taking root throughout the nation. LSCA was extended for five years, and two additional titles were added: Title III (Interlibrary Cooperation), and Title IV-A (Institutions) and Title IV-B (Physically Handicapped). The Trust Territory of the Pacific Islands was added to the list of eligible areas.

Title III was initially funded in fiscal year 1967 at approximately $400,000; and in each of the fiscal years 1968 through 1969, approximately $2 million. Title IV-A appropriations were approximately $400,000 in fiscal year 1967 and just over $2 million in each of fiscal years 1968 through 1970. Title IV-B appropriates were $250,000 in fiscal year 1967 and just over $1 million in each of fiscal years 1968 through 1970. In November 1967, a further amendment was passed by Congress to permit the renovation of an existing building for public library use as an eligible expenditure under the original Title II designated initially for new construction.[5]

Mexican Bracero Program Ends in 1964

Criticism of the Mexican Bracero Program mounted over the years since its inception in the early 1940s. In December 1963, Congress extended the Mexican Bracero Program for one year to December 1964, when the program was unilaterally terminated by the Kennedy administration in view of resistance from the American Federation of Labor-Congress of Industrial Organizations (AFL-CIO) and various Mexican American community groups, who had long been concerned about the impact of contract migratory works on American labor. In addition, the ending of the Bracero Program was one of the compromises that President Kennedy had agreed to in order to move the Congress toward increasing the world-wide ceiling on immigration.

At the program's peak, almost 500,000 Mexican Braceros were employed in the agricultural labor marker of the Southwest. A total of 4.7 million Mexican workers participated during the life of the program. Regrettably, the availability of Mexican workers significantly had depressed existing wage levels in some regions of the United States.[6] After termination of the program, Mexican workers came again in the spring of 1965—now a stream of illegal aliens constituting a new front in the coming debates over immigration.

Civil Rights and Economic Opportunity Acts of 1964

The Civil Rights Act of 1964 authorized support for institutions of higher education and school districts to provide in-service programs to assist instructional staff dealing with problems caused by desegregation. That same year, the Economic Opportunity Act was passed by Congress as the centerpiece of President Johnson's War on Poverty. The act authorized many programs with which librarians became involved, notably the Community Action programs, which funded community-staffed organizations aimed at mobilizing local resources to alleviate poverty; Volunteers in Service to America (VISTA) programs, which trained highly motivated young people to work with migrant laborers as the domestic version of the Peace Corps; and Operation Head Start programs to prepare disadvantaged preschoolers for kindergarten by teaching them school-readiness skills.

The civil rights movement, which had surged into national consciousness in the mid-1950s with the Montgomery, Alabama, bus boycott and the emergence of the Reverend Martin Luther King Jr., assaulted the discriminatory Jim Crow legal regime of the South throughout the 1960s. African American leaders were beginning to move toward political solidarity with all the world's people of color and could no longer be counted on to take the restrictionist positions taken earlier by Booker T. Washington and A. Philip Randolph.

The moral fervor of this crusade was so intense that it fanned into new life similar antidiscrimination movements among Native Americans and other ethnic minorities, feminists, and homosexuals. It was no longer tolerable to discriminate groups of people on the basis of inherited characteristics.[7]

1965 Amendments to the INA of 1952

The provisions of the 1965 act, considered amendments to the INA of 1952, were signed into law on October 3, 1965, by President Johnson in front of the Statute of Liberty in New York Harbor. Also known as the Hart-Celler Immigration Reform Act, named for its Congressional sponsors, the 1965 amendments, which would become fully operative in July 1968, eliminated both the national-origins quota system and the Asia-Pacific Triangle provisions of the 1952 act.

The 1965 amendments applied to all Eastern Hemisphere countries a complex system of eight preference categories. Visas were made available on a first-come, first-served basis to (1) unmarried children of U.S. citizens; (2) spouses and unmarried children of permanent resident aliens; (3) members of the professions and scientists and artists of exceptional ability; (4) married children of U.S. citizens; (5) siblings of U.S. citizens; (6) skilled and unskilled workers in short supply; and (7) refugees. Immediate relatives of U.S. citizens, including spouses, minor children, and parents, were to be allowed entry without numerical restriction.

The 1965 amendments maintained the principle of numerical restriction of annual worldwide immigration to the United States at 290,000 and raised the number of Eastern Hemisphere immigrants allowed to enter the United States annually from 150,000 to 170,000. Within this annual limit of 170,000 and a 20,000 maximum per-country limit, the available visas were to be granted as follows: 74 percent to nonimmediate relatives of people already in the United States; 20 percent to persons with skills and abilities sought by U.S. employers; and the remaining 6 percent to refugees, defined as aliens who had fled communist persecution or regimes.

Western Hemisphere countries, never before subject to numerical limitations, were given an annual ceiling of 120,000, with all applicants for visas being subject to the same first-come, first-served basis as Eastern Hemisphere applicants. This requirement was clearly framed to limit immigration from Mexico. West Indian immigration that had been diverted to Britain by the INA of 1952 now began to swing back to the United States, after the British adopted a restrictive immigration policy in 1962.[8]

In 1965, Canada, Mexico, the United Kingdom, and Germany headed the list of countries sending the most immigrants to the United States. In the decade after the passage of the 1965 amendments, total immigration increased by nearly 60 percent, with dramatic increases from Greece, Portugal, India, Korea, Pakistan, the Philippines, Thailand, and Vietnam. Immigration from Europe declined by over 38 percent overall. Almost 70 percent of the newcomers after 1965 settled in six states of California, New York, Florida, Texas, Illinois, and New Jersey.[9]

The 1965 act was soon outmoded in its provisions for refugees. The annual preference limit of 10,200 set for refugees was not high enough to respond to events in Cuba, Vietnam, and Haiti alone. The 1965 act's third preference for highly skilled professionals created a virtual "brain drain" from Asian countries. After 1965, the expanded demand for medical care, resulting in part from Medicare and Medicaid, brought in 75,000 foreign physicians within a decade, the bulk of them from the Philippines, Korea, Iran, India, and Thailand.

The family unification provisions of the 1965 law allowed a perfectly legal, but wholly unanticipated, pattern of immigration known as pyramiding to develop. After obtaining permanent residence status, immigrants could bring in their parents as immediate family members. A few years later, having now become citizens, the immigrants could sponsor brothers and sisters under the fifth and most heavily used preference. The siblings in turn could secure entry for their spouses and children under the second preference. The children's spouses could in turn start new pyramids, beginning with their parents.

The 1965 legislation was the perfect case study of the law of unintended consequences. Immigrant reformers had put in place a new system under which total numbers would triple and the source countries of immigration would radically shift from Europe to Latin America and Asia, exactly the two demographic results that the restrictionist campaign from the 1870s to 1929 was designed to prevent.[10]

U.S. Select Commission on Western Hemisphere Immigration of 1965

Just after the passage of the 1965 amendments, Congress approved the establishment of a U.S. Select Commission on Western Hemisphere Immigration, comprised of five presidential appointees, five senators, and five representatives to study vital hemispheric and national issues, including unemployment, immigration, security, and inter-American relations. The commission's report, issued in 1968, contained not only majority recommendations but also minority positions on immigration ceilings and Cuban refugees.[11]

Elementary, Secondary, and Higher Education Acts of 1965

The Elementary and Secondary Education Act (ESEA) of 1965, a federal law to improve public school education by direct federal intervention, provided compensatory education and counseling for at-risk students and was a boon to the development of school libraries. Title I provided funds to local education agencies (LEAs), including schools, social service agencies, and other organizations, for remedial reading and mathematics programs. Funds were apportioned according to the number of low-income children in a particular LEA's area. Title II provided $100 million in support of school libraries. In 1968, the act was amended to extend coverage to children with disabilities.

The Higher Education Act (HEA) of 1965 was for colleges, universities, and other postsecondary institutions, the federal equivalent of the ESEA of 1965. Federal grants to libraries and resource centers of higher education institutions were eligible for grants for the development and improvement of academic resources and services. It became increasingly apparent that there was a conspicuous absence of minorities in most of the white-collar professions, including librarianship.[12]

Cuban Refugees Adjusted to Permanent Resident Status

On November 2, 1966, Congress passed a law that adjusted the status of Cuban refugees to that of permanent resident aliens, chargeable to the 120,000 annual ceiling for immigrants from the Western Hemisphere. Ironically, here was a clear case of discrimination in favor of a particular nationality.

Four days later, on November 6, 1966, Congress responded to the Vietnam War, with its increasing involvement of U.S. soldiers and civilians, by passing a law to extend derivative citizenship to children born on or after December 24, 1952, of civilian U.S. citizens serving abroad. In October 1968, Congress passed a law to provide for the expeditious naturalization of noncitizens who had rendered honorable services in the U.S. armed forces during the Vietnam conflict or in other periods of military hostilities, including the Korean War, and to eliminate refugees as a category of the preference system.[13]

Model Cities Act of 1966

In 1966, Congress passed the Demonstration Cities and Metropolitan Development Act, known as the Model Cities Act. Directed by the U.S. Department of Housing and Urban Development, the act provided grants to cities to solve neighborhood problems using new ideas and involving local agencies and federal housing, education, and manpower programs.[14]

Bilingual Education Act of 1968

The Bilingual Education Act of 1968 was passed by Congress as an amendment to the ESEA of 1965. Passed with the needs of the large Mexican American community of the Southwest in mind, the 1968 act provided funds for the planning and implementation of programs to meet the special needs of children of limited English-speaking ability in schools having a high concentration of such children from families with incomes below $3,000 per year.[15]

LIBRARY SERVICES WITH MINORITIES

LSA Projects

In March 1961, the Brooklyn Public Library used LSA grants to promote its Community Coordinator Project in the Bedford-Stuyvesant, Bushwick, Brownsville, and Red Hood neighborhoods under the direction of Hardy Franklin. He collaborated with other federal projects, state and city programs, and community and social service organizations to publicize the library to those who did not know about its many services, to make the library and staff an important part of the community and family life, and to provide special materials needed for job skills training.[16]

Several libraries and library systems in South Carolina used LSA grants to develop collections and bookmobile service for rural areas to extend library services to African Americans, including the Laurens County Library, the Abbeville-Greenwood Regional Library, the Florence County Library, and the Aiken-Bamberg-Barnwell-Edgefield Regional Library. In 1963, the Wisconsin Valley Library System received an LSA grant to strengthen the reference and information resources of the Wausau Public Library in Marathon County, to extend these resources to the entire 11-county region, and to conduct training workshops for library personnel.[17]

All federal funds for public libraries were to be matched by the states on a sliding scale, according to the state's ability to pay. The availability of LSA grants prompted the development and implementation of a great variety of public library outreach services and services to the disadvantaged. Disadvantaged persons were defined as those with a need for special library services resulting from poverty, neglect, delinquency, and/or from cultural, linguistic, or other isolation from the community at large. Clearly, immigrants, African Americans, and American Indians were eligible as disadvantaged populations.

LSCA Projects

LSCA grants were used to establish special collections known as ethnic resource libraries that featured extensive collections and services for a targeted ethnic or minority group in newly constructed or remodeled facilities. Grants were used to build collections of books and other media for minorities, including library materials for classes in English as a Second Language (ESL), Adult Basic Education (ABE), and other adult literacy efforts, and to support job training and career counseling services. Bringing books to the people was a theme that was realized by the establishment of bookmobile services throughout the country. Bookmobiles provided library services to the disadvantaged, including ethnic and minority groups as well as hospitalized and institutionalized residents.

In 1964, the Multnomah County (OR) Public Library established a children's services program for migrant workers' camps. In 1965, Wisconsin's Dodge County received a 1965 LSCA grant and Door County received a U.S. Office of Employment Opportunity grant to provide library service to Spanish-speaking migrant workers and their children, primarily from Texas and Mexico, during the summer harvest season.[18]

From 1964 to 1968, the Los Angeles Public Library used LSCA grants totaling $888,836 to provide library service to the minority communities in the Lincoln Heights, Venice, and Watts communities, three culturally and economically deprived areas of Los Angeles, populated largely by African Americans and Mexican Americans, most of whom were not library users. The Los Angeles County Library's Way Out Project received LSCA grants totaling $512,712 from 1967 to 1970 to serve minorities in the lower socioeconomic classes in east and south Los Angeles County and to establish the extensive African American and Chicano reference collections at the Compton and East Los Angeles library branches, respectively. During this same period, the 49–99 Cooperative Library System of Stockton and San Joaquin County Libraries received LSCA grants totaling $42,600 to develop collections of books and other library materials in Spanish, French, German, Italian, and Portuguese to be provided through rotating deposit collections and a central collection in Stockton.[19]

From the fall of 1966 to 1974, the Oakland Public Library received LSCA grants totaling $721,080 to establish the Biblioteca Latino Americana (Latin American Library) to serve the 40,000 Mexican Americans in the Fruitvale community of Oakland. Originally located in a storefront location, it was later moved to a multiagency building constructed by the Spanish Speaking Unity Council to serve the Fruitvale community and its

Spanish-speaking residents under the direction of Barbara Wynn, its first library director, who collaborated actively with a citizens' advisory committee.[20]

During fiscal years 1966 and 1967, the North Manhattan Project of the New York Public Library, located at the Countee Cullen Branch, received LSCA grants to establish and expand library services in the Central Harlem area. Under the direction of Wendell Wray, community liaison personnel were used to reach the neighborhood residents and draw them to the library for guided tours. The Schomburg Collection, also located at the Countee Cullen Branch, was established as a research collection of materials and exhibits to foster pride in the African American culture. A similarly successful program has been the Langston Hughes Community Library and Cultural Center in Corona, Queens Borough, New York. Funded by LSCA, this program was established by black community residents, themselves operating in a storefront setting.[21]

In June 1967, the South Bronx Project, including eight branches of the New York Public Library, used an LSCA grant of $200,445 to introduce the value of library resources and services to the large Hispanic community of 200,000, mostly Puerto Ricans. The project employed Spanish-speaking staff members from Puerto Rico, Cuba, Colombia, Mexico, Peru, and Ecuador, to represent the library in local schools, churches, and community organizations. The project was carried on by the New York Public Library Office of Special Services. Both were headed until 1980 by Lillian Lopez, a Puerto Rican librarian.[22]

In June 1969, the Monmouth County (NJ) Public Library signed a contract with the Migrant Education Program under the New Jersey State Department of Education for $3,765 for services to be given to migrant worker schools and adults in the county. The services included weekly storyfilm programs at the schools plus giving books to each child enrolled in the school.[23]

ABE was defined as education for adults whose inability to speak, read, or write the English language constituted a substantial impairment of their ability to get or retain employment commensurate with their real ability. In 1965, the Cleveland Public Library's Adult Education Department was awarded an LSCA grant for experimental projects with the 50,000 Clevelanders classified as functionally illiterate adults, both white and African American, with a reading ability under fifth-grade level. In 1966, as a component of an ABE project of the Milwaukee Vocational and Adult School, the Milwaukee Public Library deposited ABE collections of high interest, low reading-level adult books in five libraries throughout the city.[24]

In October 1966, the Corpus Christi Library opened the new Green-wood Branch, which was partially built with Title II LSCA funds to serve Mexican Americans, approximately 85 percent of its patrons. Early in 1969, a group of local architects, painters, labor unions, service agencies, and trucking companies in Terre Haute, Indiana, converted a railroad car into a library facility primarily for disadvantaged young people in the Hyte section of town. The U.S. Office of Economic Opportunity helped with the staffing of the new facility, and two high school graduates provided by the Vigo County Neighborhood Youth Corps acted as attendants.[25]

Titles IV-A and IV-B of LSCA in 1966 provided matching funds to be administered by the state library agencies for library service to state institutions (IV-A) and to the blind and physically disabled (IV-B). In Louisiana, a model library at the state penitentiary was established with the allocation of $24,000 by the state library and $24,000 by the depart-ment of institutions. In New York, with a grant $20,000 in LSCA Title IV-A funds, the Kings Park State Hospital, a mental hospital with 7,500 patients, developed a model library and then conducted a carefully struc-tured demonstration on what good library service can do for the psy-chosocial development of culturally deprived and emotionally disturbed children.

A few city libraries received federal aid through the LSCA for service to patients in hospitals and at home. In 1967, with a federal grant of $53,310, the St. Louis Public Library began a pilot bookmobile program to bring library services to the 82,000 residents of housing complexes, hospitals for the aged and chronically ill, and private nursing homes of the city, who were over 65 and unable to come to the library. In 1968, the public library in Poughkeepsie, New York, established a service for senior citizens, the Literary Social Guild for the Homebound. Instead of home visits, a bus, staffed with a driver and an assistant, transported the homebound to the library for regularly scheduled programs. In 1969, the Cleveland Public Library served most of the hospitals and institutions in the city and over 12,000 homebound persons.[26]

VISTA and Community Action Projects

VISTA book kits of 150 volumes, mostly paperbacks, were prepared by the National Book Committee for use in five different situations: rural, urban, migrant, Indian, and mental-health projects manned by VISTA volunteers. Financed by $200,000 from the Ford Foundation's Fund for the Advancement of Education, 1,000 portable libraries were prepared for educationally deprived children and adults. Each state library extension agency had been alerted to the VISTA project and had assigned a staff member as liaison agent to help provide back-up resources of books and other materials. The North Dakota Library Commission, for example, worked with VISTA volunteers to establish tribal libraries and with the U.S. Office for Economic Opportunity to provide vocational training programs.[27]

In the 1960s, Baltimore's Enoch Pratt Free Library experimented with the provision of neighborhood service to reach disadvantaged adults by establishing storefront libraries and using a bookmobile to make stops in neighborhoods that were part of the library's Community Action Project. In May 1968, the St. Louis Public Library used a federal grant of $80,000, in conjunction with a bookmobile on loan from the State Library of Missouri, to provide resource materials for an inner-city African American community. By June 1969, the library had set up over 40 deposits of materials in various locations, including the African Arts and Education Center and low-cost housing complexes.[28]

In May 1969, Alex Ladenson reported that for the past two years the Chicago Public Library had planned and implemented a program to reach residents of disadvantaged areas of the city, particularly African American communities served by the Woodlawn Regional Branch, located in the heart of one of the hard-core poverty areas. Earlier in 1968, the Chicago Public Library had used a renovated old bookmobile for the special use of children in poverty areas, including African Americans and Spanish-speaking, and made stops at school playgrounds, housing projects, and a settlement house.[29]

The San Francisco Public Library began a Street Life Project in June 1968. Olive Wong had the idea of circulating books to disadvantaged patrons who did not have library cards. The purpose of the project was not to lure people into the library but to lure them into the world of information applicable to their social, economic, and political existence. Guy Bennette, director of the Fillmore Street Reference Project, also supported by the San Francisco Public Library, commented that librarians in his project saw themselves as "street librarians."[30]

Operation Head Start Projects

In the late 1960s, the Queens Borough Public Library (QBPL) used LSCA and Economic Opportunity Act grants to initiate an Operation Head Start program for preschoolers in 10 branches in disadvantaged neighborhoods. The programs took place either in the 10 branches or in public parks, playgrounds, housing developments, and other Operation Head Start centers. The project was administered by two professional librarians and approximately 40 library aides, each having a minimum of two years of college education and being trained by project supervisors and branch librarians in the 10 branches involved in the project.[31]

In the summer of 1967, the Free Library of Philadelphia used LSCA and Economic Opportunity Act grants to initiate a Reader Development Program to make available materials written on or below the eighth-grade reading level to disadvantaged adults. By April 1968, four paperback collections in Spanish had been placed in extension agencies located in Puerto Rican neighborhoods. The Biblioteca Latina (Latin Library), opened by the Boston Public Library in 1968, was housed in the Spanish-speaking Center, sponsored by the Boston Roman Catholic Church, where Operation Head Start, employment, tutorial, and similar activities shared quarters. The library had Spanish-speaking staff and volunteers and provided films, story hours for children, and bookmobile service to housing projects.[32]

Title II-B of the HEA of 1965

The Library Education and Human Resources Development Program, funded by Title II-B of the Higher Education Act of 1965, was authorized to make awards to minorities for the study of library and information science beginning in 1966. Immigrants, Mexican Americans, African Americans, and American Indians were trained as librarians using Title II-B funds.

In 1967, the School of Library and Information Services of the University of Maryland experimented with providing master's degree candidates with field, classroom, and research experience in serving the disadvantaged in Fairmount Heights, an urban, predominantly African American, community in Prince George's County, Maryland. The experimental library, known as the High John demonstration library, was directed by Richard B. Moses from the Enoch Pratt Free Library's Community Action program.

Funded by Title II-B HEA funds, with additional support from Prince George's County Library through grants from the Maryland Division of Library Extension, the High John project received mixed reviews from very favorable to very disappointing. While some library leaders, including ALA President Eric Moon, complimented the project for taking risks and working for change, others criticized the experiment as having begun without taking the time to study the community first and involving primarily white students. The experiment was later taken over by the Prince George's County Library, but, in September 1970, the building housing the High John experiment closed its doors.[33]

National Advisory Commission on Libraries

In September 1966, President Johnson issued an Executive Order creating the National Advisory Commission on Libraries and appointed Douglas Knight, President of Duke University, as chair. The commission's charge was to address and make recommendations on resources and services needed to provide adequate library and information services for formal education at all levels; bibliographic access to the nation's research and information resources; physical access to library materials throughout the nation; and trained personnel for the varied and changing demands of librarianship.

The commission's report, *Libraries at Large*, was presented to President Johnson in October 1968. Rather than giving recommendations per se, the commission called for further study that could be accomplished by a national library planning agency to be called the National Commission on Libraries and Information Science (NCLIS).[34]

Model Cities Projects

After the passage of the Model Cities Act, Eileen Cooke of the ALA Washington Office reported that there were over 21 federal departments and agencies dealing with state and local governments, with some 150 major bureaus and offices in Washington, D.C., and over 400 regional and subregional field offices. In 1966, Model Cities grants were awarded to 63 cities to develop comprehensive model neighborhoods from slum areas. Innovative library services were developed using a combination of Model Cities and LSCA grants.[35]

Joanne Coyne, a young former Peace Corps volunteer who had worked in a small village in the highlands of Peru, established Los Amigos (The Friends) Club as an informal group for Spanish-speaking mothers in the Library Neighborhood Center of the New Haven (CT) Free Public Library. The Denver Public Library had six agencies, either branches or bookmobiles, to serve the northwest section of the city, a Model Cities target area.[36]

In 1968, the Bezazian Branch in the Uptown community of Chicago was one of four Model Cities target areas in Chicago. Formerly a neighborhood of southern and eastern Europeans, the Uptown community in the early 1960s attracted a large number of American Indians from numerous tribes, and by the mid-1960s, Middle Easterners, Asians, and Latinos. Also in 1968, the Providence (RI) Public Library's South Providence Branch was selected as a Model Cities site. Richard Metts, a young African American community liaison who grew up in South Providence, worked with five white VISTA workers to produce a community newspaper and place an African American history collection in the Opportunities Industrialization Center.[37]

The Richmond (CA) Public Library received LSCA grants totaling $45,680 from 1967 to 1969 to fund the city's Service Center Library. Located in the lobby of a state service center in a largely African American district of Richmond that also housed offices for social security, employment, rehabilitation, and health services, the Service Center Library's collection focused on materials of special interest to African Americans and Mexican Americans. The Milwaukee Public Library received LSCA Title I grants of $11,396, $8,946, and $39,230 in fiscal years 1966, 1967, and 1968, respectively, to provide special library service in two disadvantaged neighborhoods, Lapham and Forest Home, often in private homes and community gathering places in areas where racial turmoil made street travel hazardous.[38]

The Westchester Library (NY) System Project used an LSCA grant to collaborate with local Community Action program centers and other anti-poverty programs to purchase library materials to deposit in the centers. In 1967, the Chemung Southern Tier Library System, which includes the Steele Memorial Library of Elmira, New York, received an LSCA grant of $14,655 for its experimental expansion of bookmobile service to include evening and Saturday special bookmobile runs within three African American wards. Known as Project Eastside, it was the first attempt of any library within this five-county area to reach this audience. In July 1969, the Racine (WI) Public Library stocked a special book room in the Racine Spanish Center and provided a trained staff of young Spanish American storytellers, who acted as supervisors.[39]

In September 1966, in Elizabeth, New Jersey, the Economic Opportunity Act's local agency, Community Action for Economic Opportunity, provided support for the establishment of the Migliore Manor Branch Library within the Migliore Manor Housing Project to serve the 250 families living in the housing complex. Also in the late 1960s, the Savannah

(GA) Public and Chatham-Effingham-Liberty Regional Libraries provided part-time library service in the African American public housing
projects in cooperation with the public library and the Housing Authority
of Savannah and Chatham County.[40]

La Biblioteca Ambulante (The Traveling Library) of the San Joaquin
Valley Library System received LSCA grants totaling $265,400 from
1967 to 1974 to provide bookmobile service to 33 locations where migrant
farm laborers resided. Director Mary Reynolds reported that the first
step in providing good library service was to de-anglicize the library by
simplifying registration and circulation procedures, building an experimental Spanish collection, and employing local bilingual staff members.
The bookmobile project was succeeded by the system's Service to Urban
Bilingual, Bicultural Disadvantaged Project, which received LSCA grants
totaling $60,000 from 1974 to 1976. The new project shifted its emphasis
from rural migrant camps to urban areas where there had been a large in-
migration of Mexican Americans.[41]

As a result of the Vietnam debate, President Johnson decided not to run
for a second term. As the extent of U.S. involvement in Southeast Asia
became a major factor in the nation's economic life and inflation increased
accordingly, there was less funding available for social and educational programs at the national level. Federal funds for libraries were used quite differently in different states: some spent the money for state-level direction
and coordination; others used it for new or improved local services. Federal
funds typically constituted one-half of a rural library's annual budget and
about 10 percent of an urban library's budget.[42]

Bilingual Education in Libraries

Bilingual services in Massachusetts for Portuguese immigrants, in New
England for French Canadians, and in Florida for Cuban refugees were
representative of programs across the country. The Casa de Saudade Branch
of the New Bedford (MA) Public Library, the first Portuguese American
public library in the United States, offered two nights weekly ESL classes
combined with citizenship preparation classes. The library also translated
notices, tests, and legal documents as a service to teachers, lawyers, and
other patrons.[43] The Lewiston (ME) Public Library served a community
of 40,000 residents, about 80 percent of whom were descendants of French
Canadians from Quebec, about 50 percent of whom were bilingual. The
library had employed a full-time outreach librarian to work with the city's
elderly, many of whom were able to speak or read only in French.[44]

In June 1962, Helga H. Eason, head of the Community Relations Department of the Miami Public Library, reported on the work of the Miami Public Library (MPL) with the Cuban refugees of the early 1960s. Prior to mass influx of Cuban refugees to southern Florida, most Miami libraries had at least a few books in Spanish to serve the many Latin Americans working and studying in the city and had employed some Spanish-speaking librarians. As more and more uprooted Cubans poured into Miami, many lacking not only the basic necessities of life but also knowledge of the English language and U.S. customs, the MPL began to offer seminars and classes for professional men, notably newspaper journalists. Classes for Cuban physicians were held at Jackson Memorial Hospital. Cuban lawyers attended the University of Miami Law School and used its law library for intensive study of American law.

At the request of the Pan-American Union, Archie L. McNeal, Director of Libraries at the University of Miami, established a clearinghouse for the placement of Cuban librarians. Some were placed, but others were not able to overcome the problem that many municipalities required employees to be American citizens. Elementary, junior, and high school libraries met the needs of refugee students by using English-speaking Cuban teachers as aides, working with teachers and pupils to bridge the language gap. Spanish-speaking librarians were employed in the Brockway Memorial Library in Miami Shores and at the Coral Gables Public Library as well as the MPL.

The MPL Foreign Language Division was developed by Alicia Godoy, a refugee from Castro's Cuba, who had master's degrees in philosophy and literature and one in library science from the University of Havana, and who had once worked in the Cuban National Library in Havana. The Reference Division assisted many Cuban refugees seeking employment with information about letters of application, names of vocational schools, colleges and universities, and correspondence courses in Spanish.

The libraries of the Miami area were assisted by Latin American radio announcers, including Robert Creus of WMET and Clarence Moore of WAEZ, and newspapermen, including Leopoldo Hernandez of the *Times of Havana,* Tony Solar of the *Miami News,* and Horacio Aguirre of *Diario las Americas,* to spread the word that the library welcomed immigrants and refugees.[45]

ALA Participation in the Civil Rights Movement

In the early 1960s, African Americans began to demand relief from local segregation laws and practices. The ALA was criticized for its lack of support and leadership. At the 1961 ALA midwinter meeting, the ALA Council approved Amendment Five to the Library Bill of Rights that declared that the rights of an individual to use a library should not be denied or abridged because of race, religion, national origins, or political views. Amendment Five was the work of the special ALA Committee on Civil Liberties appointed in 1960 to study the existing ALA statements regarding civil rights.

The ALA Intellectual Freedom Committee submitted three proposals to the ALA Executive Board: (1) to study the extent of freedom of access to libraries all over the country; (2) to deny institutional membership in ALA to segregated libraries; and (3) to study the membership in state associations and then deny chapter status to all segregated associations. The proposals were adopted at the 1962 annual conference in Miami, and the ALA Council on Library Resources pledged financial support for the proposed study. State chapters of ALA that could not guarantee rights to all members would be asked to withdraw from affiliation within three years. As a result of these pressures, segregated public libraries one by one began to disappear.[46]

The ALA contracted with the polling firm International Research Associates to survey U.S. libraries to note progress in the provision of public library services in the decade since the 1950 Public Library Inquiry. The resulting report, *Access to Public Libraries*, published in 1963 by the ALA, revealed that nonwhite neighborhoods, characterized by low educational levels and low incomes, had significantly less adequate library service than white neighborhoods of the same educational and income levels. The survey provided evidence of outright denial of access to blacks in five states of the Deep South, as well as proof of the existence of lesser barriers in the rest of the South. Ironically, the section of the report on access to foreign-language resources focused exclusively on European languages with no mention of library materials in Asian languages.

Expected as this information was, many librarians were outraged by the study's charge that although direct discrimination or complete exclusion of the members of one racial group from using a particular library or limitations on library use was confined to the 16 states classified as the South, indirect discrimination existed in libraries across the United States. Thomas F. Parker defended the findings of the 1963 study by noting that discrimination in the North resulted in the construction of more branches for the largely white suburbs than for urban areas inhabited primarily by blacks. Continued concerns within the ALA regarding the needs for integration and social justice led to the establishment of the Social Responsibilities Round Tale in 1968 at the ALA Annual Conference in Kansas City to begin to address the needs of minorities for library services.[47]

Library Service to the Disadvantaged

In 1968, the ALA Council established the Coordinating Committee on Library Service to the Disadvantaged to survey public libraries serving populations over 15,000. In 1969, the ALA published the results of its survey *Library Service to the Disadvantaged*. The committee discovered that of the 896 libraries responding, 212 reported services for the poor, 29 reported services for the functionally illiterate, 64 reported services for the aged, and 12 reported services for the Spanish speaking. Sixty percent of these programs were financed through regular library income, 15 percent financed with LSCA funds, and 12 percent financed with Community Action program funds available through the Economic Opportunity Act of 1964. The study showed that new library programs tended to focus on personal development and preparation for reading.[48]

An institute on Serving Disadvantaged Adults was held at the College of St. Catherine, St. Paul, Minnesota, on June 2–3, 1969, to address the public library service needs of American Indians, both urban and rural; African Americans; and Spanish-surnamed people, citizens, residents, and migrants. Participants at the institute learned how to develop programs for improving services to disadvantaged adults in their libraries by using community members as liaisons, setting up and listening to advisory committees from the group to be served, cooperating with local agencies, and using all possible media to communicate their messages.[49]

Border Regional Library Association (BRLA) and Project Leer

The BRLA was founded in 1966 for the promotion of library services in the metropolitan area encompassing El Paso, Las Cruces, and Ciudad Juarez. BRLA membership included librarians, paraprofessionals, media specialists, and library friends and trustees from all types of libraries in the tristate area of Trans-Pecos West Texas, southern New Mexico, and northern Chihuahua, Mexico.

Project Leer, initiated in October 1967, was a collaborative project of the Pan-American Union's Books-for-the-People Fund and the Bro-Dart Foundation. Leer, the Spanish verb "to read," served also as an acronym for Libros Elementales, Educativos, y Recreativos. The Books-for-the-People Fund provided a selection list of books in Spanish appropriate for U.S. school and public libraries, and the Bro-Dart Foundation provided library acquisition and processing services for Spanish library materials to complement other commercial library services.[50]

American Indians

During the 1966 fiscal year, the U.S. Senate Appropriations Committee surveyed federal facilities for American Indians in the Western states to determine the adequacy of state and library services and whether or not they were benefiting from the LSCA of 1964. The committee learned that of the 116 tribes or agencies surveyed, only 24 had bookmobile service. Neighboring public libraries were sometimes as far as 135 miles away, and many of those close to reservations either did not check out books to nonresidents of the city or charged a fee. Only three tribes reported receiving deposit collections from state libraries. Thirteen tribes had small community libraries, most of them consisting of donated materials collected by VISTA volunteers. Most of these collections consisted of donations of highly irrelevant materials.

Originally supported by multiagency funds, the responsibility for the Colorado River tribal library was taken over by the Colorado River Tribal Council in 1969. It was to Indians what the Peterborough, New Hampshire Library was to non-Indians, a national first.[51]

Wisconsin's Menominee County, formerly the Menominee Indian Reservation, was formed when the Menominee Tribe elected to become independent of the BIA and to maintain its own governmental services. In 1966, the State Library of Wisconsin granted the Menominee County Reference Service an LSCA grant of $8,000 to develop a library collection to serve as the basis for reference and referral, walk-in, and consultant services. The county librarian, granddaughter of a former tribal chief, built the collection primarily for the Indian children and young adults, since the number of adult readers in the country was negligible.[52]

Other early attempts in the 1960s at service to American Indians at the system and state commission levels included the Northeast Kansas Library System's efforts with the Potawatomi and Kickapoo reservations. The South Dakota Library Commission worked to provide library services at the Rosebud and Pine Ridge Sioux reservations. The Four Corners Mobile Library Service served Navajo and Apache residents in Arizona, New Mexico, Colorado, and Utah.

The Multi-County Library System in Ashland, Wisconsin, encompassing eight counties in the northwest section of Wisconsin and within its borders four reservations of Chippewa Indians, began to provide outreach services to the Chippewa. Outreach efforts of individual public libraries included the Sioux City (IA) Public Library, which pioneered with interstate cooperation in serving the Winnebago reservation in northeast Nebraska, 25 miles away; the Minot (ND) Public Library's bookmobile serving the Fort Berthold Indian Reservation, 80 miles away; and efforts by the public libraries in Tulsa, Billings, St. Paul, Cleveland, and Chicago to serve urban Indians.[53]

Haro Study on the Hispanic Community's Use of Libraries

In the late 1960s, Robert Haro interviewed 600 Mexican Americans in the Spanish-speaking communities of east Los Angeles and Sacramento. Among the attitudes he observed that distinguished Mexican Americans from other library users in the United States was their need for cultural reinforcement in literature and library service. They generally preferred to use libraries where Spanish was spoken and where Hispanic materials were available to them. Of those identified as library users, Haro detected an uneasiness about libraries in general. He explained that the resulting apathy was not so much a lack of interest as it was a lack of understanding about how libraries functioned and were administered.[54]

The 1970s witnessed the awakening of racial and ethnic awareness as evidenced by the Black Power, the Red Power, and Chicano movements. Libraries responded to these movements as well as to increased immigration from Asia and the Caribbean.

NOTES

1. U.S. Census Bureau, "No. 10: Resident Population—Selected Characteristics, 1950 to 2000, and Projections, 2025 and 2050," in *Statistical Abstract of the United States: 2001*, 121st ed. (Washington, DC: U.S. G.P.O., 2001), 13.

2. Marcia J. Nauratil, *Public Libraries and Nontraditional Clienteles: The Politics of Special Services* (Westport, CT: Greenwood Press, 1985), 101; Otis L. Graham Jr., *Unguarded Gates: A History of America's Immigration Crisis* (Lanham, MD: Rowman & Littlefield Publishers, 2004), xii.

3. Maldwyn Allen Jones, *American Immigration*, 2nd ed. (Chicago: University of Chicago Press, 1992), 246, 253, 264, 267, 277, 280–82; Robert Downs, "Signif-

icance of Foreign Materials for U.S. Collections," in *Acquisition of Foreign Materials for U.S. Libraries*, ed. Theodore Samore (Metuchen, NJ: Scarecrow Press, 1973), 4–5; Philip J. McNiff, "Cooperation in the Acquisition of Foreign Materials," in *Acquisition of Foreign Materials for U.S. Libraries*, 15; Donald F. Wisdom, "The First Two Decades of SALALM: A Personal Account," in *SALALM and the Area Studies Community: Papers of the Thirty-Seventh Annual Meeting of the Seminar on the Acquisition of Latin American Library Materials, Nettie Lee Benson Latin American Collection, University of Texas at Austin, Austin, Texas, May 30-June 4, 1992*, ed. David Block ([Albuquerque]: SALALM Secretariat, General Library, University of New Mexico, 1992), 118–52; U.S. Immigration and Naturalization Service, "Appendix 1: Immigration and Naturalization Legislation," *Statistical Yearbook of the Immigration and Naturalization Service, 1997* (Washington, DC: U.S. G.P.O., 1999), A.1–13; Michael LeMay and Elliot Robert Barkan, ed., *U.S. Immigration and Naturalization Laws and Issues: A Documentary History* (Westport, CT: Greenwood Press, 1999), 248–49; Marion T. Bennett, *American Immigration Policies: A History* (Washington, DC: Public Affairs Press, 1963), 209–11; Connie Van Fleet, "Lifelong Learning Theory and the Provision of Adult Services," in *Adult Services: An Enduring Focus for Public Libraries*, ed. Kathleen M. Heim and Danny P. Wallace (Chicago: ALA, 1990), 169; Nauratil, *Public Libraries and Nontraditional Clienteles*, 116.

4. U.S. Immigration and Naturalization Service, "Appendix 1: Immigration and Naturalization Legislation," A.1–14; E. Willard Miller and Ruby M. Miller, *United States Immigration: A Reference Handbook* (Santa Barbara, CA: ABC-CLIO, 1996), 113–14; LeMay and Barkan, *U.S. Immigration and Naturalization Laws and Issues*, 116–21; Bennett, *American Immigration Policies: A History*, 279–81.

5. R. Kathleen Molz, *The Federal Roles in Support of Public Library Services: An Overview*, prepared for the Federal Roles in Support of Public Library Services Project (Chicago: ALA, 1990), 9; Stephen Stern, "Ethnic Libraries and Librarianship in the United States: Models and Prospects," in *Advances in Librarianship*, ed. Irene P. Godden, vol. 15 (New York: Academic Press, 1991), 86–87; Tony A. Harvell, "Miami and the Cuban Revolution: Ties Across the Straits of Florida," in *SALALM and the Area Studies Community: Papers of the Thirty-Seventh Annual Meeting of the Seminar on the Acquisition of Latin American Library Materials*, 27–29; Lowell A. Martin, *Enrichment: A History of the Public Library in the United States in the Twentieth Century* (Lanham, MD: Scarecrow Press, 1998), 142–43; Gerald R. Shields, "Federal Legislation and Libraries," in *Libraries in the Political Process*, ed. E.J. Josey (Phoenix: Oryx Press, 1980), 6–7; Frank B. Sessa, "Public Libraries, International: History of the Public Library," in *Encyclopedia of Library and Information Science*, ed. Allen Kent, Harold Lancour, and Jay E. Daily, vol. 24 (New York: Marcel Dekker, 1976), 286–88; Charlene Cain, "Public Library Service to Minorities," in *Adult Services*, 218; Connie Van Fleet and Douglas Raber, "The Public Library as a Social/Cultural Institution:

Alternative Perspectives and Changing Contexts," in *Adult Services,* 488–90; Cheryl Metoyer-Duran, *Gatekeepers in Ethnolinguistic Communities* (Norwood, NJ: Ablex Publishing, 1993), 16–18; Edward G. Holley and Robert F. Schremser, *The Library Services and Construction Act: An Historical Overview from the Viewpoint of Major Participants* (Greenwich, CT: JAI Press, 1983), 147–48, 150–55; Germaine Krettek, "Library Legislation, Federal," in *Encyclopedia of Library and Information Science,* vol. 15 (New York: Marcel Dekker, 1975), 337–54.

6. U.S. Immigration and Naturalization Service, "Appendix 1: Immigration and Naturalization Legislation," A.1–14; Francesco Cordasco, "Bracero Program," in *Dictionary of American Immigration History* (Metuchen, NJ: Scarecrow Press, 1990), 91; LeMay and Barkan, *U.S. Immigration and Naturalization Laws and Issues,* 116–21, 252; Bennett, *American Immigration Policies,* 262–64; Graham, *Unguarded Gates,* 72.

7. Van Fleet, "Lifelong Learning Theory and the Provision of Adult Services," 178; Harlow G. Unger, ed., "Economic Opportunity Act (1964)," in *Encyclopedia of American Education,* 2nd ed. (New York: Facts on File, c2001, 1996), 357–59; Unger, "War on Poverty," in *Encyclopedia of American Education,* 1155–56; Cain, "Public Library Service to Minorities," 219; Xiwen Zhang, "The Anti-Affirmative Action Movement in California: Implications for Public Library Services to Asian Immigrants," in *Library Services to Latinos: An Anthology,* ed. Salvador Guerena (Jefferson, NC: McFarland, 2000), 101–2; Graham, *Unguarded Gates,* 82, 91.

8. U.S. Immigration and Naturalization Service, "Appendix 1: Immigration and Naturalization Legislation," A.1–14, A.1–15; Francesco Cordasco, "Immigration Act of 1965," in *Dictionary of American Immigration History,* 372–44; LeMay and Barkan, *U.S. Immigration and Naturalization Laws and Issues,* 256–63; M.A. Jones, *American Immigration,* 266–67, 251–53, 277–78; Thomas J. Archdeacon, *Becoming American: An Ethnic History* (New York: Free Press, 1983), 207–8; Miller and Miller, *United States Immigration: A Reference Handbook,* 95–98; Edward Prince Hutchinson, *Legislative History of American Immigration Policy, 1798–1965* (Philadelphia: Published for the Balch Institute for Ethnic Studies, by the University of Pennsylvania Press, 1981), 368–79; David M. Reimers, "Recent Immigration Policy: An Analysis," in *The Gateway: U.S. Immigration Issues and Policies,* ed. Barry R. Chiswick (Washington, DC: American Enterprise Institute for Public Policy Research, 1982), 32–42; William S. Bernard, "Immigration: History of U.S. Policy," in *Harvard Encyclopedia of American Ethnic Groups,* ed. Stephan Thernstrom, Ann Orlov, and Oscar Handlin (Cambridge: Belknap Press of Harvard University Press, 1980), 495; Reed Ueda, "Naturalization and Citizenship," in *Harvard Encyclopedia of American Ethnic Groups,* 747–48.

9. M.A. Jones, *American Immigration,* 269–78; Mary Christine Conaway, "Reaching the Unreached 'No Place' People," *Catholic Library World* 43 (Dec. 1971): 187; Walter Fogel, "Twentieth-Century Migration to the United States," in *The Gateway: U.S. Immigration Issues and Policies,* 197–200.

10. M.A. Jones, *American Immigration,* 270–71; Cordasco, "Immigration Act of 1965," in *Dictionary of American Immigration History,* 374; Francesco Cordasco, "Brain Drain," in *Dictionary of American Immigration History,* 92; Sucheng Chan, "Filipinos," in *Dictionary of American Immigration History,* 219; Graham, *Unguarded Gates,* 92.

11. Miller and Miller, *United States Immigration: A Reference Handbook,* 98; Reimers, "Recent Immigration Policy: An Analysis," 43–53.

12. Harlow G. Unger, ed., "At-risk Students," in "American Indian" in *Encyclopedia of American Education,* 102–3; Harlow G. Unger, ed., "Disadvantaged Students," in *Encyclopedia of American Education,* 334–35; Harlow G. Unger, ed., "Elementary and Secondary Education Act of 1965 (ESEA)," in *Encyclopedia of American Education,* 380; Harlow G. Unger, ed., "Higher Education Act of 1965," in *Encyclopedia of American Education,* 523; Richard Moses, "The Training of Librarians to Service the Unserved: The 'High John' Project," in *Library Service to the Unserved: Papers Presented at a Library Conference Held at the University of Wisconsin–Milwaukee, School of Library and Information Science, November 16–18, 1967,* ed. Laurence L. Sherrill, Library and Information Science Studies, no. 2 (New York: R.R. Bowker, 1970), 71–78; Richard Moses, "Hindsight on High John," in *Social Responsibilities and Libraries: A Library Journal/School Library Journal Selection,* comp. and ed. Patricia Glass Schuman (New York: R.R. Bowker, 1976), 171–75; Van Fleet, "Lifelong Learning Theory and the Provision of Adult Services," 178–79; Nancy W. Corrigan, "The Urban Negro and the Library," in *The Library's Public Revisited: By Members of the Class in The Public Library in the Political Process,* ed. Mary Lee Bundy and Sylvia Goodstein, Student Contribution Series, no. 1 (College Park: School of Library and Information Services, University of Maryland, 1967) 32–45; Jean L. Connor, "The Ripple Effect: Patterns of Library Service to the Unserved as Seen from the State Level," in *Library Service to the Unserved,* 63; Cain, "Public Library Service to Minorities," 221–22; Van Fleet, "Lifelong Learning Theory and the Provision of Adult Services," 179–80; Clara Chu, "Education for Multicultural Librarianship," in *Multiculturalism in Libraries,* by Rosemary Ruhig DuMont, Lois Buttlar, and William Caynon (Westport, CT: Greenwood Press, 1994), 129–31, 133–34; Nauratil, *Public Libraries and Nontraditional Clienteles,* 113–14.

13. U.S. Immigration and Naturalization Service, "Appendix 1: Immigration and Naturalization Legislation," A.1–15; LeMay and Barkan, *U.S. Immigration and Naturalization Laws and Issues,* 263–64; M.A. Jones, *American Immigration,* 280–83; Arnulfo D. Trejo, "Bicultural Americans with a Hispanic Tradition," *Wilson Library Bulletin* 44 (Mar. 1970): 722–23; Graham, *Unguarded Gates,* 99.

14. Charles M. Haar, *Between the Idea and the Reality: A Study in the Origin, Fate, and Legacy of the Model Cities Program* (Boston: Little, Brown, 1975).

15. Francesco Cordasco, "Bilingual Education," in *Dictionary of American Immigration History,* 78; M.A. Jones, *American Immigration,* 276–77; Francesco Cordasco, "Bilingual Education in American Schools: A Bibliographical Essay,"

Immigration History Newsletter 14 (May 1982): 1–8; Armando Rodriguez, "The Necessity of Bilingual Education," *Wilson Library Bulletin* 44 (Mar. 1970): 728; Harlow G. Unger, ed., "Bilingual/Bicultural Education," in *Encyclopedia of American Education,* 137–38; Harlow G. Unger, ed., "Bilingual Instruction," in *Encyclopedia of American Education,* 138–39; Abigail M. Thernstrom, "Language: Issues and Legislation," in *Harvard Encyclopedia of American Ethnic Groups,* 619–26.

16. Eleanor T. Smith, "Public Library Service to the Economically and Culturally Deprived: A Profile of the Brooklyn Public Library," in *The Library Reaches Out: Reports on Library Service and Community Relations by Some Leading American Librarians,* comp. and ed. Kate Coplan and Edwin Castagna (Dobbs Ferry, NY: Oceana Publications, 1965), 225–27; Cain, "Public Library Service to Minorities," 217–18; Jules Mersel, Morton H. Friedman, Emory H. Holmes, John F. Knudson, Eugene R. Streich, *An Overview of the Library Services and Construction Act-Title I* (New York: R.R. Bowker, 1969), 73–74.

17. Mersel et al., *An Overview of the Library Services and Construction Act-Title I,* 137–41, 186–87.

18. Eleanor Frances Brown, *Library Service to the Disadvantaged* (Metuchen, NJ: Scarecrow Press, 1971), 466–69; Marva L. DeLoach and Glenderlyn Johnson, "Afro-American Collections," in *Ethnic Collections in Libraries,* ed. E.J. Josey and Marva L. DeLoach (New York: Neal-Schuman Publishers, 1983), 119–49; Mersel et al., *An Overview of the Library Services and Construction Act-Title I,* 189; John C. Colson, "The United States: An Historical Critique," in *Library Services to the Disadvantaged,* ed. William Martin (Hamden, CT: Linnet Books, 1975), 70.

19. California State Library, "Special Issue: LSCA in California," in *News Notes of California Libraries* 71, no. 2 (1976): 20, 33, 34; Mersel et al., *An Overview of the Library Services and Construction Act-Title I,* 282–84; Richard Vasquez, "Libraries Lure Barrio Youth," *California Librarian* 31 (July 1970): 200–3.

20. California State Library, "Special Issue: LSCA in California," 18; William H. Farrington, "Library Services to Mexican-Americans," in *Library and Information Services for Special Groups,* ed. Joshua I Smith (New York: published in cooperation with the American Society for Information Science and the ERIC Clearinghouse on Library and Information Sciences, by Science Associates/International, 1974), 309; Brown, *Library Service to the Disadvantaged,* 406; Roberto Cabello-Argandona and Roberto P. Haro, "Library Services for the Spanish Speaking: A Systematic Review and Analysis," in *Library Services to Mexican Americans: Policies, Practices and Prospects,* ed. Roberto Urzua, Martha P. Cotera, and Emma Gonzalez Stupp, prepared by Project Staff, University of Texas, Nettie Lee Benson Latin American Collection, Mexican American Library Project (Las Cruces, NM: New Mexico State University for Educational Resources Information Center Clearinghouse on Rural Education and Small Schools, 1978), 13–14; Cain, "Public Library Service to Minorities," 225; Metoyer-Duran, *Gatekeepers in Ethnolinguistic Communities,* 17; Barbara L. Wynn, "Oakland, California: La Biblioteca Latino Americana," *Wilson Library Bulletin* 44 (Mar. 1970): 751–56;

Pauline Winnick, "The Role of the Public Library," in *Public Library Service to the Disadvantaged*, Proceedings of an Institute, December 7th and 8th, 1967 (Atlanta: Division of Librarianship, Emory University, 1969), 33; Robert P. Haro, *Developing Library and Information Services for Americans of Hispanic Origin* (Metuchen, NJ: Scarecrow Press, 1981), 32–35; Nauratil, *Public Libraries and Nontraditional Clienteles*, 116; National Citizens Emergency Committee to Save Our Public Libraries, "Serving Citizens with Special Needs: How Libraries Can Enrich Lives and Fulfill Aspirations for the Elderly and the Handicapped, the Functionally Illiterate, Hispanic Americans, Native Americans, the Homebound and Inmates of Correctional Institutions," in *The Changing Role of Public Libraries: Background Papers from the White House Conference*, comp. Whitney North Seymour Jr. (Metuchen, NJ: Scarecrow Press, 1980; copyright 1979, 1980 by the New York Public Library), 21; Mersel et al., *An Overview of the Library Services and Construction Act-Title I*, 279.

21. Brown, *Library Service to the Disadvantaged*, 245–46; Jean L. Connor, "The Ripple Effect," in *Library Service to the Unserved*, 63; E.J. Josey, "Minority Groups, Library Service for," in *Encyclopedia of Library and Information Science*, ed. Allen Kent, Harold Lancour, and Jay E. Daily, vol. 18 (New York: Marcel Dekker, 1976), 193–94; John Mackenzie Cory, "The New York Public Library," in *Encyclopedia of Library and Information Science*, vol. 19 (New York: Marcel Dekker, 1976), 385; Nauratil, *Public Libraries and Nontraditional Clienteles*, 114; Mersel et al., *An Overview of the Library Services and Construction Act-Title I*, 75–76.

22. Joseph A. Rosenthal, "Special Services for the Spanish-speaking Public Served by the Branch Libraries of the New York Public Library," in *Twelfth Seminar on the Acquisition of Latin American Library Materials, Los Angeles, California, June 22–24, 1967*, sponsored by the University of California at Los Angeles and the Pan American Union, Peter J. de la Garza, Rapporteur General, Working Paper, vol. 1, no. 11 (Washington, DC: Pan American Union, General Secretariat, Organization of American States, 1968), 259–62; Lillian Lopez, "The South Bronx Project," *Wilson Library Bulletin* 44 (Mar. 1970): 757–59; Marta Stiefel Ayala, "Lilian [i.e. Lillian] Lopez [interview]," *Wilson Library Bulletin* 53 (Nov. 1978): 249; "Pilot Project Offers Expanded Services to NYC Spanish Community," *NYLA Bulletin* 15 (Sept. 1967): 152; Brown, *Library Service to the Disadvantaged*, 403, 469; Bruni Verges, "Developing Collections on Puerto Rican Heritage," in *Ethnic Collections in Libraries*, 66, 70; Cain, "Public Library Service to Minorities," 225; Haynes McMullen, "Services to Ethnic Minorities Other than Afro-Americans and American Indians," in *A Century of Service: Librarianship in the United States and Canada*, ed. Sidney L. Jackson, Eleanor B. Herling, and E.J. Josey (Chicago: ALA, 1976), 56; "South Bronx Library Reopens," *The Bookmark* 28 (Mar. 1969): 200; Brown, *Library Service to the Disadvantaged*, 403–4; Haro, *Developing Library and Information Services for Americans of Hispanic Origin*, 28–30; Nauratil, *Public Libraries and Nontraditional Clienteles*, 116; National Citizens Emergency Committee to Save Our Public

Libraries, "Serving Citizens with Special Needs," 22; Mersel et al., *An Overview of the Library Services and Construction Act-Title I,* 76–77.

23. Brown, *Library Service to the Disadvantaged,* 470.

24. Joseph B. Olvera Jr., Evelyn Escatiola, Margaret Mercado, Benjamin Ocon, and Albert Tovar, "Chicano Collections of Library Resources," in *Ethnic Collections in Libraries,* 80; California State Library, *Catalog of Local Assistance: Library Services and Construction Act, Titles I, II, III, 1976–1989* (Sacramento: California State Library, 1988), 55; Harlow G. Unger, ed., "Adult Basic Education (ABE)," in *Encyclopedia of American Education,* 30; Brown, *Library Service to the Disadvantaged,* 254–55, 448–51; Fern Long, "New Citizens in the Library," *ALA Bulletin* 51 (Jan. 1957): 27–28; Ruth Goren, "Milwaukee Public Library," in *Encyclopedia of Library and Information Science,* vol. 18: 132–33.

25. Brown, *Library Service to the Disadvantaged,* 261, 398–99; John A. Murphey Jr., "Corpus Christi, Texas," *Wilson Library Bulletin* 44 (Mar. 1970): 765.

26. Genevieve M. Casey, "Library Service to the Handicapped and Institutionalized," *Library Trends* 20 (Oct. 1971): 354–58.

27. National Citizens Emergency Committee to Save Our Public Libraries, "Serving Citizens with Special Needs," 25.

28. Lowell A. Martin, *Baltimore Reaches Out: Library Service to the Disadvantaged,* Deiches Fund Studies of Public Library Services, no. 3 (Baltimore: Enoch Pratt Free Library, 1967); Brown, *Library Service to the Disadvantaged,* 239–43; Margaret E. Monroe, "Reader Services to the Disadvantaged in Inner Cities," in *Advances in Librarianship,* vol. 2, ed. Melvin J. Voigt (New York: Academic Press, 1971), 257–58.

29. Alex Ladenson, "Chicago: The Public Library Reaches Out," *Wilson Library Bulletin* 43 (May 1969): 875–81; Lowell A. Martin, *Library Response to Urban Change: A Study of the Chicago Public Library* (Chicago: ALA, 1969), 2–3; Brown, *Library Service to the Disadvantaged,* 401; Margaret E. Monroe, "The Cultural Role of the Public Library," in *Advances in Librarianship,* vol. 11: 18–22; Monroe, "Reader Services to the Disadvantaged in Inner Cities," 258–59.

30. Brown, *Library Service to the Disadvantaged,* 249–51; Colson, "The United States: An Historical Critique," 71.

31. Mildred L. Hennessy, "The Operation Head Start Project at the Queens Borough Public Library," in *Public Library Services to the Disadvantaged,* Proceedings of an Institute, December 7th and 8th, 1967 (Atlanta: Division of Librarianship, Emory University, 1969), 45–57; Mersel et al., *An Overview of the Library Services and Construction Act-Title I,* 74–75.

32. Brown, *Library Service to the Disadvantaged,* 243–45, 406, 410–11, 454–55; William L. Ramirez, "Libraries and the Spanish-Speaking," *Wilson Library Bulletin* 44 (Mar. 1970): 714.

33. Unger, "Elementary and Secondary Education Act of 1965 (ESEA)," 380; Unger, "Higher Education Act of 1965," 523; Moses, "The Training of Librar-

ians to Service the Unserved," 71–78; Moses, "Hindsight on High John," 171–75; Van Fleet, "Lifelong Learning Theory and the Provision of Adult Services," 178–79; Corrigan, "The Urban Negro and the Library," 32–45; Connor, "The Ripple Effect," 63; Cain, "Public Library Service to Minorities," 221–22; Van Fleet, "Lifelong Learning Theory and the Provision of Adult Services," 179–80; Clara Chu, "Education for Multicultural Librarianship," 129–31, 133–34; Nauratil, *Public Libraries and Nontraditional Clienteles,* 113–14.

34. Shields, "Federal Legislation and Libraries," in *Libraries in the Political Process,* 8; Douglas M. Knight and E. Shepley Nourse, eds., *Libraries at Large: Tradition, Innovation, and the National Interest,* Preface, by Douglas M. Knight (New York: R. R. Bowker, 1969), ix–xi; Molz, *The Federal Roles in Support of Public Library Services,* 21–22; John H. Rebenack, "Public Libraries, International: Contemporary Libraries in the United States," in *Encyclopedia of Library and Information Science,* vol. 24: 330–31; Cain, "Public Library Service to Minorities," 220; Monroe, "Reader Services to the Disadvantaged in Inner Cities," 261–62.

35. Eileen D. Cooke, "Legislation to Assist Libraries to Serve the Unserved," in *Library Service to the Unserved,* 49–53; Cain, "Public Library Service to Minorities," 219–20; Haar, *Between the Idea and the Reality,* v–x, 315–27, including Appendix 4: Demonstration Cities and Metropolitan Development Act of 1966, Title I, 315–22; Holley and Schremser, *The Library Services and Construction Act,* 76–80.

36. Joanne Coyne, "'Los Amigos' for the Spanish-speaking Mother," *Library Journal* 91 (15 Jan. 1966): 329–31; Frances A. Bucy, "Denver, Colorado: El Numero Cinco," *Wilson Library Bulletin* 44 (Mar. 1970): 765–66; Brown, *Library Service to the Disadvantaged,* 405, 457–58; Van Fleet, "Lifelong Learning Theory and the Provision of Adult Services," 178; Haro, *Developing Library and Information Services for Americans of Hispanic Origin,* 25–27; Colson, "The United States: An Historical Critique," 71.

37. Rosemary Smith Dawood, "An Informal Information Service at the Chicago Public Library's Bezazian Branch," in *Libraries and Neighborhood Information Centers,* papers presented at an Institute conducted by the University of Illinois, Graduate School of Library Science, October 25–27, 1971, 17th ser., ed. Carol L. Kronus and Linda Crowe (Urbana: University of Illinois, Graduate School of Library Science, 1972); Brown, *Library Service to the Disadvantaged,* 253–54, 403.

38. California State Library, "Special Issue: LSCA in California," 36; Metoyer-Duran, *Gatekeepers in Ethnolinguistic Communities,* 17; Mersel et al., *An Overview of the Library Services and Construction Act-Title I,* 189, 279.

39. Mersel et al., *An Overview of the Library Services and Construction Act-Title I,* 75.

40. Winnick, "The Role of the Public Library," 37.

41. Farrington, "Library Services to Mexican-Americans," 321–24; Nauratil, *Public Libraries and Nontraditional Clienteles,* 116; Mary B. Reynolds, "San

Joaquin Valley, California: La Biblioteca Ambulante," *Wilson Library Bulletin* 44 (Mar. 1970): 767; Mary Boyvey, "Library Services to Mexican Americans" *Texas Libraries* 32 (Fall 1970): 136–37; Shelah-Bell Cragin, "Mexican-Americans: A Part of The Reading Public," *Texas Libraries* 32 (Fall 1970): 139–44; Austin Hoover, "Workshop on Library Services and Materials for Mexican-Americans," *Texas Library Journal* 46 (Winter 1970): 206–8; National Citizens Emergency Committee to Save Our Public Libraries, "Serving Citizens with Special Needs," 18, 21; Mersel et al., *An Overview of the Library Services and Construction Act-Title I,* 280.

42. Holley and Schremser, *The Library Services and Construction Act,* 88–92.

43. Leo Pap, "Portuguese," in *Dictionary of American Immigration History,* 594–95; M.A. Jones, *American Immigration,* 248–49; Kathryn E. Ryan, "Libraries, Prejudice, and the Portuguese," *Current Studies in Librarianship* [Graduate Library School, University of Rhode Island] (Spring/Fall 1985): 59–64; Penelope Pillsbury and Mary Van Buren, "French Canadians in Vermont Focus of Northwest Libraries Section Meeting," *Vermont Libraries* 4 (Nov. 1975): 116–17; Jake Sherman, "Library Programs for Ethnic Americans," *The Library Scene* 4 (Dec. 1975/Mar. 1976): 11–13.

44. Richard S. Sorrell, "The Historiography of French Canadians," *Immigration History Newsletter* 11 (May 1979): 4–8; Sherman, "Library Programs for Ethnic Americans," 11–13.

45. Helga H. Eason, "Miami, Florida," *Wilson Library Bulletin* 44 (Mar. 1970): 760–62; Helga H. Eason, "More Than Money," *Wilson Library Bulletin* 36 (June 1962): 825–28; Dorothy Sinclair, "Materials to Meet Special Needs," *Library Trends* 17 (July 1968): 42; Alicia Godoy, "Miami: Two Decades of Latin Accent," *Wilson Library Bulletin* 53 (Nov. 1978): 236–37.

46. Doris Hargrett Clack, "Segregation and the Library," in *Encyclopedia of Library and Information Science,* vol. 27 (New York: Marcel Dekker, 1979), 193–94; Van Fleet, "Lifelong Learning Theory and the Provision of Adult Services," 177–78; Metoyer-Duran, *Gatekeepers in Ethnolinguistic Communities,* 2–3; Arthur Curley, "Social Responsibility and Libraries," in *Advances in Librarianship,* vol. 4: 84, 90–95.

47. International Research Associates, *Access to Public Libraries: A Research Project,* prepared for the Library Administration Division, American Library Association (Chicago: American Library Association, 1963); Vasquez, "Libraries Lure Barrio Youth," 200–203; Sinclair, "Materials to Meet Special Needs," 42; Dennis Thomison, *A History of the American Library Association, 1876–1972* (Chicago: ALA, 1978), 216–23; Josey, "Minority Groups, Library Service for," 189–93; Cain, "Public Library Service to Minorities," 218–19, 223; Metoyer-Duran, *Gatekeepers in Ethnolinguistic Communities,* 2–5; Nauratil, *Public Libraries and Nontraditional Clienteles,* 113; National Citizens Emergency Committee to Save Our Public Libraries, "Serving Citizens with Special Needs," 19; Mersel et al., *An Overview of the Library Services and Construction Act-Title I,* 189;

Monroe, "Reader Services to the Disadvantaged in Inner Cities," 254; Curley, "Social Responsibility and Libraries," 78, 83–84.

48. Vasquez, "Libraries Lure Barrio Youth," 200–203; Metoyer-Duran, *Gatekeepers in Ethnolinguistic Communities,* 2–5; Monroe, "Reader Services to the Disadvantaged in Inner Cities," 256–57.

49. Ysidro Ramon Macias, "The Chicano Movement," *Wilson Library Bulletin* 44 (Mar. 1970): 735; Brown, *Library Service to the Disadvantaged,* 419–22; Metoyer-Duran, *Gatekeepers in Ethnolinguistic Communities,* 2–5.

50. Brown, *Library Service to the Disadvantaged,* 401; Sinclair, "Materials to Meet Special Needs," 45–46; Marietta Daniels Shepard, "Reading Resources and Project LEER," *Wilson Library Bulletin* 44 (Mar. 1970): 748–50; M.A. Jones, *American Immigration,* 269–78; Conaway, "Reaching the Unreached 'No Place' People," 190; McMullen, "Services to Ethnic Minorities Other than Afro-Americans and American Indians," 57.

51. Delores J. Huff, *To Live Heroically: Institutional Racism and American Indian Education* (Albany: State University of New York, 1997), 16–21; Nauratil, *Public Libraries and Nontraditional Clienteles,* 112–13; National Citizens Emergency Committee to Save Our Public Libraries, "Serving Citizens with Special Needs," 25.

52. Mersel et al., *An Overview of the Library Services and Construction Act-Title I,* 188–89.

53. Janet N. Naumer, "Library Services to American Indians," in *Library and Information Services for Special Groups,* 38–46; Brown, *Library Service to the Disadvantaged,* 421–25; National Citizens Emergency Committee to Save Our Public Libraries, "Serving Citizens with Special Needs," 26.

54. Robert P. Haro, "How Mexican-Americans View Libraries: One-Man Survey," *Wilson Library Bulletin* 44 (Mar. 1970): 736–42; Haro, *Developing Library and Information Services for Americans of Hispanic Origin,* 1–43; Rebecca Constantino, "'It's Like a Lot of Things in America': Linguistic Minority Parents' Use of Libraries," *School Library Media Quarterly* 22 (Winter 1994): 87–89; Roberto Cabello-Argandona, "Recruiting Spanish-Speaking Library Students," in *Social Responsibilities and Libraries,* 125–30; Cabello-Argandona and Haro, "Library Services for the Spanish Speaking," 1–36; Josey, "Minority Groups, Library Service for," 195–96; Cain, "Public Library Service to Minorities," 229; Stern, "Ethnic Libraries and Librarianship in the United States," 91–92; DuMont et al., *Multiculturalism in Libraries,* 40; F. Duran, "The Chicano School Library Media Specialist," in *Opportunities for Minorities in Librarianship,* ed. E.J. Josey and Kenneth E. Peeples Jr. (Metuchen, NJ: Scarecrow Press, 1977), 29–36.

Chapter 4

PUBLIC LIBRARIES AND RACIAL AND ETHNIC AWARENESS IN THE 1970s

During the decade of the 1970s, the U.S. population was approximately 201 million, with the racial breakdown being 89 percent white, 11 percent black. The federal government did not keep statistics on American Indians and Hispanics.[1]

The hard-won battles of the civil rights movement for African Americans fueled the Black Power movement. The quality of life for Native Americans was improved by the Red Power movement, which emphasized the positive values of Indian culture and rejection of the materialism and competitiveness that were perceived to pervade white society. This movement, which was brought to national attention through the seizure of Wounded Knee, South Dakota, in 1973, has led to an increased sense of cultural pride and identity and to a greater degree of self-determination for reservation Indians and to the reclamation of tribal lands, resulting in an improved economic base for many groups of Native Americans.

The Chicano movement, which began somewhat later than the African American and Native American movements, has maintained a lower profile. Nevertheless, the formation of the United Farm Workers among the predominantly Mexican agricultural laborers of the Southwest made Cesar Chavez a national spokesman for their cause, and the voting strength of Hispanic Americans was felt in many states.[2]

LEGAL AND JUDICIAL DECISIONS AFFECTING MINORITIES

Ethnic Studies Heritage Act (ESHA) of 1972

The ESHA of June 1972, an amendment to the ESEA of 1965, provided further assistance to organizations similar in purpose to the center at Kent State University. The act provided funds that could be used to enable students to have opportunities to learn about the nature of their own cultural heritage, and to study the contributions of the cultural heritages of the other ethnic groups of the United States. U.S. Office of Education grants were made available to public and private nonprofit educational agencies, institutions, and organizations to assist them in planning, developing, and establishing and operating ethnic heritage studies programs.[3]

American higher education institutions began to increase their offerings of ethnic studies programs. African American scholars took the lead in developing such courses and established them as legitimate areas of academic concentration that led to degrees in African American studies. Following their example, scholars from other ethnic groups, notably Mexican Americans or Chicanos, lobbied for the inclusion of courses in the curricula of academic institutions to provide ethnic students the opportunity to learn about their diverse heritages. Writers, who were not members of the ethnic group studied, were considered "outsiders" and, as such, suspect. Despite this ethnocentrism, extensive bibliographies of articles, books, and periodicals were produced for every major ethnic group.[4]

Immigration from Vietnam and Southeast Asia

Before the fall of Saigon in April 1975, there had been little immigration from Indochina, except for a few thousand Vietnamese wives of American servicemen and their children. The sudden communist victory precipitated a panic-stricken flight of Vietnamese refugees, who had been associated with the U.S. presence in Vietnam, feared Vietcong reprisals, and hastened to escape.

Although some U.S. citizens feared job competition from the large influx of Vietnamese refugees and others disapproved of U.S. involvement in Vietnam, most accepted that an obligation existed toward an ally. Congress overwhelmingly approved the Indochina Migration and Refugee Assistance Act of May 1975, which amended the Migration and Refugee Assistance Act of 1962, and made $455 million available for the resettlement and education and training of refugees from Cambodia and Vietnam. The 1975 act redefined the term "refugee" to include people from Vietnam, Laos, and Cambodia (Kampuchea), because the 1962 act had been only applicable to natives of the Western Hemisphere. In June 1976, Congress passed legislation making Laotians eligible for programs and services established by the 1975 act.[5]

The Indochinese Mutual Assistance Division of the U.S. Department of Health, Education, and Welfare was established in July 1976 to provide technical assistance to the more than 100 self-help associations involved in the resettlement of Indochinese refugees. Although the U.S. government attempted to disperse the Vietnamese throughout the country, they had reassembled through secondary migrations within a few months in states like California and Texas, which had long-standing Asian communities. In October 1977, Congress passed legislation to permit adjustment to permanent resident status for Indochinese refugees, who were natives or citizens of Vietnam, Laos, or Cambodia, and were physically present in the United States for at least two years.[6]

Continuing turmoil in Southeast Asia between 1975 and 1979 led to a major new refugee crisis. In Vietnam, communist economic measures and a policy of population resettlement prompted large-scale departures of boat people, while the harassment of the country's Chinese minority had a similar effect. In Laos, a communist takeover was the signal for a mass exodus of Hmong and lowland Lao. In Cambodia (Kampuchea), Pol Pot's reign of terror created floods of refugees. By the end of 1980, the number of Indochinese refugees admitted to the United States had reached half a million.

The boat people were very different in comparison with the earlier refugees from Southeast Asia. The boat people who followed were more representative of Indochinese societies, including peasants, fishermen, and laborers. They were generally ill-educated, knew little of Western culture, rarely spoke English, and often arrived penniless. The high concentration of Indochinese in California, Texas, and Florida placed strains on local schools and social services.[7]

Caribbean Immigration

Approximately 50,000, mostly middle-class, English-speaking Caribbean immigrants, were legally entering the country annually throughout the 1970s and into the early 1980s, with thousands more entering illegally. Many of the new West Indian influx were professional, white-collar, skilled workers, but there were also numbers of unskilled workers, especially female domestic servants. The majority continued to migrate to New York City, although some settled in Miami and Los Angeles.

The simultaneous arrival of 30,000 Haitians added further to the regions' problems. Nativist hostility was intensified by the federal government's slowness in providing help and by the unfortunate fact that Castro was allowing criminals and other undesirables to leave Cuba for the United States.[8]

1976 Amendments to the INA of 1952

In September 1976, the INS announced that Cuban refugees in the United States might become permanent resident aliens without having to wait for visa numbers to become available under the Western Hemisphere quotas. Cuban refugees, who in the past were paroled into the United States, were now eligible to apply for adjustment of status after maintaining parole status for a minimum of two years. From this point forward, Cuban refugees would be able to adjust status in the United States outside the annual immigration cap for the Western Hemisphere.

In October 1976, Congress reacted to pressure from immigration restrictionists by passing further amendments to the 1965 amendments to the INA of 1952 that set annual immigration limits for both the Western and Eastern Hemispheres using the total of 20,000 per country. The 1976 amendments slightly modified the seven-category preference system and applied it to the Western Hemisphere.[9]

U.S. Select Commission on Immigration and Refugee Policy of 1978

In 1978, President Jimmy Carter appointed a bipartisan U.S. Select Commission on Immigration and Refugee Policy to make a major study of immigration and recommend changes. The 16-member commission was chaired by Father Theodore Hesburgh, president of Notre Dame University. The commission's report, not submitted to Congress until 1981, during the presidency of Ronald Reagan, would become the basis for immigration reform legislation in the 1980s. In 1979, Congress passed the Panama Canal Act of September 1979 that allowed admission as permanent residents to aliens employed on or before 1977 with the Panama Canal Company, the Canal Zone government, or the U.S. government in the Canal Zone, and their families.

The INS, in determining refugee status for Central Americans, Haitians, and South Americans, often dismissed the political causes and usually denied asylum to people with legitimate claims of having been persecuted in their native countries. Denial for admission usually meant deportation and reprisals against the individuals when they returned. The problem was that many Central Americans, especially Salvadorans and Guatemalans, not only were fleeing political repression and violence but also emigrating from extremely poor countries. Nevertheless, all but a handful of Central American refugees were turned away on the grounds that they were not genuine political refugees but simply economic migrants.[10]

Bilingual Education

The Bilingual Education Act of 1968 was renewed in 1974 and again in 1978 as amendments to the ESEA of 1965. The 1974 amendments were designed to aid areas of the country with high concentrations of persons with limited English-speaking ability. The 1974 amendment to the Bilingual Education Act created an interest in Spanish-language publishing and temporarily opened a floodgate to what turned out to be waves of inferior products and bad translations, among other problems.

The Supreme Court decision in *Lau v. Nichols* ruled in 1974 that children with a limited English-speaking ability were entitled to remedial instruction. This case was a class-action suit filed on behalf of some 1,800 non-English-speaking Chinese students against the San Francisco Unified School District.[11]

The 1978 amendments to the ESEA placed a new stress on parental involvement, instructed local schools to use personnel proficient in both the language of instruction and English, and expanded the meaning of linguistic deficiency to include both reading and writing. Eligible participants were defined by law as children with limited English proficiency as opposed to limited English-speaking ability.

In April 1978, President Jimmy Carter appointed the Commission on Foreign Languages and International Studies. In November 1979, the commission called for boosting federal subsidies for international exchange programs and training of teachers and graduate students. It also proposed the creation of 60 special-language high schools in metropolitan areas.[12]

American Indians

In 1972, the Indian Education Act authorized new educational programs for American Indians, including grants to local educational agencies and special literacy and job-training programs for Indian adults. Three years later, in 1975, Congress passed the Indian Self-Determination and Education Assistance Act to allow tribal groups to operate their own education facilities.[13]

In 1978, the Tribally Controlled Community College Assistance Act provided federal funds for the operation and improvement of tribally controlled community colleges for Indian students and empowered local Indian school boards to hire teachers and school staff without interference from the federal government. The 1978 act also provided for direct funding from the BIA for all types of Indian educational institutions.[14]

LSCA Amendments

Title I was funded at $35 million in fiscal year 1971. In December 1970, LSCA amendments were passed that emphasized services to low-income families and provided funds for strengthening state library administrative agencies and major urban resource libraries (MURLs) to serve as national or regional resource centers. Titles I, IV-A, and IV-B were consolidated as Title I. Titles II and III were continued. The new Title I (including the former Titles IV-A and IV-B) received appropriations of approximately $47 million is fiscal year 1972; $62 million in fiscal year 1973; approximately $49 million in each of fiscal years 1974 through 1976; and approximately $57 million in each of fiscal years 1977 and 1978. Title I appropriations in each of fiscal years 1979 and 1980 rose to $62.5 million.

Appropriations for Title II began at approximately $12 million in each of fiscal years 1971 and 1972, and then fell to approximately $3 million in fiscal year 1974. In fiscal years 1974 and 1975, the Title II appropriates were respectively $15 million and $4 million. Title II was not funded in fiscal years 1976 through 1980. Title III appropriations rose from approximately $2 million in fiscal year 1970 to $5 million in fiscal year 1980.

In 1973, the LSCA was amended in compliance with the Older Americans Comprehensive Services Act Amendments to add a new Title IV, Older Readers Services. Although the new Title IV was never funded, library projects for elderly readers were allowed under Title I. Also in 1973, the LSCA was amended by the National Foundation on the Arts and the Humanities Act Amendments to enlarge the definition of a public library to include research libraries that offered access to their collections and services to the general public.

In 1974, the LSCA was amended to add program priority for service to areas of high concentrations of persons of limited English-speaking ability. In 1977, further amendments added emphasis on strengthening MURLs serving African Americans, American Indians, and other minorities. This was providential for California's public libraries, since the passage of Proposition 13 in June 1978 would greatly reduce the state's property tax revenues by 57 percent.[15]

LIBRARY SERVICES WITH MINORITIES

Model Cities Projects

Model Cities Projects, the result of the 1966 enabling act, continued into the 1970s. In 1973, the Model Cities Neighborhood Library in Albuquerque was established to serve not only the Mexican Americans, who composed some 70 percent of community, but also American Indians, a developing African American population, and a poor white population. A bicycle repair class nearly took over the building and free income tax service brought people into the library for the first time in their lives. More than half of the staff was Spanish speaking and lived in the barrios or neighborhoods surrounding the library. Under the supervision of director Richard Levine, the library offered specialized services promoting an intensive interaction with the users and cultural programs with no traditional library rules and regulations in force.[16]

From 1972 to 1974, the Metropolitan Cooperative Library System received LSCA grants totaling $85,000 to improve service to African Americans in Pasadena, Altadena, and Monrovia, and Mexican Americans in Pomona, Azusa, Whittier, Santa Fe Springs, and Monterey Park. Mini-collections of books and pamphlets designed to attract nonusers to public libraries were placed in the waiting rooms of 25 local public services agencies.[17]

In 1974, the Montclair Free Public Library (NJ) opened a neighborhood information and referral (I&R) center in an economically depressed area, staffed by social workers, media specialists, and paraprofessional outreach workers, as well as professional community information librarians. In the late 1970s, the Model Cities Community Information Center in Philadelphia operated an I&R service independently of the Free Library of Philadelphia. From 1972 to 1974, the Richmond (CA) Public Library's Mobile Outreach Project (MOP) received LSCA grants totaling $45,000 to serve primarily African Americans rather than the previous targeted group of Mexican Americans and African Americans.[18]

Neighborhood Information Centers (NIC) Project

In May 1975, the Conference on Information and Referral Service in Public Libraries was held at the Detroit Public Library. The conference was sponsored by the NIC Project Consortium, consisting of the public libraries of Atlanta, Houston, Detroit, Queens Borough (New York City), and Cleveland. The project had been funded since 1972 by the Office of Library Research and Demonstration of the U.S. Department of Health, Education, and Welfare.

Prior to the receipt of federal funding in 1972, the Detroit Public Library had used its own funds to begin the development of its TIP (The Information Place) program in 1971. In June 1973, due to the dedicated administrative commitment of director Clara Stanton Jones, who influenced the planning, development, and continuance of the program, TIP was implemented in all 29 branches. After four years of staff orientation, file building, organizational change, and a comprehensive community study, Detroit decided to go public with its TIP project at the conference. In 1976, due in no small part to the originality and initial success of the TIP project, Clara Stanton Jones was elected ALA president during the ALA's Centennial Year, the first African American librarian to hold this position.

Each of the five libraries met and completed the original project objectives, but only two of the five expanded services in their communities. In Houston, director David Henington, with strong support by the mayor and city administration, extended services on a systemwide basis and received increased funding and staffing. He attributed a 50 percent budget increase, 142 new positions, and a much-improved level of credibility with city hall to the success of the library's I&R program. Despite initial commitment to the project, the other three public library systems in Atlanta, Cleveland, and Queens Borough were sidetracked by changes in administrative leadership, internal organizational restructuring, and staff resistance.

In addition to providing a model for other libraries, the Detroit Public Library began to export talent as well. In 1975, former deputy director Bob Croneberger and community social work consultant Carolyn Luck of the TIP program were appointed assistant director for public services and head of community information and referral services, respectively, at the Memphis and Shelby County Public Library and Information Center to work with C. Lamar Wallis, director, to initiate an I&R service called LINC (Library Information Center). The library had been awarded a two-year grant of $368,000 in federal revenue sharing funds to provide comprehensive I&R services. Croneberger and Luck, who had at first been advocates of decentralized I&R services, later realized that high-quality service needed to be concentrated in the central library, where the best trained, most experienced, and most knowledgeable staff were located. As part of its LINC program, the library helped Vietnamese refugees adapt to American life by providing books and tapes for learning English, as well as transportation to English classes at a local high school.[19]

Other I&R Services

During the 1970s, I&R services were developed in other public libraries or in local organizations in cooperation with public libraries across the country. In Columbus, Ohio, the public library cooperated with project CALL (Community Access Library Line), funded by United Way to provide health-line and law-line services, which incorporated audio tapes with telephone technology. In 1979, the Los Angeles County Public Library developed a CALL service, which served 10 California counties, had a database consisting of 4,000 agencies, and provided information in multiple languages on a wide range of topics.[20]

In December 1971, the Wake County (NC) Information & Referral Center was established to provide two I&R services: the Human Service Information and Referral Program and the Adult Learning Information Center. With the sponsorship of county government and in cooperation with the county department of social services, the center received federal funding from Title XX of the Social Security Act, the U.S. Office of Education's Fund for Improvement of Postsecondary Education, and LSCA.[21]

In July 1973, the Chicago Public Library established a neighborhood library, El Centro de la Causa (The Center of the Cause) to provide I&R services with grants in the amount of $147,130 from the U.S. Office of Education and the Illinois State Library. In 1974, the Peninsula Library System's Computerized Community Information Project (CIP) began as an LSCA-funded I&R services in California, with Stanford University's Stanford Public Information Retrieval System (SPIRES) providing information storage and retrieval as well as management.[22]

In 1976, Helpfile, an I&R service located in the reference division of the headquarters library of the Kalamazoo Public Library, was established with the help of an LSCA grant. In 1977, Community Answers, a volunteer-staffed I&R service located within the Greenwich (CT) Public Library, established a new organizational relationship with the statewide I&R service, Info-Line, established using Social Security Title XX grant with matching funds provided by United Way of Connecticut.[23]

Trejo and Lodwick Survey on Need for Spanish-Speaking Librarians

Under the auspices of the University of Arizona's Graduate School of Library and Information Science, Arnulfo D. Trejo and Kathleen L. Lodwick conducted a survey of library policies regarding recruiting and hiring Spanish-speaking librarians to determine if there was a need for Spanish-speaking librarians, and if such a need did exist, to determine the most effective way to recruit Spanish-speaking students to graduate library schools. The survey was based on responses to two questionnaires. The first was sent to either public library directors in towns and cities with populations of more than 5,000 persons in the states of Arizona, California, Colorado, New Mexico, and Texas, or to public library directors in selected cities in Florida, Illinois, Missouri, New Jersey, New York, Ohio, and Utah, where there are large concentrations of Spanish-speaking people and where significant pockets of Hispanic-heritage people resided. The second questionnaire was sent to 244 Hispanic-heritage librarians and media specialists in the United States and Puerto Rico.

The most significant finding was that having Spanish-speaking staff members was the best way to attract Hispanic users to the library. Although the majority of the directors responding to the questionnaire had not had any library education courses designed to help them serve the Spanish-speaking, 94 percent supported such courses. Hispanic-heritage librarians indicated that most had decided to pursue a career in librarianship after having worked in a library or after being mentored and actively recruited by a librarian.

It was evident that if Hispanic-heritage persons were to be attracted to the profession, the recruitment should begin early in high schools and colleges, preferably by assisting the students to find part-time library jobs at the clerical level to familiarize them with library work. It also seemed logical that library-school recruitment should be undertaken among those persons of Hispanic heritage who were already working in libraries. Since 490 persons in the libraries surveyed were paraprofessionals, clericals, or part-time students, there appeared to be a ready supply of potential librarians.[24]

SALALM

The demise of the Library of Congress's Latin American Cooperative Acquisitions Project (LACAP) came in 1973 after 15 years of operation. In 1974, the Public Law 480 program for the acquisition of foreign library materials was changed to the Special Foreign Currencies Program (SFCP). The SALALM continued to work collaboratively to improve the acquisition of Latin American library materials. Collection of foreign-language materials authorized by the Public Law 480 program stopped in the mid-1980s.[25]

LSCA Projects for Cataloging and Reference Services

From 1977 to 1986, the Bay Area Library and Information System (BALIS), a consortium formerly consisting of the East Bay Cooperative System and the Oakland Public Library, received LSCA grants of $2,410,194 to build a union catalog of the member libraries' Spanish-language books and develop Spanish-language access to library materials in Spanish. The resulting project was known as Hispanex, or the California Spanish Language Database.

BALIS received an LSCA grant of $68,200 in fiscal year 1987 to gather data on the reference referral process for questions from Spanish-speaking library patrons and proposed improvements in the process. The Mountain Valley Library System received an LSCA grant from 1987 to 1989 in the amount of $10,000 for staff training in reference referral and public relations for Spanish-language library users.[26]

LSCA Projects for Asian Immigrants

While residents of large Chinatowns like those in San Francisco and New York City have access to collections in their own language, most Asian Americans do not. A survey sponsored by the ALA Office for Library Service to the Disadvantaged in 1976 found that library resources and service for Asian Americans were disproportionately low in view of the percentage of Asian Americans in the total population.

The Hennepin County Library in Minnesota has used Comprehensive Employment and Training Act (CETA) money to pay a Vietnamese liaison staff to help orient refugees via lectures and information packets and to aid in selecting materials. At the Fairfax County (VA) Public Library, free legal advice has been provided by a Vietnamese attorney, and flyers printed in Vietnamese have been distributed by the Fairfax Family Service to publicize the program.[27]

Throughout the 1970s, when a large influx of Vietnamese refugees migrated to Tulsa, Inalean Mullen, adult resources coordinator at the Tulsa Public Library, came up with the idea of writing simple, basic English information pieces about living in Tulsa and recording them on audiocassettes, Oklahoman accent and all. There were plans to translate the tapes into other languages, including German, French, Spanish, and even Arabic, for the 200 students from Iraq currently attending the Spartan School of Aeronautics.[28]

The Long Beach Public Library received LSCA grants totaling $140,491 from 1971 to 1973 to establish outreach services for four branch libraries, hire five community aides, provide a bookmobile to the disadvantaged areas within its service area, and establish a Tagalog collection at the Bret Harte Branch that served as a local as well as regional resource for Filipinos.[29]

Sondra Waldrop, director of public information at Westark Community College in Fort Smith, Arkansas, reported that the influx of Vietnamese and Cambodian refugees had had quite an impact on library services in the immediate area of Fort Chaffee near Fort Smith, which was in operation as a relocation center until December 1975. Many refugees were enrolled in the ABE classes in Fort Smith and spent their evenings at the Fort Smith Public Library working for greater proficiency in English.[30]

In March 1976, the Asian Community Library, the first public library for Asian Americans, opened its doors to the public as a branch of the Oakland Public Library. Librarian Judy Yung reported that the library was funded by LSCA grants totaling $340,287 from 1975 to 1978 to offer circulating library materials in Chinese, Japanese, Filipino, Korean, and Vietnamese to residents of Oakland and also to specialize in collecting English-language materials on Asia and Asian Americans. Prior to the library's existence, most of the more than 50,000 Asian Americans residing in the Oakland Bay Area were unserved by the public library. The library, staffed by librarians speaking Asian languages, provided I&R services to other resources in the community, including where to find employment assistance, ESL and foreign-language classes, and health and social services.

In 1978, the Los Angeles Public Library established an ethnic resource center for Asian-Pacific Americans at the Montebello Branch. Jae Min

Roh, a Korean immigrant, became senior librarian at the Pio Pico Kore-atown Branch of the Los Angeles Public Library in 1984, one of the 64 branches in the library system.[31]

The Villa Regional Library of the Jefferson County (CO) Library System used a fiscal year 1981 LSCA grant of $23,000 to establish the Asian Model Library to serve the needs of immigrant Asians, including Vietnamese, Thai, Cambodian, Hmong, Laotians, Koreans, Japanese, Chinese, and Pacific Islanders. The library won the Colorado Library Association's 1981 Project of the Year Award.[32]

LSCA Projects for the Spanish Speaking

The Cleveland Public Library used an LSCA grant to fund its Project Libros to introduce and provide library service to the Spanish-speaking community, predominantly Puerto Rican, which numbered about 18,000 at that time. Deposit collections in Spanish and English dealing with Puerto Rican history and culture, and practical subjects such as homemaking and childcare, were placed in churches and community centers.[33]

In 1971, the Lorain (OH) Public Library, which had formerly provided materials in the eastern European languages, received an LSCA grant from 1971 to 1975 from the State Library of Ohio to initiate its own Project Libros to serve the needs of its Spanish-speaking community. The library cooperated with the local newspaper to publish a weekly column in both Spanish and English; with the local radio station WLRO to broadcast a weekly program; and with the local television station to present two programs to inform the non-Hispanic community of the achievements of the Spanish-speaking community. After LSCA grant funding expired, through community involvement in planning and a bilingual staff, the South Branch of the Lorain Public Library continued to serve the Spanish-speaking community by spending 20 percent of the book budget on Spanish materials that covered such topics as literacy, career preparation, and computer training.[34]

Opening in April 1978, El Centro (The Center), the Brooklyn Public Library's bilingual center, located in the Williamsburg Branch Library, used an LSCA grant to provide I&R services, ESL classes and workshops, cultural programs, and library materials for children and adults in Spanish and English. El Centro director Natalia Davis hired staff members who were bicultural as well as bilingual, including Puerto Ricans, Panamanians, Mexicans, and Dominicans. Since the ESL teachers at the center had noted that the dialectical idiosyncrasies of different countries affected the language and made communication difficult in a class where Puerto Ricans, Argentineans, and Mexicans were trying to learn together, teams of two conducted the classes, with each teacher supplementing the other's knowledge.[35]

In 1971, the El Paso Public Library, which served a border city of about 500,000 inhabitants, opened its Mexican American Services Office, and Yolanda Cuesta was hired to head this office as Mexican American Services librarian. Through her leadership, La Biblioteca del Barrio (The Library of the Neighborhood), a bookmobile program was initiated to serve the special needs of several barrios (neighborhoods) in El Paso.[36]

In 1974, the Eastern Shore Area Library of the Wicomico County Library in Salisbury, Maryland, offered a Children's Caravan "mediamobile" to serve children, mainly African American and Mexican American children of migrant agricultural workers in four Eastern Shore counties— Caroline, Dorchester, Somerset, and Wicomico. In 1976, the Los Angeles County Public Library established an ethnic resource center for Chicanos at the East Los Angeles Branch. From 1976 to 1978, the Siskiyou County (CA) Library's Tulelake-Newell Migrant Project received LSCA grants totaling $31,800 to place Spanish-language materials in migrant camp locations around Newell to reach low-income migratory workers cut off from traditional public library services.[37]

The Serra Cooperative Library System's Que Sara Project used LSCA grants totaling $130,000 from 1971 to 1974 to improve outreach to non-library users—the Mexican Americans and American Indians in San Diego and Imperial Counties living in migrant camps, barrios, and reservations—through the use of a fully equipped media van.[38] The Serra Cooperative Library System also used LSCA grants totaling $19,000 from 1971 to 1974 to improve interstate cooperation between California and Arizona. The residents of eastern Imperial County, California, received vastly improved library service through a reciprocal program between Yuma City-County Library, Arizona, and the Serra System, providing bookmobile service, materials, professional staff administration, interlibrary loans, and access to the San Diego reference center. At the end of the demonstration, Imperial County negotiated a contract with Yuma City-County to continue service to remote eastern county communities in California, including reciprocal borrowing and reference service through the Serra System to Yuma.[39]

The Peninsula Library System received an LSCA grant from 1972 to 1976 in the amount of $157,175 to improve service to the Spanish and Portuguese communities in San Mateo County through improved book collections in the local library, community involvement, story hours and puppet shows for children, ethnic festivals, and a bookmobile with bilingual materials, all under the direction of a bilingual project director.[40]

In 1978, almost two decades since the first Cubans fled the Castro Revolution in 1959, La Rama Hispanica Branch was opened in the very heart of Little Havana. The branch, staffed with qualified bilingual personnel, provided approximately 15,000 children's and adult materials, and programs and activities attuned to the community's needs. It was not an easy task to identify the library needs of Miami's Cuban community, since it continues to have generational differences, class distinctions, old and new lifestyles, and even differences in Spanish dialects.[41]

In the summer of 1973, eight public libraries in the northwest suburbs of Chicago formed the SLURP (Suburban Libraries United for Regional Planning) consortium in order to apply for a grant for shared staffing to provide centralized service for Spanish-speaking patrons. In October 1975, SLURP received a two-year LSCA grant of $63,940 for the Spanish Project, one of the first projects nationwide to serve suburban as opposed to urban Spanish-speaking communities. With only a single coordinator to work with eight separate Illinois libraries, staffing was, from the beginning, not adequate to provide equal service for each library.

In December 1976, the SLURP administrators and the project coordinator, Stephanie Ardito-Kirkland, began to discuss the project's future after October 1977. Regrettably, responsibilities for serving the Spanish-speaking never shifted to the staffs of the participating eight libraries but remained with the single coordinator. Latent prejudices surfaced when the staff questioned whether funds should be used to develop a collection of ABE materials in Spanish when collections in English seemed more important, and agencies other than the library were more prepared to teach consumer education, ESL, and reading classes. Although the project was discontinued, two valuable lessons were learned: (1) personal service that stops after two years destroys trust; and (2) there is a need to establish basic service that can be offered continuously after federal funds have been exhausted.[42]

LSCA Projects for American Indians

A landmark program, funded under HEA grants from 1971 to 75, was the National Indian Education Association (NIEA) library project. Following a survey of information needs in three western-state Indian communities, project personnel and residents planned and developed relevant library programs. At one site, a library and cultural center was established, at the second, a tribal library system, and at the third, a community school library. Circulation statistics revealed the use of printed material at rates exceeding the national average. The most telling indication of the success is that all three communities elected to maintain their libraries at the close of the demonstration period.[43]

In 1977, the New York State Legislature enacted American Indian library legislation providing an annual appropriation of $100,000, the first such special appropriation in the nation, to enable Indian libraries to become full members of the public library system. Since that time, several million dollars have supported reservation libraries, including the Mohawk's Akwesasne Library and Cultural Center in St. Regis; and the Seneca Nation's Library, serving residents of the Allegany reservation in Salamanca, the Cattaraugus reservation in Irving, and the Tonawanda Community Library in Akron.[44]

In 1978, the Tribally Controlled Community College Assistance Act provided for direct funding from the BIA for all types of Indian educational institutions, including day schools, on- and off-reservation boarding schools, tribally contracted schools, dormitories that permitted Indian students to attend nearby white public schools, and tribal libraries. Located primarily in large states in the western half of the country, these tribal community colleges have libraries that function not only as college libraries but also as public libraries. They have been given land-grant status by the U.S. Congress, which enabled them to receive funding directly from federal appropriations. As accredited institutions, the tribal colleges were required to employ qualified librarians to manage them.[45]

In October 1979, the Milwaukee Public Library received LSCA funding for its Native American library project. Aimed at the 8,000 to 10,000 Native Americans living in the city, the project was planned and implemented cooperatively with local American Indian agencies. In addition to a strong Native American collection, the Milwaukee Public Library provided a biweekly film program for elderly Native Americans, weekly films and delivery of picture books to the Indian Day Care Center, and bookmobile service for which library cards were not required and overdue fines were not charged. A community library, stocked with health education and Indian culture materials, as well as a general reading collection, was established at the Milwaukee Indian Health Center. Also in 1979, the Los Angeles Public Library established an ethnic resource center for American Indians at the Huntington Park Branch.[46]

LSCA Projects for ABE and Literacy Programs

The identification of the rural poor as a special service clientele progressed with the creation of the Appalachian Adult Education Center (AAEC) of the Bureau for Research and Development at Morehead State University in Kentucky. Funded by the U.S. Office of Education's Bureau of Library and Learning Resources, the AAEC worked with public libraries in Alabama, South Carolina, East Virginia, Ohio, Tennessee, Georgia, and Mississippi to develop guidelines for adult education and conducted institutes in public libraries in these states to design and implement library services for disadvantaged adults. The NIEA used AAEC publications to form its own guidelines. The AAEC projects demonstrated ways public libraries and ABE programs could work together to improve their services to disadvantaged adults by coordinating efforts in reader guidance, recruitment, library orientation, community referral, and the selection, use, and delivery of materials.[47]

During the late 1970s, the population of Biloxi, Mississippi, which included French, German, Greek, and Slavic immigrants and their descendants, received an influx of Vietnamese refugees, many of whom spoke little or no English. The Biloxi Public Library and Cultural Center received an LSCA grant to teach Vietnamese immigrants to read English and to encourage them to use the public library as a resource center. In January 1979, the library contacted the Catholic Social Service Agency on the Mississippi Coast, whose staff included a native of Vietnam, An Miner. With Miner's help, the library surveyed 148 Vietnamese families living in the service area to determine their library needs. Acting on input from the refugees themselves, the library obtained videotapes of many locally produced programs available from Mississippi Educational Television, which would enable the Vietnamese to adapt to the conditions under which U.S. citizens lived and worked. The library also provided high-interest, low-vocabulary books for students learning English, as well as Vietnamese newspapers and magazines.[48]

NCLIS

Following recommendations of the National Library Advisory Council of the Johnson administration, the NCLIS was created in 1970 during the administration of President Richard Nixon as a permanent, independent agency within the executive branch of the federal government to advise the president and Congress on national policy matters affecting libraries and information services. The Librarian of Congress would serve ex officio on the commission.

In 1972, President Nixon had proposed a new type of funding, revenue sharing, which provided funds for state and local governments over a five-year period to be spent for local priorities, which could include libraries. In many instances, however, local governments had other programs they preferred to fund, and some municipalities merely substituted revenue-sharing funds for local funds they had been appropriating for libraries. Libraries were forced to close some branch operations and curtail the hours of opening at main buildings.

Since 1972, initially using grants from the U.S. Office of Education, the graduate library school at Queens College had developed institute programs to train librarians to be sensitive and responsive to the needs of ethnic minorities. As part of the awakening of interest in ethnic studies across the country, David Cohen of Queens College noted that graduate library schools had begun to offer courses preparing librarians to work with immigrants and other minorities, including courses on library materials and services for ethnic and minority groups, library services for the disadvantaged and underserved, the information needs of urban residents, Asian reference sources, information resources for the Spanish speaking, and library services to the African American community.[49]

In May 1973, the NCLIS sponsored a small invitational working conference in Denver to provide a forum for the discussion and review of available research and information on the library and information service needs of a number of occupational, ethnic, and other minority groups in the United States. Data on the library needs of the disadvantaged, institutionalized, and disabled, based on questionnaires sent to state library agencies that administered LSCA grants and on-site data gathering during field-site visits and interviews, were presented by the System Development Corporation of Santa Monica, California. The conclusions were that LSCA funds had been a critical factor in projects for special clienteles, they had provided the bulk of the funds being used for innovative projects, and without them there would have been little or no innovation.

In 1974, NCLIS published its study based on the findings of the System Development Corporation study. Titled *Library and Information Service Needs of the Nation,* the report commented on the need for libraries to refocus their services to meet the needs of a growing population that had alienated libraries offering traditional services. Immigrants needed information related to survival and the satisfaction of immediate needs, including those of health, welfare, educational opportunities, vocational and career training, consumer buying, and legal and political rights.[50]

California Ethnic Services Task Force Established

During fiscal year 1977, the California State Library, under the direction of Ethel S. Crockett, used an LSCA grant to establish a 15-member California Ethnic Services Task Force to assist California librarians in establishing collections and services to meet the needs of rapidly growing ethnic populations in California. During the three years of its existence, the task force, with members representing the four major ethnic groups in California—Asian, African American, Hispanic, and American Indian—planned and implemented programs, communicated information, and prepared bibliographies on the targeted ethnic and minority groups.[51]

1979 White House Conference on Library and Information Services

As early as December 1974, President Gerald Ford had authorized what would be later referred to as the first White House Conference on Library and Information Services (WHCLIS). President Jimmy Carter declared support for the conference during his presidential campaign and, in May 1977, signed an appropriations bill that set aside $3.5 million to plan and conduct the conference under the direction of the NCLIS. The first WHCLIS was convened in Washington, District of Columbia, on November 15–19, 1979, with 806 delegates and alternates among the 3,600 persons from the United States and abroad who participated.

In order to ensure maximum participation by all citizens, 58 preconferences had been held in 49 states (all except South Dakota), 6 U.S. territories, and the District of Columbia. The preconferences included librarians, library trustees, library advocates, members of the federal library community, professional library organizations, and American Indians living on or near reservations. At these meetings, more than 100,000 citizens discussed issues, voted on resolutions, and elected delegates to the national conference.

Deliberations of the American Indian preconference were enhanced through the efforts of Mary Huffer, director of the library of the U.S. Department of the Interior. She had become concerned about the lack of library services on reservations, especially in BIA schools on reservations. She asked a small group of individuals to assist her in drafting a plan of action for her agency to improve library services. The resulting 1977 document served as a planning tool for the 1978 Indian White House Preconference.

At the conference, delegates discussed, debated, and endorsed a total of 64 resolutions, several of which had a direct effect on library services with ethnic minorities and immigrants. There were recommendations that all persons should have free access to information in public libraries, and that barriers to outreach services, whether legal, fiscal, technical, attitudinal, environmental, cultural, or geographic, must be eliminated. Delegates were concerned that all learners, regardless of age, residence (including institutions), race, disability, ethnic or cultural background, should have continuing access to the information necessary to cope with the increasing complexity of changing social, economic, and technological environments.

The conference allowed a forum for delegates to express their collective support for the future funding of the LSCA, HEA, and ESEA, and to authorize new federal funding for cultural awareness projects for rural, urban, and economically deprived areas; public, school, and academic libraries; and professional library education programs to train library personnel to work with Spanish-speaking, African American, and American Indian populations. The delegates supported the concept of regional and national centers to further international understanding, which was recommended by President Carter's 1979 Commission on Foreign Languages and International Studies.

David Cohen, director of the Institute on Ethnicity and Librarianship at the Queens College Graduate School of Library and Information Studies, City University of New York, testified at the 1979 WHCLIS. Cohen advocated the use of ethnic and ethnic-oriented staff at all levels in the library, from top administration to pages, and he believed that inclusion of ethnic needs in the planning of programs and services should be constant and automatic, and that all library staff should be interacting with the community, not just designated outreach librarians.[52]

ALA and International Organizations for Minorities

Beginning as early as the 1950s, the foreign-language book reviewing service of ALA's *Booklist* increased in momentum and frequency until the 1980s and thereafter. Librarians serving immigrant clienteles grew to depend on this journal for critical reviews of foreign-language books for adults, young adults, and children. Various ALA divisions and committees provided reviews, including the ALA Adult Services Division's Committee on Reading Improvement for Adults, the short-lived Committee on ALA Intercultural Action, the Public Library Association's Foreign Book Selection Committee, the ALA Children's Services Division's Selection of Foreign Children's Books from Various Cultures Committee (later a committee of the Association for Library Services to Children), and the Reference and Adult Services Division's Committee on Service to the Spanish Speaking. Librarians of the Donnell World Languages Center of the New York Public Library were regular reviewers and compilers of bibliographies of foreign-language library materials.[53]

The Young Adult Library Services Association (YALSA)'s Outreach Committee addressed the needs of young adults who faced barriers of access to libraries because of economic, social, cultural, or legal reasons. The Library Administration and Management Association (LAMA)'s Cultural Diversity Committee recommended efforts to improve services to culturally diverse populations and, in general, to foster the development of a culturally diverse workforce in libraries.[54]

During the 1970s and into the 1980s, the ALA sponsored caucuses for Italian Americans, Polish Americans, Armenian Americans, and Jewish Americans. Charles Townley, an American Indian, chairman of the ALA's Social Responsibilities Round Table (SRRT) Task Force on Indian Affairs, was responsible for the ALA Council's approval of its "Goals for Indian Library and Information Services" at the 1973 ALA Annual Conference in Las Vegas.[55]

The Black Caucus of ALA (BCALA) was organized by E. J. Josey at the 1970 ALA Midwinter Conference in Chicago to serve as an advocate for the development, promotion, and improvement of library services and resources to the nation's African American community and to provide leadership for the recruitment and professional development of African American librarians. The BCALA continued to meet at the ALA midwinter and annual conferences. Earlier in 1969, the ALA had established the Coretta Scott King awards for excellence in children's and young adult literature on African American themes.[56]

REFORMA, the National Association to Promote Library and Information Services to Latinos and the Spanish Speaking, was established in 1971 at the ALA Annual Conference in Dallas by Arnulfo Trejo. One of the early presidents of REFORMA, Daniel Flores Duran, moved REFORMA from being a primarily public library and a Chicano, Southwest-oriented organization to a truly national association that not only represents the needs of Chicano librarians but also of Puerto Ricans,

Cubans, and other Latino groups. Another important organization that later became a REFORMA chapter was Bibliotecas para la Gente (BPLG) (Libraries for the People), which was established in 1975 to improve library and information services to the Spanish-speaking and Latino communities of northern California. Additional chapters of REFORMA have been established in areas of the country where libraries serve Spanish-speaking communities.[57]

Martha Tome, a Cuban-born librarian, served from 1973 to 1976 as chair of ALA Adult Services Division Committee for Library Services for Spanish Speakers. In 1978 in *Library Journal*, "Guidelines for Library Services to the Spanish Speaking," was presented by Yolanda Cuesta, minority services consultant at the California State Library, and Patricia Tarin, regional audiovisual librarian with the Los Angeles County Public Library. Ten years later, the "Guidelines for Library Services to Hispanics" was prepared in 1988 by the Committee on Library Service to the Spanish Speaking of the Reference and Adult Services Division (RASD), later the Reference and User Services Association (RUSA), of the ALA. The guidelines suggested the purchase of materials in Spanish, English, and bilingually in both languages; the collaboration of the libraries with local community Hispanic organizations in the development and presentation of library programs and services; and the employment of bilingual, bicultural staff.[58]

In March 1973, the Midwest Chinese American Librarians Association was established in the Rosary College (now Dominican University) Graduate School of Library Science under the leadership of Tze-Chung Li. Another Chinese American librarians' association, headed by Irene Yeh, was formed at Stanford University in 1974. In order to create a stronger organization with a single identity, the two organizations merged in 1983 under the name of the Chinese American Librarians Association (CALA) and became an active affiliate of the ALA.[59]

Library Education for Minorities

From 1972 to 1974, the Illinois Minorities Manpower Project (IMMP), a joint effort of the ALA Office for Library Personnel Resources (OLPR) and the Illinois State Library, established the National Minority Referral Network to assist graduate library school programs in identifying qualified minority students interested in pursuing a library career. Since the ALA Office of Recruitment was then defunct, one of the IMMP recommendations was to create another task force for that purpose within ALA, which became ALA's Minority Recruitment Task Force. By 1974, a total of 22 library schools advertised active recruitment programs aimed at minorities. Studies of federal fellowship programs showed that they were successful in generating an increase in the percentage of minorities trained in library schools from 8.2 percent in 1977 to 10.1 percent in 1979.[60]

Earlier in 1968, three librarians, Elizabeth Martinez Smith, Jose G. Taylor, and David Barron, had founded the Committee to Recruit Mexican American Librarians (CRMAL) in Los Angeles in an effort to establish a means for developing library services to Spanish-speaking communities. In 1972, Patrick S. Sanchez, working with CRMAL members, proposed a Mexican American Graduate Institute of Library Science to train 15 graduate students of Mexican descent as school library media specialists at California State University, Fullerton.

The project was funded by the California State Library's Minority Recruitment and Advancement Program beginning in fiscal year 1974 at approximately $40,000 per year. As of November 1975, the graduate institute had graduated 47 Chicano librarians, with 17 having completed their master of library science (MLS) degrees in July 1975. In 1978, it was reported that the Chula Vista School District near San Diego had the highest number of Hispanic librarians and the best bilingual library services for children. Most of the librarians of the system were graduates of the Fullerton program.[61]

The Tucson-based Graduate Library Institute for Spanish-speaking Americans (GLISA) was established at the University of Arizona in 1976 under the direction of Arnulfo Trejo and continued until 1979. The GLISA program produced most of the librarians serving the Hispanic population in El Paso, with many being affiliated with either the El Paso Public Library or the El Paso Community College.[62]

From 1973 to 1978, Lotsee S. Patterson, a faculty member at the University of New Mexico, used grants from the HEA Act Title II-B funds to train library aides in the pueblos. Libraries were started either in the local school operated by the BIA or in the pueblo. Since none of the pueblos or schools had ever had a library, training personnel was a first priority in order to maintain the library after the federal grant monies were gone.

Arizona State University graduated 12 American Indian school library media specialists in 1974 and 1975, and the University of Arizona enrolled 10 American Indians in the MLS program in fiscal year 1974. Both programs were based on the normal curriculum, with supplemental counseling, internships and courses directly related to information needs of American Indians.[63]

NIEA

In the early 1970s, the University of Minnesota conducted a multiyear study that focused on information needs of selected tribes. Later taken over by the NIEA, then located in the Twin Cities, the project purchased books and other resources for geographically dispersed tribes. Under the leadership of Charles Townley, the establishment of the NIEA was one of the results of the 1978 American Indian preconference for the 1979 WHCLIS. NIEA evolved from the ALA SRRT's Task Force on Indian Affairs in the late 1960s, to the American Indian Subcommittee of the ALA Library Services to the Disadvantaged Committee in 1971.

On the St. Regis Mohawk Reservation in upper New York State, materials were placed in a tribal library in a government building near the center of tribal activity. On the Navajo reservation in Rough Rock, Arizona, books were placed in a school library with the understanding that any tribal member could use them. On the Standing Rock Sioux reservation in North Dakota, materials were given to a newly founded two-year tribal college library and to local schools.

The NIEA was also instrumental in getting federal funding from the federal government for a library project in Hogansburg, New York. The Hogansburg project was of particular interest because it fostered the first North American International Bookmobile from Hogansburg, New York to the Mohawk Indian reservation on the Canadian side of the border.[64]

Smith Study on Library Services with American Indians

In the early 1970s, in order to get an overview of library services, June Smeck Smith sent letters to all state library and education agencies in states with sizable Indian populations, cities that had large urban Indian communities, schools and colleges that had large Indian student enrollments, and the BIA. Smith documented that there were 315 distinct tribal communities in the United States.

The basic pattern revealed by this correspondence and search was that library service to Indians, whether public, school or academic, was generally an integral part of the library service being provided for students or the general public. Its weakness was that the needs of American Indians differ in many respects from the needs of the majority culture. A major exception to the general pattern was in the schools operated by the BIA. In the 1970s, the BIA operated 225 schools in 17 states, including on-reservation day schools and boarding schools, and off-reservation boarding schools, which ranged in size from one-teacher, one-room units to large secondary and postsecondary institutions. Each had a school library appropriate to its size, and there were 55 librarians employed.[65]

Haro and San Bernardino (CA) Public Library Studies Compared

In 1977, the San Bernardino (CA) Public Library found that societal changes in the past decade had warranted a reexamination of Robert Haro's findings in his 1970 survey of Mexican Americans regarding their use of libraries. The library reassessed the needs of the Spanish-speaking community for services using bilingual survey teams between December 1977 and January 1978.

Haro's earlier study had identified that the characteristic need of Mexican Americans for cultural reinforcement would make the bilingual staff and services of the neighborhood branch more attractive than the superior materials resources of the centralized main library. Such was not the case in the 1977 San Bernardino study. Fifty-two percent of those served by a neighborhood branch were Mexican Americans, who preferred the geographical accessibility of the central library and its more adequate resources.

The findings of the San Bernardino survey supported Haro's statement that Mexican Americans were without a tradition of free public library service in Mexico and Central and South America, where library service was restricted to the elite and the upper class. As in Haro's study, the San Bernardino survey supported the need for bilingual services, since 86 percent of the Mexican American community spoke some Spanish, and 16 percent were identified as solely Spanish speaking. The survey verified that the Spanish-speaking community expected the same high level of services, both in English and in Spanish, enjoyed by all segments of the community.[66]

Farrington Study of Library Services with Hispanic Americans

In 1974, William H. Farrington studied library service to Hispanic Americans in *Library and Information Services for Special Groups*. He found that librarians and project directors had learned in their service to Hispanics that all traditional library rules and regulations must be ignored.

Since the poor of whatever ethnic background were not interested in any service that might cost them money, the charging of fines for overdue and lost materials and badgering for the return of materials were self-defeating practices. He noted that successful programs were bilingual and shared the quality of flexibility, and most were media oriented, with more emphasis on nonprint rather than print resources.[67]

LSCA Bilingual Education Projects

From fiscal year 1975 to 1978, the Los Angeles County Public Library's project LIBRE (Libraries Involved in Bilingual Reading Education) received LSCA grants totaling $214,038 to establish learning centers in four county library branches. The grants were used to improve reading and language skills of ethnic and cultural minority populations, and to respond to a large influx of Asian immigrants as well as a decline in reading scores in the public schools.[68]

In 1976, after the state of New Jersey had passed a Bilingual Education Act to meet the needs of 584,494 Spanish-speaking residents in New Jersey, 65 percent of whom were Puerto Rican, the New Jersey State Library awarded an LSCA grant to the Bergenfield Public Library to offer an ESL program called Let's Talk. The project made use of student volunteers to teach English to immigrants from such diverse nations as Colombia, Czechoslovakia, Ecuador, Greece, Italy, Japan, Poland, and Portugal, and engaged a coordinator, who interviewed prospective students and matched them with tutors, led training workshops, recommended materials for acquisition, and handled publicity.[69]

In 1979, the Newark Public Library collaborated with the Newark school system and board of education to inaugurate a model program to reach Latinos in New Jersey that focused on hiring bilingual and bicultural librarians, developing Spanish-language collections, establishing a Spanish-language homework telephone hotline, and providing outreach services to the Spanish-speaking community. A year later, in 1980, this collaboration had led to the founding of La Sala Hispanoamericana, a permanent program for Latinos that offered library and information services for walk-in users and by telephone, including homework help.

Ethnic and Minority Studies Programs

In March 1971, under the auspices of the Center for the Study of Ethnic Publications in the United States, the Program for the Study of Ethnic

Publications in the United States was established at Kent State University as a result of a proposal submitted by Lubomyr R. Wynar. The center's initial research program focused on the study of ethnic periodicals and newspapers in the United States, including their historical development and current trends, and ethnic organizations, including archives, libraries, and museums. Based on its research, the center published comprehensive national surveys of ethnic newspapers and periodicals, and encyclopedic directories of ethnic newspapers, periodicals and cultural institutions.

In the 1980s, libraries became involved with promoting multiculturalism, leaving behind the primary emphases on Americanization and internationalism of prior decades.

NOTES

1. U.S. Census Bureau, "No. 10: Resident Population—Selected Characteristics, 1950 to 2000, and Projections, 2025 and 2050," in *Statistical Abstract of the United States: 2001*, 121st ed. (Washington, DC: U.S. G.P.O., 2001), 13.

2. Theodore W. Taylor, *The Bureau of Indian Affairs*, foreword by Phillip Martin (Boulder, CO: Westview Press, 1984), 27; Marcia J. Nauratil, *Public Libraries and Nontraditional Clienteles: The Politics of Special Services* (Westport, CT: Greenwood Press, 1985), 99, 103–6.

3. Francesco Cordasco, "Ethnic Studies Heritage Act," in *Dictionary of American Immigration History*, ed. Francesco Cordasco (Metuchen, NJ: Scarecrow Press, 1990), 209–10; Andrew T. Kopan, "Multicultural Education," in *Dictionary of American Immigration History*, 544; Harlow G. Unger, ed., "Ethnic Heritage Program," in *Encyclopedia of American Education*, 2nd ed. (New York: Facts on File, c2001, 1996), 397.

4. Bruni Verges, "Developing Collections on Puerto Rican Heritage," in *Ethnic Collections in Libraries*, ed. E. J. Josey and Marva L. DeLoach (New York: Neal-Schuman Publishers, 1983), 65–74; Joseph B. Olvera Jr. et al., "Chicano Collections of Library Resources," in *Ethnic Collections in Libraries*, 75–100; Wei Chi Poon, "Asian American Collections," in *Ethnic Collections in Libraries*, 180–201.

5. U.S. Immigration and Naturalization Service, "Appendix 1: Immigration and Naturalization Legislation," in *Statistical Yearbook of the Immigration and Naturalization Service, 1997*, (Washington, DC: U.S. G.P.O., 1999), A.1–16; David W. Haines, "Refugees," in *Dictionary of American Immigration History*, 612–16; Maldwyn Allen Jones, *American Immigration*, 2nd ed. (Chicago: University of Chicago Press, 1992), 282–83; Patricia Beilke and Frank J. Sciara, *Selecting Materials for and about Hispanic and East Asian Children and Young People* (Hamden, CT: Library Professional Publications, 1986), 77–80.

6. U.S. Immigration and Naturalization Service, "Appendix 1: Immigration and Naturalization Legislation," A.1–17; David Nelson Alloway, "Indochina Migration and Refugee Assistance Act," in *Dictionary of American Immigration History*, 403–4; David Nelson Alloway, "Indochinese Mutual Assistance Division of the Department of Health, Education, and Welfare," in *Dictionary of American Immigration History*, 404.

7. Sucheng Chan, "Vietnamese," in *Dictionary of American Immigration History*, 738; M.A. Jones, *American Immigration*, 282–83; Robert M. Jiobu, *Ethnicity and Assimilation* (Albany: State University New York Press, 1988), 53–58; Beilke and Sciara, *Selecting Materials for and about Hispanic and East Asian Children and Young People*, 80–83.

8. Raymond A. Mohl, "Haitians," in *Dictionary of American Immigration History*, 274–75; Raymond A. Mohl, "Cubans," in *Dictionary of American Immigration History*, 154–56; M.A. Jones, *American Immigration*, 273–74, 277–78

9. U.S. Immigration and Naturalization Service, "Appendix 1: Immigration and Naturalization Legislation," A.1–16; Michael LeMay and Elliott Robert Barkan, eds., *U.S. Immigration and Naturalization Laws and Issues: A Documentary History* (Westport, CT: Greenwood Press, 1999), 270–72.

10. U.S. Immigration and Naturalization Service, "Appendix 1: Immigration and Naturalization Legislation," A.1–18; Francesco Cordasco, "U.S. Congress, House and Senate, Committees on the Judiciary, Select Commission on Immigration and Refugee Policy," in *Dictionary of American Immigration History*, 722–23; M.A. Jones, *American Immigration*, 279–80.

11. Francesco Cordasco, "Bilingual Education," in *Dictionary of American Immigration History*, 78–80; Francesco Cordasco, "*Lau v. Nichols*," in *Dictionary of American Immigration History*, 483–85; M.A. Jones, *American Immigration*, 276–77; Salvador Guerena and Edward Erazo, "Latinos and Librarianship," *Library Trends* 49 (Summer 2000): 165; Harlow G. Unger, ed., "Bilingual/Bicultural Education," in *Encyclopedia of American Education*, 2nd ed. (New York: Facts on File, c2001, 1996), 137–38; Harlow G. Unger, ed., "Bilingual Instruction," in *Encyclopedia of American Education*, 138–39; Abigail M. Thernstrom, "Language: Issues and Legislation," in *Harvard Encyclopedia of American Ethnic Groups*, ed. Stephan Thernstrom, Ann Orlov, and Oscar Handlin (Cambridge: Belknap Press of Harvard University Press, 1980), 626–27; Esther R. Dyer, "Children's Media for a Culturally Pluralistic Society," in *Cultural Pluralism & Children's Media*, comp. Esther R. Dyer (Chicago: American Library Association, 1978), 4–6; Ruth Anne Thomas, "The Role of Media Centers in Bilingual Education," in *Cultural Pluralism & Children's Media*, 55–74.

12. California State Library, *Catalog of Local Assistance: Library Services and Construction Act, Titles I, II, III, 1976–1989* (Sacramento: California State Library, 1988), 26; Henry Drennan, "Libraries and Literacy Education," *Catholic Library World* 52 (Apr. 1981): 384; Guerena and Erazo, "Latinos and Librarianship," 167.

13. Cordasco, "Bilingual Education," 79–80; Harlow G. Unger, ed., "President's Commission on Foreign Language and International Studies," in *Encyclopedia of American Education*, 837–38.

14. Lotsee Patterson, "Historical Overview of Tribal Libraries in the Lower Forty-Eight States," in *Libraries to the People: Histories of Outreach*, ed. Robert S. Freeman and David M. Hovde, foreword by Kathleen de la Pena McCook (Jefferson, NC: McFarland & Company, 2003), 158; Taylor, *The Bureau of Indian Affairs*, 26–27; Frederick E. Hoxie, ed., "Education," in *Encyclopedia of North American Indians* (Boston: Houghton Mifflin, 1996), 178; Delores J. Huff, *To Live Heroically: Institutional Racism and American Indian Education* (Albany: State University of New York, 1997), 19; Janet N. Naumer, "Library Services to American Indians," in *Library and Information Services for Special Groups*, ed. Joshua I. Smith (New York: Published in cooperation with the American Society for Information Science and the ERIC Clearinghouse on Library and Information Sciences, by Science Associates/International, 1974), 62–64; Edward H. Spicer, "American Indians, Federal Policy Toward," in *Harvard Encyclopedia of American Ethnic Groups*, 114, 122; A. M. Thernstrom, "Language: Issues and Legislation," in 626; G. Edward Evans, "Library Resources on Native Americans," in *Ethnic Collections in Libraries*, 150–79; Nauratil, *Public Library Services with Nontraditional Clienteles*, 114–15.

15. R. Kathleen Molz, *The Federal Roles in Support of Public Library Services: An Overview*, prepared for the Federal Roles in Support of Public Library Services Project (Chicago: ALA, 1990), 10–20, 25–30; Rosemary Ruhig DuMont, Lois Buttlar, and William Caynon, *Multiculturalism in Libraries* (Westport, CT: Greenwood Press, 1994), 159–60; Ben Ocon, "Effective Outreach Strategies to the Latino Community: A Paradigm for Public Libraries," in *Library Services to Latinos: An Anthology*, ed. Salvador Guerena (Jefferson, NC: McFarland, 2000), 183; Susan Luevano-Molina, "Introduction: New Immigrants, Neo-Nativism, and the Public Library," in *Library Services to Latinos*, 9–11; JoAnn K. Aguirre, "Passport to Promise: Public Libraries as Intellectual Spaces for Immigrant Students," in *Library Services to Latinos*, 69–88; Evelyn Escatiola, "Anti-Immigrant Literature: A Selected Bibliography," in *Library Services to Latinos*, 161–81; Henry Drennan, "Libraries and Literacy Education," *Catholic Library World* 52 (Apr. 1981): 376–85; John W. Ellison and Clara DiFelice, "Libraries and Multi-Cultural Understanding," *Public Library Quarterly* 3 (Fall 1982): 23–32; Edward G. Holley and Robert F. Schremser, *The Library Services and Construction Act: An Historical Overview from the Viewpoint of Major Participants* (Greenwich, CT: JAI Press, 1983), 93–94, 147–48, 150–55; Ray M. Fry, "U.S. Department of Education Library Programs, 1984," in *Bowker Annual of Library & Book Trade Information*, 30th ed., comp. and ed. Julia Moore (New York: R.R. Bowker, 1985), 273–75.

16. William H. Farrington, "Library Services to Mexican-Americans," in *Library and Information Services for Special Groups*, ed. Joshua I. Smith (New York:

published in cooperation with the American Society for Information Science and the ERIC Clearinghouse on Library and Information Sciences, by Science Associates/International, 1974), 309, 323, 328; Guerena and Erazo, "Latinos and Librarianship," 166; Eleanor Frances Brown, *Library Service to the Disadvantaged* (Metuchen, NJ: Scarecrow Press, 1971), 397; Robert P. Haro, *Developing Library and Information Services for Americans of Hispanic Origin* (Metuchen, NJ: Scarecrow Press, 1981), 23–25.

17. California State Library, "Special Issue: LSCA in California [LSCA Projects, 1957–1976]," foreword by Ethel S. Crockett, California State Librarian, introduction by Ruth Kerstead, State Library Consultant, *News Notes of California Libraries* 71, no. 2 (1976), 68.

18. Brown, *Library Service to the Disadvantaged,* 239–43, 251–53; Arthur Curley, "Montclair Free Public Library," in *Encyclopedia of Library and Information Science,* ed. Allen Kent, Harold Lancour, and Jay E. Daily, vol. 18 (New York: Marcel Dekker, 1976), 271; National Citizens Emergency Committee to Save Our Public Libraries, "Neighborhood Information Service Centers: Public Library "Information and Referral: Provides Significant New Personal Service to the Individual Library User," in *The Changing Role of Public Libraries: Background Papers from the White House Conference,* comp. Whitney North Seymour Jr. (Metuchen, NJ: Scarecrow Press, 1980; copyright 1979, 1980 by the New York Public Library), 31–32, 42.

19. Dorothy Turick, *Community Information Services in Libraries, LJ* Special Report #5 (New York: Library Journal, 1978), 42–43; Nauratil, *Public Libraries and Nontraditional Clienteles,* 116; Robert K. Yin, Brigitte L. Kenney, and Karen B. Possner, *Neighborhood Communications Centers: Planning Information and Referral Services in the Urban Library,* prepared under a grant from the John and Mary R. Markle Foundation (Santa Monica, CA: RAND Corporation, 1974), v–ix; John Berry, "A TIP from Detroit," *Library Journal* 100 (July 1975): 1287–90; DuMont et al., *Multiculturalism in Libraries,* 105; Norbert Wiley, "Overview of the American City," in Allerton Park Institute, 17th, 1971, *Libraries and Neighborhood Information Centers,* papers presented at an Institute conducted by the University of Illinois, Graduate School of Library Science, October 25–27, 1971, ed. by Carol L. Kronus and Linda Crowe (Urbana: University of Illinois, Graduate School of Library Science, 1972), 15–29; Art Plotnik, "Summing Up After Three Years: The Success of Information and Referral Services in the Five-City Neighborhood Information Center Project," *American Libraries* 6 (July–Aug. 1975): 412–13; John H. Rebenack, "Public Libraries, International: Contemporary Libraries in the United States," in *Encyclopedia of Library and Information Science,* vol. 24 (New York: Marcel Dekker, 1976), 314–15; Charlene Cain, "Public Library Service to Minorities," in *Adult Services: An Enduring Focus for Public Libraries,* ed. Kathleen M. Heim and Danny P. Wallace (Chicago: ALA, 1990), 227; Stephen Stern, "Ethnic Libraries and Librarianship in the United States: Models and Prospects," in *Advances in Librarianship,* ed. Irene P. Godden, vol. 15

(New York: Academic Press, 1991), 89–90; Cheryl Metoyer-Duran, *Gatekeepers in Ethnolinguistic Communities* (Norwood, NJ: Ablex Publishing, 1993), 5–7; Nauratil, *Public Libraries and Nontraditional Clienteles*, 116; National Citizens Emergency Committee to Save Our Public Libraries, "Neighborhood Information Service Centers," 3–30; Alfred J. Kahn, Lawrence Grossman, Jean Bandler, Felicia Clark, Florence Galkin, and Kent Greenawalt, *Neighborhood Information Centers: A Study and Some Proposals* (New York: Columbia University School of Social Work, 1966), 110–19.

20. Metoyer-Duran, *Gatekeepers in Ethnolinguistic Communities*, 18–19; Albert J. Milo, "Reference Service to the Spanish-Speaking," in *Latino Librarianship: A Handbook for Professionals*, ed. Salvador Guerena (Jefferson, NC: McFarland, 1990), 29; National Citizens Emergency Committee to Save Our Public Libraries, "Neighborhood Information Service Centers 32–33.

21. Turick, *Community Information Services in Libraries*, 38–41.

22. Turick, *Community Information Services in Libraries*, 28–33; Kathleen Weibel, *Interagency Cooperation in Expanding Library Services to Disadvantaged Adults*, Appalachian Adult Education Center, Morehead State University, Public Library Training Institutes, Library Service Guide, no. 25 (Chicago: ALA, 1977), 17; Milo, "Reference Service to the Spanish-Speaking," 29; Gilda Baeza, "The Evolution of Educational and Public Library Services to Spanish-Speaking Children," in *Library Services for Hispanic Children: A Guide for Public and School Librarians*, ed. Adela Artola Allen (Phoenix: Oryx Press, 1987), 7, 11; Mary Ellen Michael and Leticia Encarnacion, *An Evaluation of the El Centro de la Causa Library and Information Center: August 1973–July 1974: Final Report*, ED 107291 (Washington, DC: Educational Resources Information Center, 1974); National Citizens Emergency Committee to Save Our Public Libraries, "Neighborhood Information Service Centers," 39–42.

23. Turick, *Community Information Services in Libraries*, 25–28.

24. Arnulfo D. Trejo and Kathleen L. Lodwick, "Needed: Hispanic Librarians—A Survey of Library Policies," *Wilson Library Bulletin* 53 (Nov. 1978): 259–66.

25. Robert A. Seal, "Mexican and U.S. Library Relations," in *Advances in Librarianship*, ed. Irene Godden, vol. 20: 69–121, 98–99; Edith Maureen Fisher, "Identification of Multiethnic Resources," in *Developing Library Collections for California's Emerging Majority: A Manual of Resources for Ethnic Collection Development*, produced in conjunction with the conference Developing Library Collections for California's Emerging Majority, September 22–23, 1990, San Francisco, California, ed. Katharine T.A. Scarborough (Berkeley: Bay Area Library and Information System; University Extension, University of California; School of Library and Information Studies, University of California, 1990), 53–60; Suzanne Hodgman, "SALALM Membership, 1956–1990: A Brief Overview," in *Latin American Studies into the Twenty-First Century: New Focus, New Formats, New Challenges: Papers of the Thirty-Sixth Annual Meeting of the Seminar on the Acquisi-*

tion *of Latin American Library Materials, University of California, San Diego, and San Diego State University, San Diego, California, June 1–6, 1991,* ed. Deborah L. Jakubs ([Albuquerque]: SALALM Secretariat, General Library, University of New Mexico, 1993), 215–23; Marie Zielinska and Irena Bell, "Selection and Acquisition of Library Materials in Languages Other than English: Some Guidelines for Public Libraries," *Collection Building* 2, no. 1 (1980): 7–28; Robert B. Downs and Norman B. Brown, "The Significance of Foreign Materials for U.S. Collections: Problems of Acquisitions," in *Acquisition of Foreign Materials for U.S. Libraries, ed. Theodore Samore,* 2nd ed. (Metuchen, NJ: Scarecrow Press, 1982), 8.

26. California State Library, *Catalog of Local Assistance,* 6, 21–22, 36; Roberto Cabello-Argandona and Eleanor Ross Crary, "The California Spanish Language Data Base: Development of Bilingual Access to Collections," *Catholic Library World* 52 (Apr. 1981: 372–75); Roberto Cabello-Argandona and Eleanor Ross Crary, "California Spanish Language Data Base: Bilingual Access to Collections," in *Latin American Economic Issues: Information Needs and Sources: Papers of the Twenty-Sixth Seminar on the Acquisition of Latin American Library Materials, Tulane University, New Orleans, Louisiana, April 1–4, 1981,* 287–92 ([Madison]: SALALM Secretariat, University of Wisconsin–Madison; [Los Angeles]: UCLA Latin American Center Publications, University of California, Los Angeles, 1984); Richard Chabran, "U.S. Hispanic Data Bases: Contemporary Building Blocks for Future Information Systems," in *Latin American Economic Issues,* 279–85; Cain, "Public Library Service to Minorities," 229–30; Milo, "Reference Service to the Spanish-Speaking," 26–28, 30–32; Susan A. Vega Garcia, "Latino Resources on the Web," in *Library Services to Latinos,* 207–27; Romelia Salinas, "CLNet: Redefining Latino Library Services in the Digital Era," in *Library Services to Latinos,* 228–40; Downs and Brown, "The Significance of Foreign Materials for U.S. Collections: Problems of Acquisitions," 11.

27. Nauratil, *Public Library Services with Nontraditional Clienteles,* 116–17.

28. Suzanne Boles, "Helping Vietnamese Refugees," *Unabashed Librarian,* no. 16 (Summer 1975): 5.

29. California State Library, "Special Issue: LSCA in California [LSCA Projects, 1957–1976]," 49.

30. Sondra Waldrop, "Library Service to Vietnamese Refugees," *Arkansas Libraries* 33, no. 1 (1976): 14–15.

31. Nauratil, *Public Libraries and Nontraditional Clienteles,* 116; Julie Tao Su, "Library Services in an Asian American Context," in *Diversity and Multiculturalism in Libraries,* ed. Katherine Hoover Hill (Greenwich, CT: JAI Press, 1994), 130–31; Judy Yung, "Asian Community Library," *Special Libraries* 69 (Mar. 1978): 115–17; Florence Makita Yoshiwara and Vivian Kobayashi, "The Asian American: Divergent Element of Cultural Pluralism," in *Cultural Pluralism & Children's Media,* 51; State Library of New South Wales, "Multicultural Library Services in New South Wales Public Libraries 2001, Part 8: International Case Studies,"

www.sl.nsw.gov.au/multicultural/services/case5.cfm, 8.2.5 "Los Angeles Public Library, Pio Pico Koreatown."

32. Natalia Greer, "Which Came First—The Chicken or the Egg?," *Colorado Libraries* 8 (Sept. 1982): 22–24.

33. Brown, *Library Service to the Disadvantaged*, 401; William L. Ramirez, "Libraries and the Spanish-Speaking," *Wilson Library Bulletin* 44 (Mar. 1970): 714.

34. DuMont et al., *Multiculturalism in Libraries*, 193–203.

35. Susan Malus, "El Centro Hispano de Information: A Unique Service of the Brooklyn Public Library," *Catholic Library World* 52 (Apr. 1981): 368–71.

36. Camila Alire and Orlando Archibeque, *Service to Latino Communities: A How-To-Do-It Manual for Librarians* (New York: Neal-Schuman Publishers, 1998), 172; Daphne Thompson, "Curious George in the Tomato Field: Regional Library Service to Migrant Children," *Top of the News* 30 (June 1974): 420–24; Cesar Caballero, "El Paso: The Movement Is Forward," *Wilson Library Bulletin* 53 (Nov. 1978): 232–34.

37. California State Library, *Catalog of Local Assistance*, 26, 55; Stern, "Ethnic Libraries and Librarianship in the United States: Models and Prospects," 77–78; Alire and Archibeque, *Service to Latino Communities*, 171; Guerena and Erazo, "Latinos and Librarianship," 167.

38. Guerena and Erazo, "Latinos and Librarianship," 165–66.

39. California State Library, *Catalog of Local Assistance* 52; Brown, *Library Service to the Disadvantaged*, 398.

40. California State Library, "Special Issue: LSCA in California [LSCA Projects, 1957–1976]," 75.

41. Alicia Godoy, "Miami: Two Decades of Latin Accent," *Wilson Library Bulletin* 53 (Nov. 1978): 236–37; Brown, *Library Service to the Disadvantaged*, 399–400; Lois R. Pearson, ed., "In the News [column]: From Mt. St. Helens to Miami, Librarians Face Unique Challenges of Summer, 1980," *American Libraries* 11 (Sept. 1980): 463–64; Haro, *Developing Library and Information Services for Americans of Hispanic Origin*, 12–15, 27–28; Nauratil, *Public Libraries and Nontraditional Clienteles*, 115–16.

42. Stephanie Ardito-Kirkland, "Chicago: Suburban Libraries and the Spanish Speaking," *Wilson Library Bulletin* 53 (Nov. 1978): 239–42; Haro, *Developing Library and Information Services for Americans of Hispanic Origin*, 30–32.

43. Nauratil, *Public Library Services with Nontraditional Clienteles*, 114–15.

44. Patterson, "Historical Overview of Tribal Libraries," 160–61.

45. Patterson, "Historical Overview of Tribal Libraries," 162; Taylor, *The Bureau of Indian Affairs*, 26–27; Hoxie, "Education," 178.

46. Cain, "Public Library Service to Minorities," 228–29; Nauratil, *Public Libraries and Nontraditional Clienteles*, 114–15.

47. Weibel, *Interagency Cooperation in Expanding Library Services to Disadvantaged Adults*; Cain, "Public Library Service to Minorities," 225.

48. Jamie Lynn Hengen, "Service to the Disadvantaged," *Mississippi Libraries* 43 (Autumn 1979): 155–56.

49. Molz, *The Federal Roles in Support of Public Library Services*, 21; David Cohen, "Ethnicity in Librarianship: A Rationale for Multiethnic Library Services in a Heterogeneous Society," *Library Trends* 29 (Fall 1980): 179–90; David Cohen, "Ethnicity in Librarianship: Imperatives of Library Training Programs for Minority Groups," *Catholic Library World* 51 (Mar. 1980): 342–46; Lowell A. Martin, *Enrichment: A History of the Public Library in the United States in the Twentieth Century* (Lanham, MD: Scarecrow Press, 1998), 143–44; Gerald R. Shields, "Federal Legislation and Libraries," in *Libraries in the Political Process*, ed. E.J. Josey (Phoenix: Oryx Press, 1980), 8–10; Charles H. Stevens, "National Commission on Libraries and Information Science," in *Encyclopedia of Library and Information Science*, vol. 19 (New York: Marcel Dekker, 1976), 64.

50. Donald V. Black, Herbert R. Seiden, and Ann W. Luke, *Evaluation of LSCA Services to Special Target Groups: Final Report* ([Washington, DC]: Systems Development Corporation, 1973), [i], I-1–3, II-1–6, IV-3, 23, 92–97, 146–51; U.S. National Commission on Libraries and Information Science, *Library and Information Services Needs of the Nation: Proceedings of a Conference on the Needs of Occupational, Ethnic, and Other Groups in the United States* (Washington, DC: U.S. G.P.O., 1974); Donald V. Black, "Library Needs of the Disadvantaged," in *Library and Information Services Needs of the Nation*, 281–314; Manuel E. Velez, "Library and Information Needs of the Mexican-American Community," in *Library and Information Services Needs of the Nation*, 223–25; Stern, "Ethnic Libraries and Librarianship in the United States: Models and Prospects," 89–91; Shields, "Federal Legislation and Libraries," 8–10; Stevens, "National Commission on Libraries and Information Science," 70–71.

51. Sylva N. Manoogian, "The Importance of Ethnic Collections in Libraries," in *Ethnic Collections in Libraries*, 7; Vivian Kobayashi and Irene Yeh, coords., *Asian Languages Library Materials: Chinese, Philipino, Vietnamese Bibliographies* (Sacramento: California Ethnic Services Task Force, California State Library, 1979).

52. Beilke and Sciara, *Selecting Materials for and about Hispanic and East Asian Children and Young People*, 5, 8; National Citizens Emergency Committee to Save Our Public Libraries, "Neighborhood Information Service Centers," iii–v; National Citizens Emergency Committee to Save Our Public Libraries, "Continuing Education Services: How Public Libraries Can Expand Educational Horizons for All Americans, in *The Changing Role of Public Libraries*, 1–46; National Citizens Emergency Committee to Save Our Public Libraries, "Neighborhood Information Service Centers," 1–46; National Citizens Emergency Committee to Save Our Public Libraries, "Serving Citizens with Special Needs: How Libraries Can Enrich Lives and Fulfill Aspirations for the Elderly and the Handicapped, the Functionally Illiterate, Hispanic Americans, Native Americans, the Homebound and Inmates of Correctional Institutions," in *The Changing Role of Public Libraries*, 1–46; National Citizens Emergency Commit-

tee to Save Our Public Libraries, "Strengthening the Library Profession: New Approaches Are Needed in the Recruiting and Training of America's Future Librarians," in *The Changing Role of Public Libraries,* 1–46; Robert D. Stueart, ed., *Information Needs of the 80s: Libraries and Information Services Role, in 'Bringing Information to People,' Based on the Deliberations of the White House Conference on Library and Information Services,* Foundations in Library and Information Science, vol. 15 (Greenwich, CT: JAI Press, 1982); Van Fleet, "Lifelong Learning Theory and the Provision of Adult Services," 180–81; Shields, "Federal Legislation and Libraries," 10–11; *Book Reading and Library Usage; A Study of Habits and Perceptions,* conducted for the American Library Association (Princeton: Gallup Organization, 1978); Elizabeth Rountree, "Users and Nonusers Disclose Their Needs: New Orleans Public Library Survey," *American Libraries* 10 (Sept. 1979): 486–87; Cain, "Public Library Service to Minorities," 231; Cohen, "Ethnicity in Librarianship" 179–90; Alex Ladenson, *Library Law and Legislation in the United States* (Metuchen, NJ: Scarecrow Press, 1982), 129–36; Stueart, *Information Needs of the 80s,* xv–xxi, 145–69.

53. Danilo H. Figueredo, "Love's Labour's Not Lost: Latino Publishing," *MultiCultural Review* 7 (Sept. 1998): 24–33; Dorothy Sinclair, "Materials to Meet Special Needs," *Library Trends* 17 (July 1968): 42–43; Mary Lou White, "Ethnic Literature for Children: A View from the Heartland," *Catholic Library World* 51 (Mar. 1980): 326–29; Cain, "Public Library Service to Minorities," 212–44, 228; Oralia Garza de Cortes, "Developing the Spanish Children's Collection," in *Library Services to Latinos,* 75–90; Hector Marino, "Considerations for the Development of Spanish Language Collections in School Libraries," in *Library Services to Latinos,* 91–108.

54. Alire and Archibeque, *Service to Latino Communities,* 243–44; Kay Britto, "What Language Do You Speak?," *Voice of Youth Advocates* 10 (Apr. 1987): 19–20.

55. Carmine Michael Diodati Jr., "Ethnic Groups, Library Service to: Italian Americans," in *ALA Yearbook 1978: A Review of Library Events, 1977* (Chicago: ALA, 1978), 123–24; Diodati, "Identifying Ethnic Communities," *Catholic Library World* 51 (Mar. 1980): 347–49; Diodati, "Italian-Americans," in *ALA Yearbook 1977,* 121; Diodati, "Italian Americans," in *ALA Yearbook 1979,* 147–48; Diodati, "Italian Americans," in *ALA Yearbook 1980,* 179–80; Diodati, "Italian-Americans and Libraries," in *ALA Yearbook 1976,* 201–3; Diodati, "Italian Americans and Libraries," in *ALA Yearbook 1981,* 164–65; Diodati, "Italian Americans and Libraries," in *ALA Yearbook 1982,* 156–57; Diodati, "Italian Americans and Libraries," in *ALA Yearbook 1983,* 157–58; Diodati, "Italian Americans and Libraries," in *ALA Yearbook of Library and Information Services, 1984,* 174–75; Diodati, "Italian Americans and Libraries," in *ALA Yearbook of Library and Information Services, 1985,* 165; Max Celnik and David Aronovitch, "Ethnic Groups, Library Service to: Jewish Americans," in *ALA Yearbook 1978,* 124–25; Max Celnik and David Aronovitch, "Jewish Americans," in *ALA Yearbook 1977,* 121–23; Edith

Maureen Fisher, "Ethnic Materials and Information Exchange Round Table," in *ALA Yearbook of Library and Information Services, 1988,* 129–30; Fisher, "Ethnic Materials Information Exchange Round Table," in *ALA Yearbook of Library and Information Services, 1987,* 128–29; Susan J. Freiband, "Ethnic Materials Information Exchange Round Table," in *ALA Yearbook of Library and Information Services, 1986,* 135; Victoria M. Gala, "Ethnic Groups, Library Service to: Polish Americans, in *ALA Yearbook 1978,* 125–26; Victoria M. Gala, "Polish Americans," in *ALA Yearbook 1977,* 124; Victoria M. Gala, "Polish Americans," in *ALA Yearbook 1979,* 206–7; Edith Lubetski, "Association of Jewish Libraries," in *ALA Yearbook of Library and Information Services, 1986,* 66–67; Marie Zielinska, "Ethnic Materials Information Exchange Round Table," in *ALA Yearbook of Library and Information Services, 1989,* 108–9; Marie Zielinksa, "Ethnic Materials Information Exchange Round Table," in *ALA Yearbook of Library and Information Services, 1990,* 111–12.

56. Black Caucus of the American Library Association, http://www.bcala.org/history;about.htm; Coretta Scott King Award, http://www.ala.org/ala/srrt/corettascottking/abouttheaward/aboutaward.htm.

57. Daniel Flores Duran, "Non-English Speaking, Library Service to the," in *ALA Yearbook 1976,* 250; Duran, "REFORMA," in *ALA Yearbook 1979,* 237–38; Duran, "REFORMA," in *ALA Yearbook 1980,* 266–67; Marta Stiefel Ayala, "Daniel Flores Duran [Interview]," *Wilson Library Bulletin* 53 (Nov. 1978): 235; Cesar Caballero, "REFORMA," in *ALA Yearbook 1981,* 249–50; Marta Stiefel Ayala, "Luis Chaparro [Interview]," *Wilson Library Bulletin* 53 (Nov. 1978): 267; Baeza, "The Evolution of Educational and Public Library Services to Spanish-Speaking Children," 6–7; John L. Ayala, "REFORMA," in *ALA Yearbook 1976,* 304; Ingrid Betancourt, "REFORMA," in *ALA Yearbook of Library and Information Services, 1989,* 206–8; Patrick Jose Dawson, "The History and Role of REFORMA," in *Latino Librarianship,* 121–34; Salvador Guerena, "REFORMA," in *ALA Yearbook of Library and Information Services, 1985,* 241–42; Luis Herrera, "REFORMA," in *ALA Yearbook 1982,* 236–38; Rhonda Rios Kravitz, "REFORMA," in *ALA Yearbook of Library and Information Services, 1990,* 211–13; Susan C. Luevano, "REFORMA," in *ALA Yearbook of Library and Information Services, 1986,* 269–70; Liz Rodriguez Miller, "REFORMA," in *ALA Yearbook of Library and Information Services, 1988,* 283–84; Albert J. Milo, "REFORMA," in *ALA Yearbook 1983,* 237 (Chicago: ALA, 1983); Albert J. Milo, "REFORMA," in *ALA Yearbook of Library and Information Services, 1984,* 245–46; Jose Taylor, "REFORMA," in *ALA Yearbook 1977,* 280–81; Elena Tscherny, "REFORMA," in *ALA Yearbook of Library and Information Services, 1987,* 264–65; Guerena and Erazo, "Latinos and Librarianship," 155–57; Dawson, "The History and Role of REFORMA," 121–34; Beilke and Sciara, *Selecting Materials for and about Hispanic and East Asian Children and Young People,* 11–12.

58. Marta Stiefel Ayala, "Martha Tome [Interview]," *Wilson Library Bulletin* 53 (Nov. 1978): 243; Yolanda J. Cuesta, "Ethnic Groups, Library Service to: Hispanic Americans," in *ALA Yearbook 1978*, 122–23; Yolanda J. Cuesta and Patricia Tarin, "Guidelines for Library Services to the Spanish Speaking," *Library Journal* 103 (July 1978): 1354–55; ALA Reference and Adult Services Division, Committee on Library Services to the Spanish Speaking, "Guidelines for Library Services to Hispanics," *RQ* 27 (Summer 1988): 491–93, also published in *Journal of Multicultural Librarianship* 2 (Mar. 1988): 57–60; R. Errol Lam, "The Reference Interview: Some Intercultural Considerations," *RQ* 27 (Spring 1988): 390–95; D. Bryan Stansfield, "Serving Hispanic Persons: The Cross-Cultural Border Library Experience at Fabens," *RQ* 27 (Summer 1988): 547–61; Eugene Estrada, "Changing Latino Demographics and American Libraries," in *Latino Librarianship*, 12–13; Milo, "Reference Service to the Spanish-Speaking," 30; Beilke and Sciara, *Selecting Materials for and about Hispanic and East Asian Children and Young People*, 11–12.

59. Tze-Chung Li, "Chinese American Librarians Association," in *ALA Yearbook 1978*, 92–93; Li, "Chinese American Librarians Association," in *ALA Yearbook 1979*, 83; Li, "Chinese American Librarians Association," in *ALA Yearbook 1980*, 115; Li, "Chinese American Librarians Association," in *ALA Yearbook 1981*, 104; Li, "Chinese American Librarians Association," in *ALA Yearbook 1982*, 95; Amy Seetoo Wilson, "Chinese-American Librarians Association," in *ALA Yearbook of Library and Information Services, 1985*, 98–99; Wilson, "Chinese-American Librarians Association," in *ALA Yearbook of Library and Information Services, 1986*, 117–18; Wilson, "Chinese-American Librarians Association," in *ALA Yearbook of Library and Information Services, 1988*, 116; Wilson, "Chinese-American Librarians Association," in *ALA Yearbook of Library and Information Services, 1987*, 114–15; Wilson, "Chinese-American Librarians Association (CALA)," in *ALA Yearbook of Library and Information Services, 1989*, 98; Eveline L. Yang, "Chinese-American Librarians Association (CALA)," in *ALA Yearbook of Library and Information Services, 1990*, 100–1; John Yung-Hsiang Lai, "Chinese American Librarians Association," in *ALA Yearbook 1983*, 90–91; Lai, "Chinese-American Librarians Association," in *ALA Yearbook of Library and Information Services, 1984*, 109; Mengxiong Liu, "The History and Status of Chinese Americans in Librarianship," *Library Trends* 49 (Summer 2000): 109–37; Norine Chiu, "Library Service to the Chinese-American Community," *Journal and Library & Information Science* 5 (Apr. 1979): 16–42; Julie Tao Su, "Library Services in an Asian American Context," in *Diversity and Multiculturalism in Libraries*, 124.

60. Roberto Cabello-Argandona, "Academic Librarianship and the Chicano," in *Opportunities for Minorities in Librarianship*, ed. E. J. Josey and Kenneth E. Peeples Jr. (Metuchen, NJ: Scarecrow Press, 1977), 42–43; Roberto Cabello-Argandona, "Recruiting Spanish-Speaking Library Students," in *Social Responsibilities and Libraries: A Library Journal/School Library Journal Selection*, comp. and ed.

Patricia Glass Schuman (New York: R. R. Bowker, 1976), 125–30; Cain, "Public Library Service to Minorities," 226.

61. Cabello-Argandona, "Academic Librarianship and the Chicano," 53–54; California State Library, "Special Issue: LSCA in California [LSCA Projects, 1957–1976]," 87; Baeza, "The Evolution of Educational and Public Library Services to Spanish-Speaking Children," 5–6; Guerena and Erazo, "Latinos and Librarianship," 155.

62. Baeza, "The Evolution of Educational and Public Library Services to Spanish-Speaking Children," 5–6; National Citizens Emergency Committee to Save Our Public Libraries, "Serving Citizens with Special Needs," 22.

63. National Citizens Emergency Committee to Save Our Public Libraries, "Serving Citizens with Special Needs," 31.

64. Naumer, "Library Services to American Indians," 24, 63–64; E.J. Josey, "Minority Groups, Library Service for," in *Encyclopedia of Library and Information Science*, vol. 18, 192–93; Nauratil, *Public Libraries and Nontraditional Clienteles*, 115; National Citizens Emergency Committee to Save Our Public Libraries, "Serving Citizens with Special Needs," 28–32.

65. Huff, *To Live Heroically: Institutional Racism and American Indian Education*, 10–13; June Smeck Smith, "Library Service to American Indians," *Library Trends* 20 (Oct. 1971): 223–38; DuMont et al., *Multiculturalism in Libraries*, 40–41, 55–56.

66. Michael Gonzalez, Bill Greeley, and Stephen Whitney, "Assessing the Library Needs of the Spanish-Speaking," *Library Journal* 105 (1 Apr. 1980): 786–89; Roberto P. Haro, "How Mexican-Americans View Libraries: One-Man Survey," *Wilson Library Bulletin* 44 (Mar. 1970): 736–42; Stansfield, "Serving Hispanic Persons," 547–61; Haro, *Developing Library and Information Services for Americans of Hispanic Origin*, 1–43.

67. Farrington, "Library Services to Mexican-Americans," 309; National Citizens Emergency Committee to Save Our Public Libraries, "Serving Citizens with Special Needs," 18–21.

68. California State Library, *Catalog of Local Assistance*, 26.

69. Karen Sanudo, "A Case for Bilingual Librarianship in New Jersey," *New Jersey Libraries* 12 (Feb. 1979): 3–9; "Bilingual Program at Newark Public Library Wins Approval of the Florence John Schumann Foundation & the Victoria Foundation," *New Jersey Libraries* 12 (Feb. 1979): 28; "Bergenfield Public Teaches English," *Wilson Library Bulletin* 55 (Dec. 1980): 253; Martha Powers Williams, "Doing It: Migrant Workers Library," in *Revolting Librarians*, ed. Celeste West and Elizabeth Katz (San Francisco: Booklegger Press, 1972), 63–67; Martha Power Williams, "The Migrants: 'Library Project for Migrant Workers,'" *New Jersey Libraries* 7 (Feb. 1974): 1–4; New Jersey Library Association, Committee on Service to the Disadvantaged, "Service to Migrant Workers," *New Jersey Libraries* 7 (Feb. 1974): 4.

Chapter 5

PUBLIC LIBRARIES AND MULTICULTURALISM IN THE 1980s

During the decade of the 1980s, the U.S. population was approximately 221 million, with approximately 88 percent white. While black Americans made up approximately 12 percent of the total population, their political power had only begun to be felt through the election of black mayors and legislators. Native Americans numbered 1.4 million, representing barely 0.6 percent of the total population.

Three out of four American Indians were located west of the Mississippi, mostly in Arizona, New Mexico, Oklahoma, California, and Alaska. While nearly 500 different tribes had been identified, the majority belonged to 10 tribes, of which the Navajo, Cherokee, Sioux, and Chippewa were the largest.

The Spanish-speaking community numbered 14.6 million, or 6 percent of the population. Of these, Mexican Americans, or Chicanos, were by far the largest group and had also been in the United States the longest time.[1]

LEGISLATIVE AND JUDICIAL DECISIONS AFFECTING MINORITIES

Refugee Act of 1980

Confronted with the fall of South Vietnam, Cambodia, and Laos to Communist forces and the hundreds of thousands of refugees, Congress passed the

Refugee Act of March 1980, the first systematic procedure for the admission and effective resettlement of refugees to the United States. Besides eliminating the parole authority of the president, the 1980 act provided that refugees formerly admitted in limited numbers as seventh-preference immigrants would now come in under a special refugee quota set at 50,000 per year.

The 1980 act also provided for the first time the admission of 5,000 asylum seekers annually. It set up a system for reimbursement to states and voluntary associations for financial and medical assistance they provided to refugees, and it established a comprehensive program for their domestic resettlement. Over 90 percent of the refugees admitted between 1945 and 1980 had come from countries with Marxist governments, including 875,000 Cubans, 750,000 Indochinese, at least 600,000 eastern Europeans from behind the iron curtain, and others from Yemen, Afghanistan, and Ethiopia.

The Refugee Education Assistance Act of October 1980 established a program of formula grants to state education agencies for basic education of refugee children. It also provided for services to Cuban and Haitian entrants identical to those for refugees under the Refugee Act of 1980. In June 1981, Congress reduced previously appropriated funds for migration and refugee assistance, including funds provided for the processing of Cuban and Haitian entrants, and, in August 1981, restricted the access of aliens to various publicly funded benefits, including the Aid to Families with Dependent Children program.[2]

1981 Report of the 1978 U.S. Select Commission of Immigration and Refugee Policy

In 1981, the bipartisan U.S. Select Commission of Immigration and Refugee Policy (SCIRP) of 1978 released its report that affirmed the positive value of legal immigration but advocated a new device and approach to control illegal immigration. The commission advocated enacting employer sanctions that would make it illegal to hire an undocumented alien worker and suggested an amnesty program to provide legalization to permanent resident alien status to an estimated 3 million illegal aliens then in the country. The jobs magnet should be cut off.[3]

Sanctuary Movement

Outraged by the INS's almost systematic and arbitrary deportation of Central Americans, with over 50,000 Salvadorans being deported in 1981 alone, sympathetic citizens throughout the United States took it upon themselves to offer sanctuary to Central Americans fleeing terror at home but denied entry to the United States. In 1982, the Sanctuary movement, estimated at about 100,000 participants, established a network of approximately 250 churches, synagogues, and Quaker meeting houses, began to provide transportation, shelter, and protection for hundreds of Central Americans who would have otherwise been deported to an almost certain death at home. The Reagan administration devoted much energy to undermining the Sanctuary movement. In 1984, Sanctuary members in Arizona and Texas were prosecuted and convicted for sheltering refugees, but the movement attracted nationwide support.[4]

In 1983, the INS apprehended and deported over 1.25 million illegal immigrants, about double the number of a decade earlier, and officials believed that just as many had escaped detection. It became increasingly clear that the United States could not control its 5,000 miles of border adequately. Although there was broad support for a new policy and a bipartisan effort to enact one, bills combining amnesty for illegal aliens with sanctions against those who employed them were defeated in Congress on three occasions between 1982 and 1984.[5]

By 1985, three cities, Miami, Los Angeles, and New York, had populations of whom more than 25 percent were foreign born. More than 50 percent of the residents were those born abroad and their children. Miami was overwhelmingly Hispanic, mostly Cuban. Los Angeles was more cosmopolitan, including Iranians, Salvadorans, Armenians, Chinese, Koreans, Vietnamese, Filipinos, and Arabs; more than two-thirds were Hispanic, with Mexicans easily the largest group. In New York City, for example, the mix was broad with no group predominating, including more Dominicans than in any city but Santo Domingo, more Haitians than anywhere but Port-au-Prince, more Greeks than anywhere but Athens, more Jamaicans than anywhere outside Jamaica, more Russians (mostly Jewish) than anywhere outside the Soviet Union, and more Chinese and Taiwanese than anywhere outside mainland China and Taiwan.[6]

Immigration Reform and Control Act (IRCA) of 1986

The IRCA, also known as the Simpson-Rodino Act for its Congressional sponsors, authorized permanent resident status for illegal aliens who had resided in the United States since January 1, 1982. It created sanctions prohibiting the employment of illegal aliens while at the same time granted amnesty to illegal aliens and special agricultural workers (SAWs) who had resided in the United States since January 1, 1972.

The 1986 act authorized adjustment to permanent resident status for Cubans and Haitians who entered the United States on parole without inspection and had continuously resided in the country since January 1982. It increased the numerical limitation for immigrants admitted under the preference system for dependent areas from 600 to 5,000 beginning in fiscal year 1988. It allocated 5,000 nonpreference visas in each of fiscal years 1987 and 1988 for aliens born in countries from which immigration was adversely affected by the 1965 act.

Response to the amnesty program was initially sluggish. Many undocumented aliens feared a trap, and even more were worried that families might be split up if some members were eligible and others who had entered after the 1982 cutoff date were not. It was difficult for people who had tried for years to hide all evidence of their existence in the United States to produce proof of residence. After a last-minute rush, only about 1.5 million out of perhaps 3 million or 4 million who were eligible had applied for legal status by the time the act expired on May 4, 1988. In addition, some 400,000 people had claimed amnesty under the clause relating to SAWs.

Ironically, the 1986 act failed to stem the flow of illegal aliens. A federal government crackdown on illegal immigrants, involving expanded border patrols, chain-link fences, closed-circuit television monitors, electronic sensors, and a 14-foot ditch along the border, deterred the entry of only a small fraction. Equally ineffectual were the sanctions against hiring them. Although offending employers were fined a total of 1 million dollars during the first two years of the act, many continued to hire aliens whose documents were false.[7]

Kennedy-Donnelly Act of 1988

Those unable to benefit from the 1986 amnesty because they had arrived in the United States since the 1982 cutoff date were large numbers of new Irish, who had fallen on hard times when the Irish economy suddenly dipped. Like other Europeans with little recent history of emigration, they had been all but excluded by the family-preference system and had consequently entered the country as tourists, staying on when their visas expired. Estimated to number 150,000, illegal Irish were better educated and less rural than their nineteenth-century predecessors, but most were employed in unskilled jobs.

An Irish Immigration Reform Movement, aimed at changes in the immigration laws, succeeded in 1987 in obtaining 10,000 additional visas to be awarded by lottery to 36 countries disadvantaged by the 1965 act. Well-organized Irish applicants sent in a disproportionate number of claims and secured 40 percent of the total as well as two-thirds of the 15,000 visas made available by the Kennedy-Donnelly Act of 1988, named for its supporters in the Congress. The sponsors of the so-called Irish Bill saw it as a stopgap measure and continued to press for more comprehensive changes. They held that more weight should be given to what they could contribute than to whether they had American-based relatives.[8]

Soviet Immigration

The changing face of Soviet Communism in the late 1980s created a refugee emergency, which posed considerable problems for the United States. For more than 20 years, American administrations had been pressing the Soviet Union to allow its people, specifically its Jews, to emigrate freely. Except for a brief period in the early 1970s when the Leonid Brezhnev regime had permitted some 30,000 Jews to depart, this pressure had had little effect. When Mikhail Gorbachev relaxed exit restrictions in 1987, approximately 80 percent of those wishing to emigrate were Jews.

The overwhelming majority of Russian emigrants wanted to go to the United States, and a growing number were able to do so, although bureaucratic delays in obtaining exit and immigrant visas, the limited number of direct flights to American destinations, and the requirement that emigrants could take with them no more than $140, together slowed the process considerably. The number of Soviet Jewish refugees entering the United States rose from a mere handful in the early and mid-1980s to 8,000 in 1987, 19,000 in 1988, and 43,500 in 1989.

As early as the summer of 1988, the American embassy in Moscow was inundated by applications from Jews and other Soviet refugees eager to leave and was forced to suspend the issue of refugee visas temporarily. Before then, Soviet Jews, once out of their country, had been automatically accepted by the United States as refugees. Now every Soviet Jewish applicant for refugee status, like other would-be refugees, had to convince American immigration officials that he or she had a well-grounded fear of persecution if not allowed to emigrate or if forced to return to the Soviet Union.

Fewer than 20 percent of Soviet Jewish applications were rejected, and many were later accepted on appeal. The expiring Reagan administration continued to seek ways of dealing with the growing Soviet influx. President Reagan reallocated existing quotas in January 1989, expanding the number of Soviet refugees permitted to enter in 1989 by 40 percent and offsetting the increase by a corresponding reduction in the number of places reserved for other refugee groups. This policy produced an outcry from organizations concerned with the welfare of Southeast Asian and Latin American refugees.

There was similar criticism when President George Herbert Walker Bush asked Congress in April 1989 to create a new category of special-interest immigrant visas to permit 150,000 additional immigrants in the next five years. The search for a new refugee policy culminated six months later in a decision whose effect was to exclude many Soviet Jews who might otherwise have been able to enter. Until then, Soviet Jews wishing to immigrate to the United States had commonly obtained exit visas for Israel. Once outside the Soviet Union, they had made their way to Vienna and Rome, where they languished in camps until American immigration officials considered their applications for refugee status.

In September 1989, the Bush administration announced that all such applications must be made directly to the American embassy in Moscow and that the Vienna and Rome facilities would be closed. These changes in screening procedures channeled a large proportion of Soviet Jewish emigration to Israel. In 1990, the United States admitted just over 50,000 refugees from the Soviet Union, four-fifths of them Jews, and a further 30,000 Soviet refugees, also largely Jewish, under the new special-interest refugee category. The immigration of Soviet Jews to Israel, on the other hand negligible for most of the 1980s, rose to 13,000 in 1989 and then soared to an estimated 175,000 in 1990.

Many of the newly arrived Soviet Armenians settled in Los Angeles, which had a long-established Armenian community. Soviet Jews gravitated instead to East Coast cities, half of them to New York, especially to Brighton Beach at the southern tip of Brooklyn, whose Jewish character dated back to the 1930s. They were generously helped by Jewish American organizations such as the New York Association of New Americans (NYANA), which provided financial, English instructional, housing, medical assistance, job training, and placement services.[9]

Bilingual Education

By the late 1980s, ESL classes were being conducted in 80 different languages and reaching 500,000 children, approximately 70 percent of them Spanish speaking. By 1988, 17 states had passed laws making English the official language, but bilingual education persisted in many localities despite sharp cuts in funding during the Reagan administrations.[10]

LSCA Amendments

In October 1984, Congress reauthorized LSCA with a five-year extension, and President Reagan signed the enabling law. The extension reauthorized Titles I, II, and III, and added three new titles: Title IV, Library Services for Indian Tribes and Hawaiian Natives (to establish and improve American Indian tribal libraries and library services with Hawaiian natives); Title V, Foreign Language Materials Acquisition; and Title VI, Library Literacy Programs (for librarian training and outreach programs for illiterate and functionally illiterate adults). The U.S. Department of Education reported that from fiscal year 1957 through 1985, more than $1 billion had been spent on Title I alone.

Under LSCA Title I, funds went to 54 state library administrative agencies in fiscal year 1984 to establish, extend, and improve public library services. According to the U.S. Department of Education, 140 MURLs were funded and services provided to approximately 3 million disadvantaged persons, 2 million limited English-speaking individuals, just under 800,000 blind and physically disabled persons, just over 800,000 persons in state institutions, and over 700,000 elderly persons. During fiscal year 1984, Title I was funded at $65 million; Title II at approximately $22 million; and Title III at $15 million.

Under LSCA Title II in fiscal years 1983 and 1984, a total of 51 state agencies received approximately $50 million for more than 500 construction projects, including new buildings, additions to existing buildings, and remodeling projects. Under Title III, 6,000 public libraries received funding to support networks and consortia to improve services for readers.

Funding for LSCA Title IV was determined by setting aside 2 percent of the appropriations for LSCA Titles I, II, and III, with 1.5 percent allocated for Indian tribes and 0.5 percent for Hawaiian natives. In fiscal year 1985, the amounts set aside for Title IV were $1.77 million for awards to Indian tribes and $590,000 for Hawaiian natives.

Two types of discretionary awards were available: basic and special projects grants. The basic grant for Indian tribes was computed by dividing the annual appropriation available by the number of federally recognized entities. Monies that remained from tribes that did not apply or that did not qualify for funding were used to make special projects grants on a competitive basis. Only tribes that received basic grants were eligible to apply for special projects grants. Special projects grantees were required to share a minimum of 20 percent of the total cost of the project, and a librarian was required to administer the grant funds. In fiscal year 1985, 130 basic grant awards at an established amount of $43,498 were made to Indian tribes in 26 states, and one basic grant of $590,000 was made to Alu Like, Inc. of Honolulu, Hawaii, on behalf of Hawaiian natives. The remaining funds were used to award 18 special projects grants to 17 tribes in 10 states.[11]

LIBRARY SERVICES WITH MINORITIES

A common feature among the more successful programs for minority groups has been group members' active participation in their planning and operation. Too often, well-intentioned librarians have carefully developed programs to help the disadvantaged only to find, to their surprise, that their services are unwanted.

Successful programs have been consistent with the goals of self-determination and have actively involved minority group members, both librarians and community residents, to establish relevant library service for the targeted minority group or groups. Many projects have included developing a core collection of multiethnic, multimedia materials; setting up deposit collections in community centers; producing bilingual promotion media; coordinating with community organizations and schools; and providing in-service training programs for public service personnel.[12]

American Indians

In 1980, the Chicago Public Library opened a Native American I&R center with a grant from the Illinois State Library. Chicago's population included an estimated 20,000 Native Americans representing more than 100 different tribes. The unemployment rate for this group reached as high as 80 percent. An I&R center housed a book and periodical collection and provided telephone reference service. A microcomputer was utilized to provide current information on organizations that served Native Americans, including employment agencies, child welfare groups, and medical services.[13]

African Americans

Black History Month in February of each year has inspired programs in a number of libraries. In 1981, the Muncie (IN) Public Library mounted an extensive multisite exhibit of photographs on the theme of local black heritage.

In 1983, for example, the Seattle Public Library cosponsored with the City Art Works several programs on the role of black artists in the development of visual art styles in America. The Akron-Summit County (OH) Public Library celebrated Black History Month 1983 with a presentation of folk tales in Swahili and Zulu, and a performance to the accompaniment of conga drums, talking drums, maracas, flute, and foot bells. At the Baltimore County Public Library, a festival of art, dance, drama, poetry, and music was held, honoring the work of black artists such as Billie Holiday, Paul Dunbar, and Langston Hughes.[14]

Partnerships for Change Grants from the California State Library

Beginning in fiscal year 1989, the California State Library established the Partnerships for Change (PFC) grant program for libraries that served changing populations with diverse needs and that were committed to assessing their communities' needs—undertaking innovative library services, forming community coalitions, and developing public relations strategies to promote library services to their communities, particularly Spanish-speaking and Southeast Asian immigrants.

The Echo Park Branch of the Los Angeles Public Library, located in the urban community 1 mile west of downtown Los Angeles, received a PFC grant for its Biblioteca para Todos (Library for Everyone) program to improve Spanish, ESL, and citizenship collections and to provide outreach to the Spanish-speaking community, including public school students. The Logan Heights Branch of the San Diego Public Library used its PFC grant to expand its Spanish-language collection on issues such as drug abuse, parenting, immigration, career education, and self-improvement, in addition to its ESL and citizenship-related materials. Targeting its services to 5- to 16-year-olds, the branch advertised in local Spanish-language media, published a bilingual newsletter and brochures, and produced Spanish-language videos to introduce Latinos to the library.

The Santa Ana Public Library used its PFC grant to develop a program called Vietnamese Voices at the Newhope Branch, which is located next to the largest Vietnamese community in the United States. The branch focused on building the Vietnamese-language collection, hiring bilingual clerical staff and tutors, and sponsoring an oral history project to collect the memoirs of Vietnamese immigrants, who reflected on their experiences in Orange County. The Linda Vista Branch of the San Diego Public Library used its PFC grant to develop services for the 55,000 Southeast Asians residing in the surrounding area, principally Vietnamese but also Hmong, Lao, and Pacific Islanders. Collaboration with the Vietnamese Federation,

Vietnamese bookstores, and the Lao Family Community Center proved to be very helpful in cultural programming and expanding collections of materials in Indochinese languages, ESL materials, and materials in English about Southeast Asian subjects.[15]

LSCA Projects for Asians

The Asia Model Library of the Villa Regional Library of the Jefferson County (CO) Library System used a fiscal year 1982 LSCA grant of $25,000 to organize its Asian-language material into machine-readable vernacular language and bilingual cataloging records access. The University of California, Riverside received a fiscal year 1988 LSCA grant of $13,222 for the conversion of 4,900 Spanish language titles to machine-readable form and added them to OCLC. The San Jose Public Library received a fiscal year 1988 LSCA grant of $2,500 for the online conversion of 1,000 Chinese-language fiction titles to machine-readable form and added them to the OCLC. Established in 1967, the OCLC was by the mid-1970s the bibliographic utility used by 1,250 public, academic, school, and special libraries in 45 states, the District of Columbia, Canada, and Puerto Rico.[16]

The South State Cooperative Library System received an LSCA grant of $278,900 from 1981 to 1989 to continue a program of cooperative acquisitions, cataloging, and processing of materials in Asian languages (Chinese, Japanese, Korean, Vietnamese) for contracting libraries subscribing to its Project ASIA (Asian Shared Information and Access).[17]

The Monterey County (CA) Library's Thu-Vien Project received a fiscal year 1986 LSCA grant of $66,500 to develop quality library service for Vietnamese residents through staff training, addition of language materials, and a public information program. The library received a fiscal year 1988 LSCA grant of $4,950 for the online conversion of 2,000 Spanish-language book titles to machine-readable form and added them to the OCLC bibliographic database.[18]

LSCA Projects for Polish Immigrants

In 1984, rising Polish immigration caused the Portage-Cragin Branch of the Chicago Public Library to begin amassing Polish-language materials and items in English about history and culture. In 1987, the Joyce Foundation provided funds for Polish-language books and materials and in 1992 received an LSCA grant of $150,000 to fund the creation of a Polish Information Center with a full-time bilingual librarian. At the end of the 1990s, the collection had more than 4,000 books and more than 400 videos.[19]

LSCA Projects for Spanish-Speaking Immigrants

In the late 1980s, the Houston Public Library received two LSCA grants for intergenerational programs for Hispanic preschool children and their parents at the Stanaker Branch. The first was for a parents' reading program in fiscal year 1988 that emphasized reading aloud to children, child development, and the positive use of educational toys that mothers and fathers could make at home. The second grant allowed the branch to present a computer literacy program for parents and preschoolers and an after-school homework tutoring program staffed by volunteers.[20]

Quadrus and Friends Visit the Library was the name of a creative program sponsored by the Free Library of Philadelphia during 1980 to break down stereotypes of the library and to stimulate reading and library use among the 60,000 8- to 14-year-olds in the city's African American and Hispanic neighborhoods. Underwritten by a $25,000 LSCA grant, 50,000 English- and Spanish-language comic books featuring characters from various ethnic groups were distributed. The comic books were used to encourage participation in library programs. Quadrus was publicized through a citywide media campaign. Libraries reported both a substantial increase in library registration and circulation figures and an improved relationship with the targeted children.[21]

LSCA Projects for New Americans and Preparation for Citizenship

In the 1980s, the New Americans Project (NAP) of the Queens Borough Public Library, established in 1977, was offering 57 ESL classes annually. Approximately 2,000 New Americans enrolled, representing 60 countries and speaking 35 different languages. In January 1985, the NAP became part of the newly formed Outreach Services Department. One of its most popular programs has been the Books-By-Mail Service, which makes available through loan foreign-language materials in Greek, Italian, Korean, Russian, Spanish, French (primarily for the Haitian community), and Chinese.[22]

In March 1982, the Whitman County (WA) Library System and the Neill Public Library in Pullman, the county seat and site of Washington

State University, together received an LSCA grant of $11,920 from the Washington State Library to publicize existing ESL activities, provide library materials for them, and coordinate class space and tutor training. Included in Pullman's population of 23,000, were more than 1,000 individuals representing 35 countries. Of these 1,000, some were drawn by educational opportunities at the university and some were refugees sponsored by local churches or families.[23]

The Merced County (CA) Library received a fiscal year 1989 LSCA grant of $79,650 for its Library Services for New Americans program to aid the Southeast Asian population in adapting to American culture through workshops, library tours, collection building, and staff training.[24]

The Chicago Public Library received a fiscal year 1988 LSCA grant of $136,970 for its Year of the New Reader program, which targeted Chicago's new Asian, Hispanic, Middle Eastern, and Polish residents. Six bilingual professional librarians, representing Colombian, Iraqi, Greek, Polish, Korean, and Vietnamese cultures, presented an intercultural workshop early in the program for some 90 librarians. The librarians emphasized that the public library was a refuge for newcomers and stressed the timidity of immigrants, their ignorance of the library system, and their reticence toward public institutions.[25]

Since 1988, the Franklin Learning Center (FLC) of Minneapolis has been providing a community-based computer-learning program to fill a critical literacy education gap. It serves the Phillips neighborhood, which, in 1988, had the highest percentage of families receiving public assistance in Minnesota and the highest unemployment rate in Minneapolis, with more than half of the residents being New Americans, American Indians, and members of other ethnic and minority groups. The FLC offers services in four major areas: (1) ABE for adults having few or no reading skills, (2) General Equivalency Development (GED) preparation of students who have not completed high school and read at or above the ninth-grade level, (3) a reading skills enhancement program to build reading skills, and (4) ESL classes for intermediate and advanced levels of learners from 39 countries.[26]

LSCA Projects for Soviet Immigrants

The Glendale (CO) Public Library, a branch of the Arapahoe Regional Library, was located on an island completely surrounded by Denver. Director Annette Choszczyk reports that in 1988, changes in immigration rules and regulations brought many Russian-speaking refugee families into the neighborhood around the library, including a library manager from the former Soviet Union, who volunteered to help these new arrivals. LSCA grants provided the funds for the development of a popular Russian-language collection, the addition of ESL and vocational materials, and the hiring of the Russian volunteer as a paid staff member. The Glendale Public Library evolved into a bilingual branch with more than 60 percent of library use by Russian-speaking users.[27]

LSCA Construction Projects

The Los Angeles Public Library received a fiscal year 1986 LSCA grant of $114,075 for the construction of the Chinatown Branch. The Langston Hughes Library and Cultural Center in Corona, Queens Borough, New York, and the Vivian G. Harsh Collection of Afro-American History and Literature of the Chicago Public Library, located at Carter G. Woodson Regional Library, were noted for their extensive collections on African American history and culture.

The construction of the Rudy Lozano Branch Library, which was dedicated in 1989, helped provide a new focus for the library's efforts to serve the Hispanic community. Since 1989, the branch has had the largest Spanish-language collection in the Chicago Public Library System, which has been cited as a national model for library services to Hispanic communities. The branch, located in the West Side's Pilsen neighborhood, was once an enclave of Czech immigrants. By 1989, the neighborhood was almost entirely Hispanic, including 87.9 percent of the 45,403 residents, and heavily Mexican American. About 32 percent of the population did not speak English or spoke it poorly.[28]

The Cesar Chavez Library, a branch of the Salinas (CA) Public Library, was located in a neighborhood where approximately 70 percent of residents were agricultural workers, many of them migrants from Mexico. With the help of an LSCA grant, the library offered a Families for Literacy program featuring a bilingual storytime program geared to young parents and their children up to five years old as part of a family-oriented approach to reading in partnership with the Salinas Adult Reading Program and the local Special Supplemental Nutrition Program for the Women, Infants, and Children (WIC) program. The library has sponsored an annual Latino festival and book fair offering English, Spanish, and bilingual Spanish-English multicultural and multimedia materials that draws interested community members as well as teachers and librarians from throughout California.[29]

LSCA Projects to Address U.S.-Mexico Border Issues

The San Diego State University, Imperial Valley, received a fiscal year 1989 LSCA grant of $39,700 to interview 100 border scholars and survey 25 resource centers to determine needs and resources for a study of border-related issues of the United States and Mexico.[30]

The California-Mexico border was the site of the first and second binational Conferences on Libraries of the Californias. The first one was held in Tijuana in 1984, organized by the Latino Services Project of the Serra Cooperative Library System, and the second in 1985 in Calexico, California, and Mexicali, Baja California, organized by the Institute for Border Studies of San Diego State University. Each attracted over 400 librarians. They were funded through LSCA grants awarded by the California State Library and had as their purpose the convening of librarians from both sides of the U.S. and Mexico border to discuss their common problems as well as to set goals to provide better library services to border populations.[31]

ALA and Affiliated Organizations for Minorities

The Ethnic Materials and Information Exchange (EMIE) Task Force of the ALA Social Responsibilities Round Table was elevated to the status of Round Table at the ALA annual conference held in Philadelphia in 1982. The ALA Council Committee on Minority Concerns and the Advisory Committee to the ALA Office of Library Outreach Services supported the elevation of the Task Force to Round Table status, and ALA Council approval came in January 1983. The EMIE Round Table continued to address issues of multiculturalism and ethnic studies that affected the development of ethnic collections to serve the increasingly diverse clientele of all types of libraries.[32]

The Asian/Pacific American Librarians Association (APALA) was established at the 1980 ALA annual conference in New York to support the aspirations of Asian/Pacific American librarians, the only minority librarians who have a larger percentage of representation in the library profession than the percentage of Asian Americans in the general population. APALA was incorporated in the state of Illinois in 1981 and became an ALA affiliate organization in 1982. The predecessor of APALA, the Asian American Librarians Caucus (AALC), was founded under the leadership of Janet M. Suzuki at the 1975 ALA annual conference in San Francisco as a caucus supported by the ALA Office for Library Service to the Disadvantaged (OLSD).[33]

Guadalajara International Book Fair

The Guadalajara International Book Fair (Feria Internacional del Libro) (FIL), organized in 1986 by the University of Guadalajara in Guadalajara, Jalisco, Mexico, brings together library professionals and representatives from Spanish-language publishing houses, distributors, and booksellers from all over the world. The fair is held annually for a week during the last weekend in November. Exhibits feature Spanish-language books, although a number of American exhibitors show college texts, children's books, and language-teaching materials. A series of professional seminars complement the activities available to professional visitors.

One of the world's richest literary prizes is awarded during this event: the $100,000 Juan Rulfo Prize for Latin American and Caribbean Literature. ALA organizes a delegation of American librarians to attend the book fair and provides significant financial support.[34]

New York State Department of Education and Minority Education

In November 1987, Thomas Sobol, Commissioner of Education and president of the University of the State of New York, convened a Task Force on Minorities to review the curriculum and instruction guides issued by the New York State Education Department to see whether they adequately reflected the pluralistic nature of U.S. society and to identify areas where changes or additions might be needed. Both the task force members and curriculum consultants found that the materials used included a systematic bias toward European culture and its derivatives, and their report documented how the contributions of non-European cultures had been systematically distorted, marginalized, or omitted.

The task force recommended that new conditions of teacher and school administrator certification in the state of New York should include appropriate competence and thorough knowledge of African American, Asian American, Latino, and Native American contributions to U.S. society, as well as European American contributions to it. The task force further recommended that the New York State Education Department work with all school districts and colleges and universities to develop and implement effective recruitment programs to increase the number of cultures represented in their faculties and staff.[35]

NCLIS Cultural Minorities Task Force

In 1980, NCLIS established a 16-member Task Force on Improving Library and Information Services to Cultural Minorities, also referred to as the NCLIS Cultural Minorities Task Force. E.J. Josey was appointed chair of the task force. The task force held its first meeting in November 1980 and by February 1981 had agreed to the goal to explore the status of library information services, resources, and programs, concentrating on four minority groups—American Indians, Asians, African Americans, and Hispanics. The task force, which was to report back to the commission in June 1982 with recommendations, held two hearings at the 1981 ALA annual conference in San Francisco to receive testimony from librarians and representatives of ethnic and minority groups. Only 22 persons participated directly in the hearings, but others, who were unable to attend either of the hearings, submitted written testimony.

The task force's 1982 report to NCLIS, published in 1983, affirmed the concepts that a multilingual and multicultural society is desirable and that libraries play an important role in the integration of cultural differences within the community. The task force found that funds for services for minorities had come primarily from federal dollars and that, due to severe budgetary cutbacks, many library programs for minorities had been eliminated by library administrators.

The report also included a study of the library and information needs of the Asian American community in the United States, undertaken by APALA members Henry Chang and Suzine Har-Nicolescu. They surveyed 240 public libraries in urban areas likely to have large Asian populations. Their research indicated that too much responsibility for multicultural service in public libraries was placed on minority librarians alone. Providing only ethnic specialists to deal with ethnic minorities was criticized on the grounds that service to minorities should be offered by all members of the staff at all times. Ethnicity in itself was not the only factor for successful librarianship in minority communities. An understanding of the ethnic and racial makeup of communities, language fluency in appropriate situations, and a positive attitude of service were equally important.[36]

Bezugloff Survey of Public Library Multilingual Services

In 1980, over 50 years since the 1926 and 1927 ALA surveys of library services in the United States, Natalia B. Bezugloff, Head of the Foreign

Literature Department of the Cleveland Public Library, surveyed 127 public libraries offering multilingual library services in 50 states. She received only 102 responses, representing an 80-percent return rate. Of these 102 libraries, 72 had foreign-language collections of various sizes in more than 70 foreign languages.

The largest foreign-language collections were located in urban industrial centers. Libraries with collections of more than 20,000 volumes included the Los Angeles Public Library, with 192,982 volumes; the Cleveland Public Library, with 191,536; the Detroit Public Library, with 65,000; the Donnell Library Center of the New York Public Library, with 46,408; the San Francisco Public Library, with 43,057; the Chicago Public Library, with 36,811; the Saint Louis Public Library, with 31,380; the Rochester (NY) Public Library, with 31,100; the Minneapolis Public Library and Information Center, with 28,200; the Seattle Public Library, with 26,529; the Hawaii State Library System, with an estimated 29,273; and the Milwaukee Public Library, with an estimated 22,634.

Of the 45 libraries that reported the age of their collections, 10 were started before 1900, 13 in the early 1900s before World War I, and 22 since World War I. Eight libraries had multilingual departments administered separately from other subject departments, including the Los Angeles Public Library, the San Francisco Public Library, the Atlanta Public Library, the Detroit Public Library, the Brooklyn Public Library; the Cleveland Public Library; the New York Public Library's Donnell Library Center; and the Cumberland County (NC) Public Library System, headquarters of the North Carolina Foreign Language Center, established in 1976.

The great majority of foreign-language collections did not have language specialists to service them. In most cases, professionals with some language skills within the library systems were consulted. On the other hand, proficiency in foreign languages was a prerequisite for the staff in the multilingual departments. The largest linguistically skilled staff was in the New York Public Library's Donnell World Languages Library Center, consisting of five professionals and two nonprofessionals. The Los Angeles Public Library was next with four professionals and 3.75 full-time-equivalent nonprofessionals. Altogether, there were about 30 languages in which library staffs were proficient, with the most widespread language ability being in Spanish.

Forty-five libraries provided reference services to members of ethnic communities. Other services included readers' advisory service; outreach; long- and short-term loans to and from branches; referrals to social and other agencies in the community; online database searching; visits to and materials for ESL and citizenship classes; maintenance of files regarding members in the community who spoke, translated, or taught foreign languages; and provision of language-learning materials. The survey indicated a renaissance of ethnic consciousness as evidenced by a marked increase in interest by second- and third-generation descendants of immigrants in foreign-language and language-learning materials.[37]

Reports of the RAND Corporation and California State Library

The 1988 RAND Corporation report, *Public Libraries Face California's Ethnic and Racial Diversity*, reported on the California State Library's State of Change Conference in May 1988 to consider the implications of California's diversity for all libraries in the state. Stanford University received an LSCA grant of $347,259 from 1986 to 1988 to plan and present the conference. The RAND Corporation, assisted by members of the California State Library Ethnic Services Conference Planning Committee, including its co-chairs, Yolanda J. Cuesta and Roberto G. Trujillo, reported that it could find no systematic empirical evidence of barriers to public-library access to minorities in California.[38]

Reacting negatively toward the RAND Corporation report, the Center for Policy Development of the California State Library found that there were indeed barriers—including cultural and ethnic racial barriers—when library staffs and programs were not sympathetic to groups and individuals who differed from the middle class (Anglo clientele most familiar to them) and when reading itself was a barrier to a significant portion of our adult population who are functionally illiterate. Fiscal barriers prevented free access to libraries. Widespread geographical barriers existed when branches were too far away, bookmobile stops were too infrequent, or the library was inadequate to meet the needs of the community. Inertial barriers perpetuated inadequate services, collections, and disinterested staffs. Efforts at special programming had been flawed and ultimately failed due to underfunding, lack of community involvement, insufficient understanding of the life experience of target clienteles, and a reluctance to structure services to meet collective as well as individual needs.[39]

In a similar vein, the South Bay Cooperative Library System in Northern California used a 1985 LSCA grant to produce a guide, *Promoting Library Awareness in Ethnic Communities*. The California Library Information Project for the Pacific received a fiscal year 1986 LSCA grant of $24,300 for a consultant to study Pacific Rim peoples in California and offer recommendations on service to them. The Stockton-San Joaquin

County Public Library used a fiscal year 1989 LSCA grant of $16,890 to present three symposia on social trends and community analysis to improve development of library collections to meet changing community needs.[40]

Library Education for Minorities

Since the inception of the Library Career Training Program, Title II-B of the Higher Education Act of 1965, the program had made grants that enabled members of underrepresented minorities to pursue graduate degrees in librarianship. In a seven-year study from the years 1985 to 1991 along, 88 doctoral, 17 post-master's, and 223 master's fellowships alone were awarded, and the amount of federal funds awarded was $3,399,300.

In fiscal year 1985, another Title II-B program, the Library Research and Demonstration Program, funded in the amount of just over $200,000 a project titled Leadership Training, Guidance, and Direction for the Improvement of Public Library and Information Services to Native American Tribes. Under the direction of Lotsee Smith (later, Patterson) of the University of Oklahoma, the demonstration project to train and retain persons in the principles and practices of and in the development and improvement of public library and information services to Native Americans.[41]

In 1980, the ALA Office for Library Service to the Disadvantaged (OLSD) became the Office for Library Outreach Service (OLOS). Its purview included promotion of services to all minority groups, the economically disadvantaged, and the illiterate. In 1984, ALA president-elect E.J. Josey appointed a special ALA President's Committee on Library Services to Minorities, co-chaired by Elizabeth Martinez Smith and Binnie Tate Wilkin during fiscal year 1985, and Marva DeLoach and Albert Milo during fiscal year 1986. At the 1986 ALA midwinter meeting, there was an open hearing of the ALA Office for Library Personnel Resources (OLPR) Advisory Committee on Minority Recruitment.

At the ALA annual conference in New York in June 1986, the committee presented its report, *Equity at Issue: Library Services to the Nation's Four Major Minority Groups, 1985–86,* which was accepted by ALA Council and the ALA Executive Board. The report provided a historical and problem-oriented analysis of the status of library services to minorities in all types of libraries. It included 22 recommendations for action by ALA and its constituent and affiliated units and groups, and it urged adoption of the eight recommendations not previously accepted by NCLIS in their

1982 *Report of the Task Force on Library and Information Services to Cultural Minorities.*

The eight recommendations that NCLIS did not intend to implement related to research on library personnel, publication of minority materials free of stereotyping, state financing for minority programs in libraries, and fees as barriers to service, especially in minority communities. Although the NCLIS task force had urged publishers and producers to work toward the elimination of the negative stereotypical images of cultural minorities that had appeared in print and nonprint materials, the NCLIS commissioners voted not to accept this recommendation on the grounds that such action would imply support of censorship.

A 1986 survey by the Library Education Task Force of the ALA Ethnic Materials Information Exchange Round Table indicated that ethnicity was treated at core course levels in elective courses such as advanced reference, government documents, and services to children, young adults, or adults. Thirty-five percent of the schools surveyed answered that ethnicity was not included in those courses designed specifically to prepare specialists to work with various ethnic groups. These were usually taught on a once-a-year schedule or every two years. Courses in this category included library services to special population groups, services to ethnic minorities, multicultural librarianship, and information resources in languages other than English. Of the respondents, 64 percent responded that such courses were not included in their curriculum.[42]

At the 1987 ALA midwinter conference, the ALA Council's Committee on Minority Concerns issued a preliminary report to the ALA Council in response to the *Equity at Issue* report. The committee recommended that all ALA divisions and units be urged to cooperate on specific goals within their charges and with the major priorities of ALA as they related to minorities. It further recommended that relationships with legislative groups, professional organizations in all levels of education, and other library associations be strengthened or established toward the attainment of these goals. The ALA Executive Board and the ALA Council reviewed the report and approved the implementation priorities recommended.

Also at the 1987 ALA midwinter conference, the OLPR advisory committee held another hearing on recruitment to discuss strategies for recruitment and funding sources. At the 1987 ALA annual conference in San Francisco, OLPR presented a program to initiate its expanded focus on recruitment, with speakers from the California Library School Recruitment Project, the REFORMA/UCLA Mentor Project, and the Recruitment Committee of the Association of Library and Information Science Education (ALISE).[43]

At the 1988 ALA midwinter conference, William E. Moen and Kathleen Heim (later, de la Pena McCook) presented a report on minority recruitment based on Moen's survey, Library and Information Science Student Attitudes, Demographics and Aspirations (LISSADA) conducted in the spring of 1988. The survey, based on almost 3,500 returned questionnaires representing 54 ALA-accredited graduate library schools, was conducted under the auspices of the OLPR in preparation for its Preconference on Recruitment scheduled for the ALA annual conference in New Orleans in July 1988. Moen and Heim reported the ethnic breakdown of library school students to be 93.7 percent white, 3.7 black, 1.1 percent Asian/Pacific Islander, 0.8 percent Hispanic, and 0.6 American Indian/Alaskan Native.

In 1990, Sybil E. Moses wrote a report of ALA activities addressing ethnic and cultural diversity. She included over 40 preconference and conference programs, as well as projects and publications during the years 1986 through 1989. She included the ALA Minority Concerns Policy, which focused on the needs of African Americans, Hispanic Americans, Asian Americans, and American Indians.[44]

Survey of Library Adult Education Services

Proposals for a study of adult services in public libraries to update Helen Lyman Smith's *Adult Education Activities in Public Libraries* of 1954 were discussed at the midwinter and annual conference sessions of the Reference at the ALA annual conferences and Adult Services Division's Services to Adults Committee in 1984 and 1985. In December 1984, a questionnaire based on Smith's 1952–53 survey was sent with a detailed instruction booklet to a group of interested individuals selected from the *ALA Handbook of Organization* and attendance sheets from the Adult Services in the Eighties (ASE) open assemblies at the 1984 ALA midwinter meeting. The fourth and final version of the questionnaire was distributed to 1,758 library systems, representing more than 8,000 single-unit libraries, central libraries, and branches. Responses were received from 4,215 individual libraries representing 1,114 systems.

The results of the ASE questionnaire indicated that the majority of programming for Native Americans, Asians, and Hispanics took place in California (Native American, 52; Asian, 9; Hispanic, 52). States reporting 10 or more libraries offering programming to blacks included California, with 23; Florida, Illinois, North Carolina, New York, and Ohio, with 13 each; and Georgia, with 10. Two hundred ninety-one library programs were designed for minorities and initiated in 1985.

Of these, 110 focused on black history, culture, and issues. Hispanic culture, especially food and music, was the subject of 28, while 24 programs centered on Asian concerns and 6 on Native American culture. There were 72 programs offering instruction in ESL, usually cosponsored by local boards of education and colleges or funded through LSCA grants. Many of these ESL programs were designed for specific minorities, especially Hispanics and Asians.

Public libraries had organized 18 programs based on general ethnic concerns, including multicultural understanding, business operations, tax help, genealogical research, and political issues. Those states that offered 10 or more programs either for specific minorities or based on minority concerns included California, with 66; New York and Illinois, with 27 each; Texas, with 26; and Massachusetts, with 11. Only 504 libraries out of the 4,215 responding institutions reported programming aimed at the activation of minority clienteles.[45]

The 1990s were an era of globalization prompting a reexamination of immigration laws. Federal aid for libraries moved from funding for library services and construction of library facilities to funding for library services and technology.

NOTES

1. U.S. Census Bureau, "No. 10: Resident Population—Selected Characteristics, 1950 to 2000, and Projections, 2025 and 2050," in *Statistical Abstract of the United States: 2001*, 121st ed. (Washington, DC: U.S. G.P.O., 2001), 13; Marcia J. Nauratil, *Public Libraries and Nontraditional Clienteles: The Politics of Special Services* (Westport, CT: Greenwood Press, 1985), 102–3.

2. U.S. Immigration and Naturalization Service, "Appendix 1: Immigration and Naturalization Legislation," *Statistical Yearbook of the Immigration and Naturalization Service, 1997,* (Washington, DC: U.S. G.P.O., 1999), A.1–18; David Nelson Alloway, "Refugee Act of 1980," in *Dictionary of American Immigration History,* ed. Francesco Cordasco (Metuchen, NJ: Scarecrow Press, 1990), 609–10; David W. Haines, "Refugees," in *Dictionary of American Immigration History,* 615–16; Michael LeMay and Elliott Robert Barkan, eds., *U.S. Immigration and Naturalization Laws and Issues: A Documentary History* (Westport, CT: Greenwood Press, 1999), 272–75; Maldwyn Allen Jones, *American Immigration,* 2nd ed. (Chicago: University of Chicago Press, 1992), 279; David M. Reimers, "Recent Immigration Policy: An Analysis," in *The Gateway: U.S. Immigration Issues and Policies,* ed. Barry R. Chiswick (Washington, DC: American Enterprise Institute for Public Policy Research, 1982), 13–53; E. Willard Miller and Ruby M. Miller,

United States Immigration: A Reference Handbook (Santa Barbara, CA: ABC-CLIO, 1996), 114–17.

3. Francesco Cordasco, "U.S. Congress, U.S. Immigration Policy and the National Interest," in *Dictionary of American Immigration History*, 723–24; LeMay and Barkan, *U.S. Immigration and Naturalization Laws and Issues*, 275–79; M.A. Jones, *American Immigration*, 287; Guy E. Poitras, "Issues in Immigration Policy for the 1980s," in *Latin American Economic Issues: Information Needs and Sources: Papers of the Twenty-Sixth Seminar on the Acquisition of Latin American Library Materials, Tulane University, New Orleans, Louisiana, April 1–4, 1981* ([Madison]: SALALM Secretariat, University of Wisconsin–Madison; [Los Angeles]: UCLA Latin American Center Publications, University of California, Los Angeles, 1984), 22–28; Otis L. Graham Jr., *Unguarded Gates: A History of America's Immigration Crisis* (Lanham, MD: Rowman & Littlefield Publishers, 2004), 107.

4. Felix Masud-Piloto, "Central Americans," in *Dictionary of American Immigration History*, 121; M.A. Jones, *American Immigration*, 279–80.

5. M.A. Jones, *American Immigration*, 287; Miller and Miller, *United States Immigration: A Reference Handbook*, 118–19.

6. M.A. Jones, *American Immigration*, 269–70.

7. U.S. Immigration and Naturalization Service, "Appendix 1: Immigration and Naturalization Legislation," A.1–19; Francesco Cordasco, "Immigration Reform and Control Act of 1986," in *Dictionary of American Immigration History*, 391–96; LeMay and Barkan, *U.S. Immigration and Naturalization Laws and Issues*, 282–88; M.A. Jones, *American Immigration*, 288–89; Mary Elizabeth Brown "Alan K. Simpson (1931-): There Can Be No Perfect Immigrant Reform Bill," in *Shapers of the Great Debate on Immigration: A Biographical Dictionary* (Westport, CT: Greenwood Press, 1999), 247–260; Miller and Miller, *United States Immigration: A Reference Handbook*, 98–102; Thomas J. Archdeacon, "Immigration Law," in *Oxford Companion to United States History*, ed. Paul S. Boyer and Melvyn Dubofsky (New York: Oxford University Press, 2001), 365.

8. M.A. Jones, *American Immigration*, 289–90; Mary Elizabeth Brown, "Edward M. Kennedy (1932-): Immigration as a Solution to Other Problems," in *Shapers of the Great Debate on Immigration*, 219–32; Miller and Miller, *United States Immigration: A Reference Handbook*, 102–3.

9. M.A. Jones, *American Immigration*, 283–87; Miller and Miller, *United States Immigration: A Reference Handbook*, 102–3.

10. Ardela Artola Allen, "Library Services for Hispanic Young Adults," *Library Trends* 37 (Summer 1988): 80–94; Andrew T. Kopan, "Multicultural Education," in *Dictionary of American Immigration History*, 543; Harlow G. Unger, ed., "Bilingual/Bicultural Education," in *Encyclopedia of American Education,* 2nd ed. (New York: Facts on File, c2001, 1996), 137–38; Harlow G. Unger, ed., "Bilingual Instruction," in *Encyclopedia of American Education*, 138–39; Harlow G. Unger, ed., "English as a Second Language (ESL)," in *Encyclopedia of American Education*, 389–90; Salva-

dor Guerena, "The English-Only Movement: A Selected Bibliography," in *Latino Librarianship: A Handbook for Professionals*, ed. Salvador Guerena (Jefferson, NC: McFarland, 1990), 135–44; Marlene S. Kamm, and Tracey Heskett, " 'So Juan Can't Speak English': The Library's Role in a Multicultural and Multilingual Society," *Illinois Libraries* 62 (Dec. 1980): 886–90; Harriet Quimby and Margaret Dennehy, "Creative Connection: School Library Resources for the E.S.L. Child," *Catholic Library World* 52 (Apr. 1981): 387–91; Alfredo H. Benavides, "Social Responsibility: A Bilingual/Multicultural Perspective," in *Social Responsibility in Librarianship: Essays on Equality*, ed. Donnarae MacCann (Jefferson, NC: McFarland, 1989), 43–52.

11. R. Kathleen Molz, *The Federal Roles in Support of Public Library Services: An Overview*, prepared for the Federal Roles in Support of Public Library Services Project (Chicago: ALA, 1990), 10–20, 25–30; Edward G. Holley and Robert F. Schremser, *The Library Services and Construction Act: An Historical Overview from the Viewpoint of Major Participants* (Greenwich, CT: JAI Press, 1983), 93–94, 147–48, 150–55; Ray M. Fry, "U.S. Department of Education Library Programs, 1984," in *Bowker Annual of Library & Book Trade Information 1985*, 30th ed., comp. and ed. Julia Moore (New York: R. R. Bowker, 1985), 273–75; Ray M. Fry, "U.S. Department of Education Library Programs, 1985," in *Bowker Annual of Library & Book Trade Information 1986*, 31st ed. (New York: R. R. Bowker, 1986), 251–53.

12. Nauratil, *Public Library Services to Nontraditional Clienteles*, 117–18.

13. Ibid., 115.

14. Ibid., 114.

15. Cheryl Metoyer-Duran, *Gatekeepers in Ethnolinguistic Communities* (Norwood, NJ: Ablex Publishing, 1993), 22; Rosemary Ruhig DuMont, Lois Buttlar, and William Caynon, *Multiculturalism in Libraries* (Westport, CT: Greenwood Press, 1994), 171–75; Camila Alire and Orlando Archibeque, *Service to Latino Communities: A How-To-Do-It Manual for Librarians* (New York: Neal-Schuman Publishers, 1998), 170–1, 173; Stephanie Asch, "Urban Libraries Confront Linguistic Minorities: Programs That Work," in *Literacy, Access, and Libraries Among the Language Minority Population*, ed. Rebecca Constantino (Lanham, MD: Scarecrow Press, 1998), 74–86; Luis Herrera and Albert J. Milo, "Managing Administrative Change for Ethnic Collection Development," in *Developing Library Collections for California's Emerging Majority: A Manual of Resources for Ethnic Collection Development*, produced in conjunction with the conference Developing Library Collections for California's Emerging Majority, September 22–23, 1990, San Francisco, California, ed. Katharine T.A. Scarborough (Berkeley: Bay Area Library and Information System; University Extension, University of California; School of Library and Information Studies, University of California, 1990), 14–21; Susan Luevano-Molina, "Ethnographic Perspectives on Trans-National Mexican Immigrant Library Users," in *Library Services to Latinos: An Anthology*, ed. Salvador Guerena (Jefferson, NC: McFarland, 2000), 169–80; Susan Luevano-Molina, "Mexican/Latino Immigrants and the Santa Ana Public Library: An

Urban Ethnography," in *Library Services to Latinos,* 43–63; Kenneth M. Knox, "Santa Ana Public Library Staff Perceptions of Immigrant Language Usage," in *Library Services to Latinos,* 65–68; JoAnn K. Aguirre, "Passport to Promise: Public Libraries as Intellectual Spaces for Immigrant Students," in *Library Services to Latinos,* 69–88; Xiwen Zhang, "The Anti-Affirmative Action Movement in California: Implications for Public Library Services to Asian Immigrants," in *Library Services to Latinos,* 117–18; Sherry Shiuan Su and Charles William Conaway, "Information and a Forgotten Minority: Elderly Chinese Immigrants," *Library and Information Science Research* 17, no. 1 (1995): 69–86; Xiwen Zhang, "The Practice and Politics of Public Library Services to Asian Immigrants," in *Library Services to Latinos,* 141–50; Keum Chu Halpin, "The Hinomoto Library of Los Angeles," *California Librarian* 33 (Oct. 1972): 216–19.

16. DuMont et al., *Multiculturalism in Libraries,* 171–72; California State Library, *Catalog of Local Assistance: Library Services and Construction Act, Titles I, II, III, 1976–1989* (Sacramento: California State Library, 1988), 56.

17. DuMont et al., *Multiculturalism in Libraries,* 38–39; California State Library, *Catalog of Local Assistance,* 64; Charlene Cain, "Public Library Service to Minorities," in *Adult Services: An Enduring Focus for Public Libraries,* ed. Kathleen M. Heim and Danny P. Wallace (Chicago: ALA, 1990), 229–30.

18. California State Library, *Catalog of Local Assistance,* 35.

19. State Library of New South Wales, "Multicultural Library Services in New South Wales Public Libraries 2001, Part 8: International Case Studies," www.sl.nsw.gov.au/multicultural/services/case5.cfm, 8.2 "Chicago Public Library (CPL)—Collections and Outreach in Partnership with the Community."

20. Louise Yarian Zwick and Oralia Garza de Cortes, "Library Programs for Hispanic Children," *Texas Libraries* 50 (Spring 1989): 12–16.

21. Nauratil, *Public Library Services to Nontraditional Clienteles,* 116–17.

22. Renee Tjoumas, "Giving New Americans A Green Light in Life: A Paradigm for Serving Immigrant Communities," *Public Libraries* 26 (Fall 1987): 103–8; Renee Tjoumas, "Opening Doorways to New Immigrants: Queens Borough Public Library's Coping Skills Component," *Public Library Quarterly* 14, no. 4 (1995): 5–19; DuMont et al., *Multiculturalism in Libraries,* 105; Alire and Archibeque, *Service to Latino Communities,* 171; Beilke and Sciara, *Selecting Materials for and about Hispanic and East Asian Children and Young People,* 10.

23. Dollahite Benson, "Welcome to America From the Library," *Public Libraries* 22 (Summer 1983): 54–56.

24. California State Library, *Catalog of Local Assistance,* 30.

25. Tamiye Fujibayashi Trejo and Mary Kaye, "The Library as a Port of Entry: Library Professionals Get Professional Advice on Helping New Citizens Discover U.S.-Style Service," *American Libraries* 19 (Nov. 1988): 890–92.

26. State Library of New South Wales, "Multicultural Library Services in New South Wales Public Libraries 2001, Part 8: International Case Studies," available

at: www.sl.nsw.gov.au/multicultural/services/case5.cfm, 8.2.4 "Minnesota: Minneapolis Public Library—Franklin Learning Center (FLC)."

27. Kathleen de la Pena McCook, *A Place at the Table: Participating in Community Building* (Chicago: ALA, 2000), 56–59; Debra D. Ratliff, "The Refugees in Our Midst," *Colorado Libraries* 16 (Sept. 1990): 18–19.

28. Mary Ellen Quinn, "Hispanic Collections in the Public Library: The Chicago Public Library Experience," in *Multicultural Acquisitions,* ed. Karen Parrish and Bill Katz (New York: Haworth Press, 1993), 223; State Library of New South Wales, "Multicultural Library Services in New South Wales Public Libraries 2001, Part 8"; California State Library, *Catalog of Local Assistance,* 29.

29. State Library of New South Wales, "Multicultural Library Services in New South Wales Public Libraries 2001, Part 8." available at: www.sl.nsw.gov.au/multicultural/services/case5.cfm, 8.3.1 "Salinas Public Library—Cesar Chavez Library."

30. California State Library, *Catalog of Local Assistance,* 52.

31. Salvador Guerena and Edward Erazo, "Latinos and Librarianship," *Library Trends* 49 (Summer 2000): 162, 167–68; Albert J. Milo, "Reference Service to the Spanish-Speaking," in *Latino Librarianship,* 24–34, 33.

32. J.B. Petty, "Reflections on the Role of EMIERT in the Past and in the Future: A Message from the Chair," *EMIE (Ethnic and Multicultural Information Exchange Round Table) Bulletin* 17 (Spring 2001): 1, 3, 13.

33. Suzine Har-Nicolescu, "Asian/Pacific American Librarians Association," in *ALA Yearbook of Library and Information Services, 1987* (Chicago: ALA, 1987), 60; Victor Okim, "Asian/Pacific American Librarians Association," in *ALA Yearbook of Library and Information Services, 1986,* 61–62; Conchita J. Pineda, "Asian/Pacific American Librarians Association," in *ALA Yearbook of Library and Information Services, 1989,* 48–49; Betty L. Tsai, "Asian Pacific American Librarians Association," in *ALA Yearbook of Library and Information Services, 1988,* 51–52; Kenneth A. Yamashita, "Asian/Pacific American Librarians Association—A History of APALA and Its Founders," *Library Trends* 49 (Summer 2000): 88–109; Bernard Kreissman, "Asian/Pacific American Librarians: An American Perspective," in *Asian/Pacific American Librarians: A Cross Cultural Perspective,* Papers of the 1984 Program of the Asian/Pacific American Librarians Association, June 25, 1984, Dallas, Texas, ed. Lourdes Y. Collantes (New York: Asian/Pacific American Librarians Association, 1985), 3–5, 13–22, 26–30; Minja P. Lee, "An Assessment of Asian/Pacific American Librarians' Status and Achievement," in *Asian/Pacific American Librarians,* 13–22; Sucheng Chan, "Asians in California: A Selected Bibliography on Chinese, Japanese, Korean, Filipino, Asian Indian, and Vietnamese Immigrants and Their Descendants," *Immigration History Newsletter* 18 (Nov. 1986): 2–12; Henry C. Chang, "Asian/Pacific American Librarians: A Profile," in *Asian/Pacific American Librarians,* 3–5; Cain, "Public Library Service to Minorities," 229–30; Suzanne Lo and Susan Ma, "Resources for Asian/Southeast Asian Collection Development," in

Developing Library Collections for California's Emerging Majority: A Manual of Resources for Ethnic Collection Development, produced in conjunction with the conference Developing Library Collections for California's Emerging Majority, September 22–23, 1990, San Francisco, California, ed. Katharine T. A. Scarborough (Berkeley: Bay Area Library and Information System; University Extension, University of California; School of Library and Information Studies, University of California, 1990), 172–214; Julie Tao Su, "Library Services in an Asian American Context," in *Diversity and Multiculturalism in Libraries,* ed. Katherine Hoover Hill (Greenwich, CT: JAI Press, 1994), 124.

34. Alire and Archibeque, *Service to Latino Communities,* 244; Quinn, "Hispanic Collections in the Public Library," 230; Milo, "Reference Service to the Spanish-Speaking," 33; Fred Kobrak, "Fairs Around the World: A User's Guide," in *Bowker Annual 1993: Library and Book Trade Almanac,* 38th ed. (New Providence, NJ: R. R. Bowker, 1993), 121; Guadalajara International Book Fair, *FIL: A Cultural Bridge,* http://www.fil.com.mx/ingles/i_que_es/i_que_his.asp.

35. New York State Education Department, Task Force on Minorities, *"A Curriculum of Inclusion": A Report to the Commissioner of Education by the Task Force on Minorities: Equity and Excellence* (Albany: New York State Education Dept., 1989), i–viii, 1–13; New York State Education Department, Social Studies Review and Development Committee, *One Nation, Many Peoples: A Declaration of Cultural Independence: The Report of the New York State Social Studies Review and Development Committee* (Albany: New York State Education Dept., 1991), vi–x, 29–31, 35–36, 45–47; Ruth Ghering Biro, "Multicultural Resources for Libraries," *Catholic Library World* 51 (Mar. 1980): 331–35; Mary Lou White, "Ethnic Literature for Children: A View from the Heartland," *Catholic Library World* 51 (March 1980): 326–29; Marcia A. Wratcher, "Integrating Ethnic Studies into the Curriculum," *Catholic Library World* 51 (Mar. 1980): 336–41; Gillian D. Leonard, "Multiculturalism and Library Services," in *Multicultural Acquisitions,* 7–10; Regina McCormick, "Ethnic Studies Materials for School Libraries: How to Choose and Use Them," *Catholic Library World* 51 (Mar. 1980): 339–41.

36. U.S. National Commission on Libraries and Information Science, Task Force on Library and Information Services to Cultural Minorities, *Report of the Task Force on Library and Information Services to Cultural Minorities* (Washington, DC: NCLIS, 1983), ix–xx, 100–106; "National Commission on Libraries and Information Science Establishes Cultural Minorities Task Force," *School Library Media Quarterly* 9 (Spring 1981): 139–40; "NCLIS Appoints Minority Task Force," *Wilson Library Bulletin* 55 (May 1981): 650; Beilke and Sciara, *Selecting Materials for and about Hispanic and East Asian Children and Young People,* 6–8; Henry Chang and Suzine Har-Nicolescu, "Needs Assessment of Library Information Service for Asian American Community Members in the United States," in National Commission on Libraries and Information Science, Task Force on Library and Information Services to Cultural Minorities, *Report of the Task Force on Library and Information Services to Cultural Minorities,* 79–87; Chang,

"Asian/Pacific American Librarians: A Profile," 3–5; David B. Carlson, Arabella Martinez, Sarah A. Curtis, Janet Coles, and Nicholas A. Valenzuela, *Adrift in a Sea of Change: California's Public Libraries Struggle to Meet the Information Needs of Multicultural Communities* (Sacramento: California State Library, Center for Policy Development, 1990), 76–77; DuMont et al., *Multiculturalism in Libraries*, 107; Cain, "Public Library Service to Minorities," 228, 230, 232–33; Stern, "Ethnic Libraries and Librarianship in the United States: Models and Prospects," in *Advances in Librarianship*, vol. 15: 92–95; "National Commission on Libraries and Information Science Establishes Cultural Minorities Task Force," 139–40; "NCLIS Appoints Minority Task Force," *Wilson Library Bulletin* 55 (May 1981): 650; Nauratil, *Public Libraries and Nontraditional Clienteles*, 117–18; Allen, "Library Services for Hispanic Young Adults," 88–94.

37. Natalia B. Bezugloff, "Library Services to Non-English-Language Ethnic Minorities in the United States," *Library Trends* 29 (Fall 1980): 259–74; Patrick M. Valentine, "The North Carolina Foreign Language Center: A Public Library Service," *Public Library Quarterly* 5 (Winter 1984): 47–61.

38. Judith Payne, Martha Samulon, Peter Morrison, Carole Oken, Rick Eden, and Larry Picus, *Public Libraries Face California's Ethnic and Racial Diversity*, prepared for the Stanford University Libraries with a grant from the California State Library (Santa Monica, CA: RAND Corporation, 1988), iii, v–xviii, 1–4, 10–47, 79; Stern, "Ethnic Libraries and Librarianship in the United States: Models and Prospects," 98–99; Metoyer-Duran, *Gatekeepers in Ethnolinguistic Communities*, 21–23; DuMont et al., *Multiculturalism in Libraries*, 102, 161–63; Eugene Estrada, "Changing Latino Demographics and American Libraries," in *Latino Librarianship*, 12–13; Milo, "Reference Service to the Spanish-Speaking," 27–28.

39. Carlson et al., *Adrift in a Sea of Change*, 108–11; John T. Eastlick and Theodore A. Schmidt, "The Impact of Serving the Unserved on Public Library Budgets," *Library Trends* 23 (Apr. 1975): 603–15; Ruhig DuMont et al., *Multiculturalism in Libraries*, 103.

40. Grace F. Liu, *Promoting Library Awareness in Ethnic Communities: Based on the Experiences of the South Bay Cooperative Library System, 1984–1985* (Sacramento: Underserved Community Library Awareness Project, California State Library, 1985), 1–11, 72–82; Stern, "Ethnic Libraries and Librarianship in the United States," 96–99; Rebecca Constantino, " 'It's Like a Lot of Things in America': Linguistic Minority Parents' Use of Libraries," *School Library Media Quarterly* 22 (Winter 1994): 87–89; Su and Conaway, "Information and a Forgotten Minority," 69–86.

41. Guerena and Erazo, "Latinos and Librarianship," 163–64; Fry, "U.S. Department of Education Library Programs, 1985," 253–59.

42. ALA, Ethnic and Multicultural Information Exchange Round Table, Library Education Task Force, "Ethnic and Minority Concerns in Library Education," *EMIE Bulletin* 6 (Summer 1989): 6–10; Ismail Abdullahi, "Library Services to Multicultural Populations," in *Encyclopedia of Library and Information Science*, vol. 48

(New York: Marcel Dekker, 1976), 266–67; Clara Chu, "Education for Multicultural Librarianship," in *Multiculturalism in Libraries*, 141, 144–45.

43. Cain, "Public Library Service to Minorities," 235–37; Van Fleet, "Lifelong Learning Theory and the Provision of Adult Services," 169; Connie Van Fleet and Douglas Raber, "The Public Library as a Social/Cultural Institution: Alternative Perspectives and Changing Contexts," in *Adult Services*, 467–69.

44. *Equity at Issue: Library Services to the Nation's Four Major Minority Groups, 1985–86: Report of the President's Committee on Library Services to Minorities* (Chicago: ALA, 1986); Stern, "Ethnic Libraries and Librarianship in the United States: Models and Prospects," 78; Ann Knight Randall, "Library Service to Minorities," in *Bowker Annual of Library & Book Trade Information*, 32nd ed. (New York: R. R. Bowker, 1987), 86–93; Cain, "Public Library Service to Minorities," 233–34; Van Fleet and Raber, "The Public Library as a Social/Cultural Institution: Alternative Perspectives and Changing Contexts," 490–93; DuMont et al., *Multiculturalism in Libraries*, 31–32; Xiwen Zhang, "The Anti-Affirmative Action Movement in California," 118.

45. William E. Moen and Kathleen M. Heim, eds., *Librarians for the New Millennium* (Chicago: ALA, Office for Library Personnel Resources, 1988); William E. Moen, "Library and Information Science Student Attitudes, Demographics and Aspirations Survey: Who We Are and Why We Are Here," in *Librarians for the New Millennium*, 94–109; Ann Knight Randall, "Minority Recruitment in Librarianship," in *Librarians for the New Millennium*, 11–25; Leonard, "Multiculturalism and Library Services," in *Multicultural Acquisitions*, 3–4; DuMont et al., *Multiculturalism in Libraries*, 118; Chu, "Education for Multicultural Librarianship," 139.

Chapter 6

PUBLIC LIBRARIES AND GLOBALIZATION IN THE 1990s

In 1990, the U.S. population was approximately 239 million, with 77 percent white, 11 percent black, 0.8 percent American Indians, Eskimos, and Aleuts, 2.8 percent Asians and Pacific Islanders, and 8 percent of Hispanic origin. Throughout the 1990s, the U.S. population in the 1990s would grow by 32.7 million to 281 million, the largest gain in history and the equivalent of adding the entire population of Canada. This record total included approximately 14 million immigrants. If the children of immigrants born to them once in the United States were added to this figure, immigration total would represent approximately 21 million or two-thirds of the growth. In California alone, the growth in the immigration population was 96 percent.[1]

LEGAL AND JUDICIAL DECISIONS AFFECTING MINORITIES

Immigration Act of 1990

The Immigration Act of November 1990 was in part a response to complaints from the majority of immigration states to pass legislation to deal with the illegal immigration issue. The act raised the annual ceiling on immigration, not counting refugees, from 490,000 in 1991 to 700,000 from 1992 to 1994, and then dropped to 675,000 in 1995. The 675,000 level to be enforced in 1995 was to consist of 480,000 family-sponsored,

140,000 employment-based, and 55,000 so-called diversity immigrants from traditional sources of immigration such as Ireland, Italy, and Poland. It transferred the exclusive jurisdiction to naturalize aliens from the federal and state courts to the attorney general.

The 1990 act provided safe haven to Salvadoran refugees and eliminated barriers against the entry of homosexuals, sufferers from AIDS, and Communists. The 1990 law set up a Commission on Legal Immigration Reform and enacted special provisions concerned with Central American refugees and persons seeking to leave Hong Kong.[2]

Soviet Scientists Immigration Act of 1992

The Soviet Scientists Immigration Act of October 1992 conferred permanent resident status as employment-based immigrants on a maximum of 750 scientists, not including spouses and children, from the independent states of the former Soviet Union and the Baltic states. It stipulated that employment must be in the biological, chemical, or nuclear technical field, or work in conjunction with high technology defense projects.

California's Proposition 187

In 1992, California's Proposition 187 to withhold social services from illegal immigrants passed by a resounding vote of 59 percent for and 41 percent against. Most Hispanic voters favored the measure in early polling, though only 31 percent voted for it after a long campaign in which Hispanic political leaders branded it as anti-Hispanic. Proposition 187 was almost immediately tied up in court proceedings.[3]

North American Free-Trade Agreement (NAFTA) of 1993

The NAFTA Implementation Act of December 8, 1993, superseded the United States-Canada Free-Trade Agreement Act of September 28, 1988. It facilitated temporary entry on a reciprocal basis between the United States and Canada and Mexico for professionals to render services for remuneration. For Canadians, there was no limit to number of admissions; for Mexicans, a limit was set for a transition period for up to 10 years at 5,500 initial petition approvals per year.[4]

Violent Crime Control and Law Enforcement Act of 1994

The Violent Crime Control and Law Enforcement Act of September 1994 authorized the establishment of a criminal-alien tracking center. It established a new nonimmigrant classification for aliens providing counterterrorism information. It provided for expeditious deportation for denied asylum applicants and provided for improved border management through increased resources and strengthened penalties for passport and visa offenses. The Antiterrorism and Effective Death Penalty Act of April 1996 expedited procedures for the removal of alien terrorists.[5]

U.S. Commission on Immigration Reform of 1995

In March 1995, President Bill Clinton appointed the U.S. Commission on Immigration Reform. Chaired by African American former congresswoman Barbara Jordan, the commission finished its work in 1997. The commission's report included recommendations to cut overall legal immigration to 550,000 or 40 percent, to shift selection criteria toward skills needed in the United States, and to end chain migration of families by eliminating the preferences for brothers and sisters and adult children of new immigrant citizens.

Illegal immigration was condemned, as well as the idea of a large-scale agricultural guest-worker program. The commission asked for increased border security and pilot programs toward establishing a national computerized registry based on social security data as a basis for an employment verification system for all citizens. No one charged the commission with racism or disputed its findings.

In 1996, U.S. immigration policy admitted 916,000 legal immigrants joined by perhaps 500,000 illegal immigrants, the largest cohort since 1914. The booming American economy of the 1990s was a magnet, drawing ever-larger numbers of unskilled laborers across both southern and northern borders. Many of the skilled foreign computer programmers, doctors, nurses, and university students, who came by air on temporary visas, overstayed to blend in to American society. In many cases, taking advantage of the loophole of marriage to an American granted them status as resident aliens rather than merely visa holders.

Personal Responsibility and Work Opportunity Reconciliation Act of 1996

The Personal Responsibility and Work Opportunity Reconciliation Act of August 1996 barred legal immigrants from obtaining food stamps and Supplemental Security Income (SSI) and barred legal immigrants entering the United States after date of enactment from most federal means-tested programs for five years. It provided states with broad flexibility in setting public-benefit eligibility rules for legal immigrants by allowing states to bar current legal immigrants from both major federal programs and state programs. It barred illegal aliens from most federal, state, and local public benefits, and required the INS to verify immigration status in order for aliens to receive most federal public benefits.[6]

A year later, the Balanced Budget Act of August 1997 and, shortly thereafter, the Agricultural Research Reform Act of February 1998, continued or partially restored eligibility benefits to legal aliens who had been restricted by the Personal Responsibility and Work Opportunity Reconciliation Act of 1996. Such restrictions no longer applied to qualified aliens, including aliens who had become citizens through naturalization, legal permanent residents, refugees, aliens granted asylum or similar relief, aliens paroled into the United States for at least one year, and veterans or active-duty personnel and their close families.[7]

Illegal Immigration Reform and Immigrant Responsibility Act of 1996

The Illegal Immigration Reform and Immigrant Responsibility Act of September 1996 was designed to address a variety of issues related to illegal undocumented aliens, Central American refugees, the requirements for sponsoring immigrants, and the centralization and reform of naturalization procedures. The act provided for the employment of additional Border Patrol and INS agents to investigate and prosecute illegal immigrants.[8]

Nicaraguan Adjustment and Central American Relief Act of 1997

The Nicaraguan Adjustment and Central American Relief Act of November 1997 pertained to Central American and other aliens, who were long-term illegal residents in the United States, when hardship relief rules were made more stringent when the 1996 act was passed. It allowed approximately 150,000 Nicaraguans and 5,000 Cubans adjustment to permanent resident status and approximately 200,000 Salvadorans and 50,000 Guatemalans, as well as aliens from the former Soviet Union, to seek hardship relief.[9]

LSCA Amendments

LSCA regulations required that when the total appropriation for Title I exceeded $60 million, each state had to reserve a percentage of these funds under the MURLs program for urban libraries whose collections and services were used beyond their local jurisdiction. In fiscal year 1999, there were 185 cities, excluding the District of Columbia, with a population of 1,000 or more in the United Sates, plus five cities in the commonwealth of Puerto Rico, for a total of 190 cities that were eligible for MURL funds.

In fiscal year 1967, Congress had first appropriated $375,000 for LSCA Title II for planning purposes. From that time through fiscal year 1992, a total of over $238 million was appropriated to encourage state library administrative agencies to plan for, establish, operate, and expand programs involving all types of libraries. In fiscal year 1990, the appropriation for Title III was just over $19 million.

In fiscal year 1991, Congress appropriated $976,000 for a new Title V of the LSCA, known as the Foreign Language Materials Acquisition Program. Ironically, Title V had been established in 1984 but was not funded until fiscal year 1991. By September 1992, 29 grants totaling $976,000 were awarded to public libraries in 11 states. Funds were used to enhance library services to emerging ethnic groups, to respond to the diverse needs of the community by obtaining materials in a variety of formats, and to introduce new languages, services, and materials to library branches and collections. Before the availability of Title V, libraries sought LSCA Title I grants to develop foreign-language collections, to hire staff to direct programs, and to retrofit collections and train staff to meet the needs of targeted user groups. Title V was funded for three fiscal years, from 1991 to 1993, but no funds were appropriated in fiscal year 1994.

LSCA Title VI was the Library Literacy Program to support adult literacy programs in state and local public libraries. The program received an appropriation of over $8 million in fiscal year 1992. By September 1992, 256 grants totaling over $8 million were awarded to 246 local public libraries and 10 state libraries. Individual grants ranged from approximately $5,000 to the maximum amount of $35,000.[10]

LIBRARY SERVICES WITH MINORITIES

1991 WHCLIS

The second WHCLIS was authorized by President Reagan in August 1988 but was not held until July 9–13, 1991, in Washington, D.C. At the time when the conference was convened, there were more than 115,000 libraries in the United States: 8,865 public libraries with 6,350 branches; 92,539 school library media centers; 3,398 academic libraries; and 10,263 special libraries, serving corporate, hospital, medical, and governmental organizations.

In preparation for the 1991 WHCLIS, there had been preconference forums in all 50 states, the District of Columbia, and 7 U.S. territories. Over 100,000 Americans, including representatives of Native American tribes and the federal library and networking community, participated in these forums, and thousands of ideas and resolutions were approved and submitted to the state preconference planners.

There were 984 delegates and alternatives, as well as 1,000 nonvoting honorary delegates, 64 at-large delegates, and 300 volunteers, including library and information professionals, government officials, and trustees and friends of libraries. After considerable debate, the 2,500 recommendations generated at the preconferences were reduced to 95 recommendations that were endorsed and subsequently published in 1992 by the NCLIS as *Information 2000: Library and Information Services for the 21st Century.*

Delegates hoped that the 95 recommendations would serve to inform and educate national policy makers on the needs of U.S. citizens for library and information services. They called for strengthening and expanding existing LSCA, HEA, and ESEA legislation, and supported yet-to-be-drafted legislation to develop a National Information Infrastructure (NII), one of the goals of the Clinton administration. Delegates were concerned about strengthening library collections and framing library access policies to accommodate diverse user needs, while ensuring no-fee and improved access to information to multicultural and multilingual populations.

In the area of expanding networks and access to information, there was a recommendation to focus on the needs of Native Americans. Delegates made resolutions affirming the need for educating and hiring ethnic and minority librarians for traditional library services, as well as special outreach programs, and calling for the establishment of a national coalition for information literacy.[11]

California State Library's Center for Policy Development Study

In 1900, the Center for Policy Development of the California State Library published a study, *Adrift in a Sea of Change,* which documented the condition of California's public libraries. The study noted that budgets for non-English and other materials directed to serve information needs of minorities were typically a small portion of total library budgets, despite the relative portions of minorities within the community.

One of the crucial issues at the core of the study was whether special efforts, like Ethnic Resource Centers that had been established throughout California using LSCA and other federal funds, were effective in meeting the needs of minorities or whether they actually hindered needed efforts to improve services to minorities. The study involved field visits to 15 public libraries, including some of the largest in the state, all with heavy concentrations of minority populations, and a mail survey to more than 150 libraries that were not visited and all 15 cooperative library systems.

The study showed that three-quarters of the 15 libraries visited, plus most of those responding to the survey, had no current data regarding the use of the library by minorities. Budgets for non-English and other materials directed to serve perceived minority information needs had been typically a small portion of total library budgets, despite the relative proportions of minorities within the community. While libraries have relied principally upon flyers and printed materials for outreach, they have not believed these are effective as word of mouth, community newspapers, or non-English-language radio.[12]

In 1990, the BALIS, and University Extension and the School of Library and Information Studies of the University of California, Berkeley, developed a manual titled *Developing Library Collections for California's Emerging Majority: A Manual of Resources for Ethnic Collection Development* to address the library needs of California's emerging majority populations, including African American, American Indian, Asian and Pacific American, and Latino. The manual was made available at a conference on the same theme presented by the Public Library Association conference in San Diego in March 1991.[13]

Padilla Study

Amado M. Padilla's 1991 study *Public Library Services for Immigrant Populations in California* surveyed librarians serving immigrant communities to determine if they could do a better job if they had a bilingual staff member with knowledge and interest in servicing immigrants. One finding was that immigrants and foreign students alike had little familiarity with libraries in their countries of origin, and their perceptions of libraries differed from how libraries were perceived in the United States.

The study demonstrated that libraries need to go beyond the traditional services and seek ways to network and collaborate with other community organizations and agencies working with immigrants. Immigrants expressed disappointment in visiting libraries advertising a non-English collection if they then discovered that the books were very dated and on a random assortment of topics. It was pointed out that delicate balance exists between now much constitutes a special collection and what should be collected. These two issues were best resolved through a joint collaboration of library professionals in charge of acquisitions and consultation from immigrant populations. California libraries visited were the San Jose Public Library, the Mission Branch Library in San Francisco, the East Palo Alto Library Branch of San Mateo County, and the Fremont Public Library of Alameda County.[14]

ALA Organizations for Minorities

In 1990, the ALA International Relations Committee created a new Subcommittee on U.S.-Mexico libraries to coordinate efforts by individuals and groups in the United States, who were already working with Mexican colleagues, as well as to provide an opportunity for new projects and interactions. In the summer of 1994, the subcommittee was incorporated into a new Subcommittee on Relations with Libraries in Latin America and the Caribbean. In 1995, the subcommittee announced its intent to work with SALALM's Outreach/Enlace program to cosponsor an internship project involving Latin American and Caribbean librarians.[15]

The Public Library Association conference in San Diego in March 1991 included a program on United States-Mexico library cooperation sponsored by the Subcommittee on U.S.-Mexico Libraries of the ALA International Relations Committee. The Committee on Library Services to the Spanish Speaking of the Reference and Adult Services Division presented a program on Developing Collections for the Spanish Speaking at the 1994 ALA annual conference in Miami Beach. The Texas Library Association's (TLA) Exchange Program a small but successful program of U.S.-Mexico library exchanges, was initiated in 1994 by the Texas-Mexico Relations Subcommittee of the TLA College and University Library Division.

In 1992, the ALA Ethnic and Multicultural Information Exchange Round Table (EMIERT) published the first edition of *Ventures into Cultures.* That same year, the ALISE, at its annual conference held in San Antonio, studied the issue of whether cultural diversity should be infused throughout the curriculum or addressed in specialized courses. Although approaches differed, it was agreed that to develop new courses as the only strategy to accommodate cultural diversity would mean that existing courses would not require multicultural perspectives. Multiculturalism does not introduce new topics but new approaches to teaching old topics. The Ethnic, Multicultural, and Humanistic Concerns Special Interest Group (SIG) established at the 1991 ALISE annual conference held its first workshop at the 1992 annual conference. Discussions continued at the 1993 annual conference workshop on Enhancing Diversity in Library Schools.[16]

U.S.-Mexico Cooperative Library Education Programs

A program was offered in the early 1990s by the School of Library and Information Science of the University of Wisconsin, Milwaukee, for the head librarians of the 26 campuses of the Instituto Tecnologica y de Estudios Superiores de Monterrey (TESM), the largest private university system in Mexico. Collaboration between the University of North Texas School of Library and Information Sciences and the Escuela Nacional de Biblioteconomia y Archivonomia (National School of Library and Archival Science) (ENBA) took place in 1994.

The University of Arizona offers a Master of Arts degree with an emphasis in library science through its distance education program. Beginning in the summer of 1995, the School of Information Resources and Library Science (SIRLS) initiated a partnership with the Universidad de las Americas in Pueblo to offer the program's courses to librarians in Mexico and throughout Latin America.[17]

Center for the Study of Books in Spanish for Children and Adolescents

The Center for the Study of Books in Spanish for Children and Adolescents, a resource center of books in Spanish and in English about Latinos for children and young adults, is located at California State University, San Marcos. Director Isabel Schon is a leading authority on the subject, with many books, articles, and book reviews to her credit, including many reviews in ALA's *Booklist* of Spanish-language books for young adults and children.[18]

Trejo Foster Foundation

The Trejo Foster Foundation for Hispanic Library Education was established by Arnulfo Trejo, the first president of REFORMA, and named for himself and his late wife Annette M. Foster Trejo. The foundation serves as a think tank for issues concerning library and information services for persons of Hispanic heritage in the United States and provides support to finance research as well as seminars, workshops, and other activities that will promote and enhance library education for Hispanics. The Trejo Foster Foundation became the clearinghouse for REFORMITA, a student club organized to empower children, especially of low-income Hispanic families, with reading and library skills to give them self-confidence, appreciation for academic achievement, and respect for family values.

The foundation has sponsored four institutes since 1993, each focusing on a topic of interest to Spanish-speaking and Hispanic-culture librarians. The first institute, Status of Hispanic Library and Information Services: A National Institute for Educational Change, was held July 29–31, 1993, at the University of Arizona's School of Information Resources and Library Science. The second, Latino Populations and the Public Library Conference, was held November 12–15, 1995, at the Graduate School of Library and Information Science of the University of Texas, Austin. The third, Hispanic Leadership in Libraries, was held August 8–10, 1997, at the School of Communication, Information and Library Studies at Rutgers University. The fourth, Library Services to Youth of Hispanic Heritage, was held March 12–14, 1999, at the School of Library and Information Science of the University of South Florida, Tampa.[19]

LSCA Projects

Title I funds were used in many states to fund programs for illiterate and limited-English-speaking adults. In fiscal year 1993, each state spent, on the average, 2.8 percent of its LSCA Title I funds on literacy and 1.42 percent for limited-English speakers. Several states exceeded these national-average expenditures. For literacy programs, the District of Columbia at 49 percent led the list, followed by Illinois at 12 percent, Massachusetts at

9 percent, Idaho at 8 percent, and New Jersey and Texas, both at 6 percent. For programs for limited-English speakers, Illinois and North Carolina led the list at 10 percent each, followed by the District of Columbia and Massachusetts at 5 percent, and California and New Jersey at 4 percent each. In fiscal year 1993, the Illinois State Library's Advisory Committee made family literacy a priority. Using approximately $400,000 in LSCA Title I funds, 14 projects were funded.

Illinois LSCA funds were also used to meet the need for materials and programs aimed at those who spoke languages other than English. The Chicago Public Library sponsored a project titled We Speak Your Language that produced a videotape introducing the American public library and provided multimedia materials for the study of English. The video was produced in Spanish, Polish, Korean, and Chinese to present the generic public library as an informational place for all citizens. The Portage-Cragin Branch of the Chicago Public Library established a reference and referral center for Polish-language materials. The North Suburban Library System designed a project called Beyond the Library Card to link ESL teachers and classes with the library.

The West Springfield (MA) Public Library established a program called ESL for Those at Home to teach over 80 non-English speakers, including those who spoke Russian, Polish, Vietnamese, Chinese, and Spanish, to learn English. The Lawrence (MA) Public Library conducted a library ESL/Job Survival Skills literacy program of interactive lessons, combining digitized video and movies with voice-annotated text, to teach listening skills needed for job interviews and employability skills. The ABE office at the Martin Luther King Library in the District of Columbia noted an increase in the number of technical assistance requests from city literacy providers, as well as an increase in the number of requests for the Spanish-speaking and literacy-related videos.

During fiscal year 1992, the Flagstaff City-Coconino County (AZ) Public Library received approximately $35,000 to expand its adult literacy program to provide literacy instruction to 70 Native American adults at the Tuba City Public Library, located on a Navajo reservation where only 34 percent of the adults were high school graduates. The Broward County (FL) Library received over $32,000 to hire a student services coordinator to help the READ campaign be responsive to its 1,000 adult literacy students. The East Providence (RI) Public Library received just over $29,000 to develop collections of literacy materials in four libraries in neighboring towns and to write and produce a practical guide for librarians on establishing and using literacy collections.

The conversion of bibliographic records to machine-readable form has continued to be a significant activity for Title III grants. In fiscal year 1990, the Tougaloo (MS) College received a Title III grant in the amount of approximately $10,000 to add the library's holdings to the computerized Mississippi Union Catalog, providing access to a significant collection of African American history.

During the fiscal year 1992, LSCA Title V grants for the Foreign Language Materials Acquisition program were granted to 29 libraries in 11 states for library materials in Japanese, Chinese, Korean, Vietnamese, Tagalog, Hindi, Spanish, Farsi, and Russian. The size of grants ranged from $35,000 to the Chemeketa Cooperative Regional Library Service in Salem, Oregon, for Spanish materials, to over $100,000 to the Chicago Public Library for materials in Chinese, Korean, and Vietnamese.

The Boston Public Library received an LSCA Title I MURL grant of approximately $25,000 in fiscal year 1990 to respond to patron requests in multisubject and multilingual areas. Foreign titles were acquired in French, Italian, Spanish, German, Finnish, and other languages. The Detroit Public Library received just over $46,000 to support and enhance the resources of the Detroit Associated Libraries (DAL) for cooperative online database searching, career and employment information materials for all branch libraries in the DAL regional area, and Black Americana and ethnic materials for the main library, branch libraries, and bookmobile services. The New York Public Library branch libraries received a fiscal year 1990 MURL grant in excess of $200,000 to add recordings, films, video and audio cassettes, instructional software, ESL materials, microforms, and print materials to specialized subject collections at the Donnell World Languages Center, the Library of the Performing Arts at Lincoln Center, and the Mid-Manhattan Library.[20]

Also in 1991, Adrian Tandler, head of the NAP at the Queens Borough Public Library, received an LSCA grant of $12,772 from the State Library of New York to help develop two new Korean-language collections. The library's Coping Skills Program targeted Spanish, Chinese, and Korean speakers. Bilingual lawyers, teachers, and counselors offered programs to help immigrants adjust to life in the United States, such as starting a new small business, parenting, and dealing with stress.

The Queens Borough Public Library also initiated its World LinQ system comprised of a multilingual Internet Web-based information system that provides access to local and global electronic information resources in English, Spanish, Chinese, Korean, and Russian, with the goal being to cover all major immigrant languages spoken in Queens. The library used a Native Language Technology grant from the New York State Library under the Library Services and Technology Act (LSTA) to initiate training in using the system.[21]

In the early 1990s, the Lexington Branch Library of the Saint Paul (MN) Public Library, under the leadership of librarian Annette Salo, established a cooperative program with Lao Family Community of Minnesota, a mutual assistance organization, to introduce over 800 families to library services. The Friends of the Saint Paul Public Library granted $30,000 for a three-year period to build collections in Asian languages and purchased a mobile unit to serve the more than 76 percent of public-housing community residents who were Southeast Asian.

In July 1991, using funds from the Southeast Asian Access Project of the federal Community Revitalization Program, the Lexington Branch Library hired a Hmong management trainee to assist with the library's translation service and to help facilitate the use of the library among Hmong immigrants. The library established the Book Buddy Project, staffed by volunteers who read to children at a downtown family shelter, to promote reading and literacy among homeless children. The project received a National Achievement citation from the Public Library Association, a division of the ALA, in 1992.[22]

The Rolling Meadows (IL) Library's Biblioteca del Centro (Library of the Center), located in a Chicago suburb in an apartment complex inhabited largely by immigrants, was established in the early 1990s both to serve the needs of the newcomers and to encourage them to visit the main library. Resembling the Model Cities library projects of the 1960s and 1970s, the Biblioteca was part of an apartment complex's Neighborhood Resource Center, containing a free health clinic, computer laboratory and classroom, and a police desk. With an onsite social worker, the center offered various services that New Americans needed, including ESL, citizenship preparation, job-skills training, and computer-literacy training.[23]

Beginning in 1991, the Newark (NJ) Public Library has operated the Multilingual Materials Acquisition Center, commonly referred to as MultiMac, which was funded in part by an LSCA grant from the New Jersey State Library. It has provided a team of expert librarians who offer all New Jersey libraries, not just public libraries, workshops, consultations, and materials to improve multilingual and multicultural services and collections and sensitivity to diverse populations.[24]

In 1992, the Pio Pico-Koreatown Library of the Los Angeles Public Library system used a Partnerships for Change grant of nearly $200,000 from the California State Library to increase its Korean materials collection threefold, launch a major publicity campaign, develop new programs, and hire two more Korean-speaking staff members. According to Jae Min Roh, senior librarian of the Pio Pica Koreatown Branch, because there is not a strong public library tradition in Korea, Korean immigrants need to be educated about U.S. public libraries.

In 1993, Project Colorin-Colorado was started in the Miami-Dade Public Library System to create and perform special programs in small- and medium-sized libraries celebrating Hispanic Heritage Month. Comprised of 14 members of whom only 8 were of Hispanic heritage, the project concentrated on creating new puppet shows adapted from well-known Hispanic tales. Marta Garcia, the children's department manager at the West Dade Regional Library and leader of the group, had worked for several years at the New York Public Library, where she learned the art of storytelling and puppet-making from Pura Belpre.

In April 1994, Spanish-speaking West Kendall Regional Library staff member Nubya Sanchez of the Miami-Dade Public Library System initiated La Hora de Cuentos, a Spanish story-hour program. She developed the program, which Spanish speakers viewed as a way to preserve their language and traditions and non-Spanish speakers viewed as a way for their children to learn Spanish. The program was regularly attended by Colombians, Cubans, Venezuelans, Nicaraguans, Peruvians, and Argentinians.[25]

In June 1994, the Albany Park Branch of the Chicago Public Library opened its Korean Room, the largest circulating Korean-language collection in the Midwest, containing approximately 16,000 books and 15 periodicals, as well as videos, slides, and CD-ROMs. Also in 1994, the Sumner Community Library in Minneapolis initiated library services for the Hmong, who had immigrated to the United States after the Vietnam War. The library hired an outreach consultant who surveyed the community and met with Hmong families. The Hmong wanted to develop fluency in the Hmong language and familiarity with their distinctive way of viewing the world. They needed ESL materials, information about other ethnic groups, and simple English and bilingual materials dealing with their current areas of interest.[26]

In Washington state, the first citizenship class to be held in the Lower Columbia area took place in the Longview Public Library on February 22, 1995, as part of an INS pilot project begun in 1994. Twelve of the twenty immigrants, representing Mexico, Cambodia, Vietnam, China, Indonesia, India, Germany, Canada, and Norway, became new citizens on May 11, 1995, at a special ceremony held prior to the Longview City Council meeting in the Longview Council Chambers. The class, one of 15 programs offered statewide, was designed to decentralize the naturalization process and administer it at the community level. This citizenship program collaborated with Project Read, the library's adult literacy program, and the ABE program at Lower Columbia College, to assist area residents who wanted to attain U.S. citizenship.[27]

Begun in September 1995, the Lea Por Vida (Read for Life) program was jointly administered by the WIC program of a local health clinic and the Las Palmas Branch of the San Antonio Public Library to combine health education with an introduction to library services. Doctors and nurses at a health clinic in a Latino neighborhood gave patients personalized "reading prescriptions"—packets of materials that addressed their specific health concerns—and directed them to gather further information at the library. Included in each packet was a library-card application form in Spanish, which gave program participants access to the enhanced collections of health-related materials that could be checked out at the branch.[28]

In 1996, the San Francisco Public Library opened its International Center, which included materials in approximately 40 languages, including Chinese and Tagalog, and a staff that spoke a wide variety of foreign languages. The San Francisco Community Connection database included information in English about agencies and institutions that provided social services in San Francisco, including ESL and citizenship classes, legal help, housing, and medical assistance.[29]

Also in 1996, the Forsyth County (NC) Public Library and Durham County (NC) Public Library used LSCA grants to develop library services and multimedia collections and to network with other organizations to reach growing Spanish-speaking communities, many of which were migrant agricultural workers. The libraries surveyed the Spanish-speaking migrant communities in their service areas and found that newly arrived migrants needed information about learning English, as well as about health issues and legal matters, as opposed to the popular fiction materials preferred by more settled Latinos. The libraries used public service announcements in Spanish on local radio and television stations, as well as bookmobile services, to promote library use.

During the 2000 fiscal year, the State Library of North Carolina, using LSCA funds, contracted with Rincon & Associates to gather data and conduct a demographic analysis of the Hispanic community in North Carolina. The data was gathered to guide the development and implementation of programs at the state level.[30]

Margaret Steinfurth and Rodrigo Diaz were the only two full-time librarians in the late 1990s at the Ruskin Branch Library of the Tampa-Hillsborough County Public Library System, which served a large population of approximately 26,000 seasonal agricultural workers, mostly from Mexico. Diaz, born and raised in Tampa, where her Cuban grandparents had come to work in the city's cigar industry, is a Spanish speaker with the cultural skills to work with users at housing centers and recreation centers where Spanish-speaking patrons lived. Diaz and Steinfurth attended meetings of the Ruskin Civic Association, Chamber of Commerce, and other community-based organizations to provide information about library services.[31]

The Bensonville Community (IL) Public Library was involved in a multiple partnership program, the Bensonville Intergovernmental Groups' Lifelong Learning Community, which included city departments and the elementary, junior high, and high schools. Each partner established its version of a lifelong learning center. The library's center has focused its efforts on combating illiteracy in the Latino community. The library formed the Family Literacy Council, which has worked on literacy issues with churches, schools, Operation Head Start programs, social services agencies, and various community organizations.[32]

LSTA of 1996

On September 30, 1995, the LSCA, administered by the U.S. Department of Education, expired. During the final fiscal year of 1995, LSCA grants amounted to $17,436,000. At that time, LSCA was replaced by the LSTA.

On September 30, 1996, the Museum and Library Services Act signed into law by President Clinton established a new government agency, the Institute of Museum and Library Services (IMLS). On December 18, 1998, the IMLS was given the authority to disperse $135,366,938 in LSTA grants to library agencies nationwide to support the use of technology to share information resources, and library outreach to the underserved urban and rural populations.

The focus of the LSTA shifted from the construction of libraries to the provision of the infrastructure to enable the use of electronic information and to help communities exploit the most current information technology. Emphasizing electronic networking and targeting the underserved, LSTA grants are available to all types of libraries, not just public libraries as was the case with LSCA. LSTA grants are awarded out of two major program areas, the National Leadership Program funded over $5 million in fiscal year 1998, and the Native American Library Services Program funded just over $2.5 million, with approximately $366,000 of this latter figure reserved for Native Hawaiians. Within the Native American Library Services Program, grants are made directly to Indian tribes as a result of the technical amendments signed by President Bill Clinton on December 1, 1997. There are three types of grants: basic library services grants, technical assistance grants, and enhancement grants.

LSTA state program grants were made to each state or territory according to a population-based formula and administered by each state or territory's library administrative agency, usually the state library, with each state providing at least $1 for every $2 of federal funds. The fiscal year 1999 awards ranged from $14,263,331 to the California State Library to $547,003 to the Vermont Department of Libraries and were matched by $1 at the state level for every $3 of federal funds expended.[33]

LSTA and HEA Title II-B Projects

In late 1997, after the LSCA had been replaced by the LSTA, the State Library of North Carolina and the public library leadership of North Carolina mutually decided not to fund the North Carolina Foreign Language Center, located in the headquarters library of the Cumberland County (NC) Public Library and Information Center, which had served as a model for statewide multilingual library service since its inception in 1976.[34]

During fiscal year 1997, HEA Title II-B (Library Education and Human Resource Development Program) fellowship awards included several to train librarians to work with minorities, each funded at $88,000. Florida State University's Library Training Program for Master's Fellows gave preference to training Asian, Native American, Hispanic, and African American librarians. Wayne State University's Master's Level Fellowships for Library Education program recruited ethnic minorities traditionally underrepresented in the library profession, giving preference to applicants wishing to specialize in school media, children's services, and young adult services, as well as applicants interested in information acquisition and transfer and the management of communication technology. The University of Oklahoma's Education for Minorities in Targeted Areas of Library and Information Science fellowships were used to prepare qualified minority students in three areas of current shortage: cataloging, school media, and science reference. Texas Woman's University's Educating Librarians to Serve Young People fellowships focused on addressing the need for diversity in the profession of librarianship. Queens College of the City University of New York used a $32,000 grant to address the shortage of minority librarians in the areas of school media and children's and young adult library services to serve the New York City area. The University of Wisconsin–Milwaukee's Multicultural Children's and Young Adult Librarianship fellowships focused on training minority librarians to serve children and young adults in racially and ethnically diverse populations.

HEA Title II-B continued to grant funds for librarian institute programs. In fiscal year 1997, the University of Oklahoma's School of Library and Information Studies received an institute grant in the amount of approximately $29,000. The grant was used to sponsor the Summer Institute for Tribal Librarians: Training for Internet-Based Resources. The institute trained 16 tribal library personnel, recruited from reservations and Indian country throughout the nation, to serve the information needs of elderly, illiterate, or disadvantaged Native Americans who lived in rural America, by effectively tapping Internet-based resources.[35]

Bilingual Education

In 1994, a bilingual education study in New York City found that most recent immigrants who took most of their classes in English fared better academically than students in bilingual programs where they could speak their native tongues. New York City offered bilingual education in Spanish, Chinese, Haitian Creole, Russian, Korean, Vietnamese, French, Greek, Arabic, and Bengali, at a cost of more than $400 million a year.

By the beginning of 1998, limited-English-speaking students made up more than 6 percent of the total elementary and secondary school student population in the United States. Most were residents of California, Texas, New York, Florida, and Illinois. In 1995, California passed a law establishing English as the official state language. In 1996, a group of economically deprived Hispanic parents voted to boycott a local elementary school in Los Angeles until authorities agreed to teach their children in English and thus improve their long-term chances of attending college and getting jobs. In June 1998, California voters overwhelmingly approved a measure that banned bilingual education in public schools and replaced it with a year of intensive English instruction or the traditional immersion programs for learning foreign languages.

By 1999, nearly one in five children born in the United States had at least one foreign-born parent. The number of children who spoke a language other than English at home made up 5 percent of all school-age children, as did the number of children who had difficulty speaking English. Two-thirds of all immigrants had arrived from Latin America, and 40 percent found themselves in the lower 20 percent in terms of income and had two years fewer schooling than the average native-born American. California and Arizona have banned bilingual education in state public schools. In its place, these schools have introduced new programs of at least one year of intensive instruction in English to promote assimilation.[36]

Americans with Disabilities and National Literacy Acts

The Americans with Disabilities Act of 1990 prohibited discrimination against persons with disabilities regardless of racial or ethnic background. The National Literacy Act of 1991 established the National Institute for Literacy. An inability to read or write, according to the national Adult Literacy Survey released in the late 1990s, affected between 21 percent and 23 percent of the adult citizens of the United States. Because the Adult Literacy Survey is given in English only, it does not determine whether non-English-Speaking test takers might be literate in their native languages. Commissioned by the U.S. Department of Education and conducted by the Educational Testing Service, the test was administered to 25,000 randomly selected Americans above the age of 15.

Goals 2000: Educate America Act of 1993

In 1993, Congress passed the Goals 2000: Educate America Act to establish nationwide educational goals for the year 2000 and provide federal grants to states and local communities to reform the nation's education system in an effort to achieve those goals. The Goals 2000 program provided for the first national certification, albeit voluntary, of state and local education standards and assessments.[37]

Continued Immigration from the Americas

In 2000, Hispanics became the largest minority in the United States, increasing 61.6 percent over the previous 10 years to a total of 35.3 million or 12.5 percent of all Americans. In 1990, African Americans had been the largest minority, and while their numbers increased 21.5 percent in the 10 years that followed, the new total of just under 34.7 million comprised only 12.1 percent of the American population.

More than 63 percent of Hispanics in the continental United States were of Mexican origin, and just under 11 percent of mainland Hispanics were of Puerto Rican descent. More than half lived in two states—California, where Hispanics, mostly of Mexican origin, made up just over 30 percent of the population and whites constituted a minority, and Texas, where they made up nearly 29 percent, largely of Mexican origin. Also in 2000, Hispanics made up 14 percent of the population of New York, where the majority were of Puerto Rican origin, and about 14 percent of the population of Florida, where the majority were of Cuban origin.

Unlike immigrants of previous generations, only about one-third of the new arrivals in the 1990s, both legal and illegal, applied for citizenship. Estimated at about 10 million and growing, the new alien population resisted assimilation because of the ease with which jet air travel and efficient long-distance telephone service allowed them to maintain ties to families and cultures in their native countries. Unlike immigrants of the past, the new immigrants were able to create subcultures that were unattached to the larger American society.[38]

Library Services with American Indians

From the early 1980s into the 1990s, the Native American Committee of the NCLIS took the lead in championing tribal libraries and in gathering and documenting information related to the needs for library and information services on reservations. In addition to site visits to reservations, the commission held hearings throughout the country on the need for improved library services to American Indians.

In fiscal year 1992, LSCA Title IV grants for the Library Services for Indian Tribes and Hawaiian Natives Program were awarded to 225 Indian tribes and 170,000 Hawaiian natives. Funds were used in 28 states to support a variety of library activities, including salaries and training of library staff, the purchase of library materials, and the renovation or construction of library facilities. Approximately $900,000 was awarded under the Basic Grant Program, and just over $900,000 was used for Special Projects Grants. Eleven Indian tribes successfully competed for Special Projects Grants, with grants ranging from more than $21,000 to the Red Lake Band of Chippewa in Minnesota to pay the salary of a library technician, to $160,000 to the Otoe Missouria tribe of Oklahoma for the construction of a new library facility. The Fort Peck Assiniboine and Sioux Tribes in Montana will use their award of $120,474 to improve community understanding of the special health and medical needs on the reservation. The

Native Community of Tuluksak, Alaska, with the assistance of the Yupiit School District, used its $162,000 grant to build a 2,100-square-foot community and school library.

In December 1992, the NCLIS published *Pathways to Excellence: A Report on Improving Library and Information Services for Native American Peoples.* The report provided 10 major challenges involving federal, state, and local governments and agencies, the tribes themselves, and the nation at large. Among these were strengthening technical assistance to Native American communities by improving access and strengthening cooperative activities.

In 1999, under the direction of Ben Wakashige, State Librarian, the State Library of New Mexico established the Native American Libraries Project. Funded by the state's legislature for two years in 1994, the project focused on technology and the Internet. In 1997, the State Library received additional funding from the New Mexico state legislature to establish a resource and training center on the Navajo reservation and to place computer equipment in 33 communities, including 14 pueblos, several communities on the Navajo reservation, and the state's 2 Apache tribes, the Jicarilla and the Mescalero. State funding was used for library acquisitions, library skills training workshops, and professional consultation on meeting library standards.[39]

Ayalas' Study on Public Library Services to the Latino Community

In June 1994, *The Report Card on Public Library Services to the Latino Community* by Reynaldo Ayala and Marta Stiefel Ayala was published as a result of a project initiated and sponsored by REFORMA but funded by a grant from the W.K. Kellogg Foundation of Battle Creek, Michigan. Based on data collected from December 1993 to May 1994 from 134 libraries, 252 Latino library users and community leaders, 91 library directors, and 59 bilingual and bicultural Latino library professionals, it was observed by the Ayalas that the rapid growth of the Latino population, and especially of Latino children, demanded that public libraries improve their services to this population. They pointed out that there were few Latino librarians—only 1.8 percent of all librarians—and, of those, even less were bilingual or served in Latino community libraries.

Their findings revealed that major budget cuts in public libraries had caused a deterioration of services through reduced staffing, materials, and programming. The study recommended that the American library community should increase recruitment, retention, and mentoring of bilingual and bicultural Latino personnel; should include members of the Latino community in the process of planning library services for the community as a whole; and should foster networking among libraries providing service to the Latino community.[40]

ALA Goals 2000 Program

The ALA, almost 60,000 strong in membership in the early 1990s, adopted a Goals 2000 program to guide library and information policy into the new century, with an emphasis on fitting libraries into the information culture. The Washington Office of ALA was expanded and a new office for Information Technology Policy was established.

The 1997 report *Equal Voices, Many Choices: Ethnic Library Organizations Respond to ALA's Goal 2000* was published under the direction of ALA Executive Director Elizabeth Martinez to elicit the reaction of ethnic minority library leaders. REFORMA leaders Edward Erazo and Sandra Balderrama made the point that libraries must seek to involve members of the Latino community so that they may access electronic resources and access basic traditional library services.

As ALA Executive Director from 1994 to 1997, Martinez instituted a variety of major programs in such areas as national information technology policy; created a library support foundation, the Fund for Libraries, to seek additional funds to bring libraries into the Digital Age; established strong partnerships with the corporate sector; and helped found the National Coalition for Literacy. Martinez was also responsible for the creation in 1998 of the Spectrum Initiative, an ALA-sponsored $1.35 million three-year project that awarded scholarships to people of color.[41]

ALA Spectrum Initiative

The purpose of the ALA Spectrum Initiative was to recruit minority libraries and provide fifty $5,000 scholarships per year for three years of graduate study in library and information science. These 150 scholarships were to be awarded to members of racial and ethnic minority groups, substantially increasing the number of minority librarians. Scholarship recipients needed to be citizens or permanent U.S. or Canadian residents and be from one of four specified underrepresented groups: African American or African Canadian, Asian or Pacific Islander, Latino, or Native American or Canadian.

The Spectrum Initiative has been closing the gap in fellowship funding created when the federal funding for institutes ceased and only funding of fellowships continued. The successful institutional models of the California State University at Fullerton program and the University of Arizona have never been replicated.[42]

Library Education for Minorities

During fiscal year 1994, Congress appropriated approximately $5 million for the HEA Title II-B Library Education and Human Resource Development Program to assist institutions of higher education and other library organizations and agencies in training persons in library and information science and to establish, develop, and expand programs of library and information science. Grants are made for fellowships and traineeships at the master's and doctoral levels, as well as for training institutes for librarians.

During fiscal year 1994, 64 fellowship awards were made to 37 institutions to support 167 fellowships, including 18 new doctoral, 95 continuing doctoral, and 54 master's. Stipends were $14,000 for all fellowship candidates, based on economic need. For each fellowship, institutions received $8,000 for master's-level and $10,000 for doctoral-level studies. Between fiscal years 1966 and 1994, institutions of higher education were awarded a total of 5,267 awards: including 1,474 doctoral, 282 post-master's, 3,365 master's, 16 bachelor's, and 53 associate's fellowships; and 7 traineeships.

Under HEA Title II-C (Improving Access to Research Library Resources Program), Congress appropriated approximately $6 million to institutions to make accessible collections that were rare, exclusively held, and of interest to a national research audience. Since its establishment in 1977, approximately $99 million was awarded to acquire rare and unique materials, to augment special collections in demand by researchers, to preserve fragile and deteriorating materials not generally available elsewhere, and to provide access to research collections by converting bibliographic information into machine-readable form and entering the records into national databases. During fiscal year 1994, the Chicago Historical Society received an HEA Title II-C grant of approximately $116 million to preserve and make available to researchers manuscript collections that illuminated major, national civil liberties and civil rights issues of the mid- to late-twentieth century.

Fiscal year 1994 HEA Title II-B (Library Education and Human Resource Development Program) fellowship grants were awarded to several institutions to train librarians to work with ethnically diverse communities. Clark Atlanta University, a historically black university, received a master's fellowship grant to train a librarian to provide services to ethnically and racially diverse populations. The Inter American University of Puerto Rico received two master's fellowship grants to train libraries to provide services to Hispanic populations. Simmons College was awarded three master's fellowships to train librarians to serve ethnically diverse communities. HEA Title II-B institute grants included at least five specifically for training librarians to provide services to minorities and other special populations. San Jose State University received an HEA Title II-B institute grant in the amount of approximately $52,000 to sponsor an institute titled Information Needs and Behaviors of Diverse Populations: Research and Methodology. The University of California at Berkeley received approximately $110,000 for an Institute for the Recruitment, Education, and (Re)Training of Minorities in Academic Libraries. Montana State University received over $36,000 for a Tribal College Librarians' Professional Development Institute, and the University of Oklahoma received over $33,000 for a Tribal Librarians' Summer Institute for School Readiness. Pennsylvania State University received over $83,000 for the Pennsylvania Library Institute: Meeting the Information and Educational Needs of Special Populations.

According to 1996–97 data from the ALA Office for Library Personnel Resources, the ALA awarded its accredited master's degree 193 (4.4%) African Americans; a post-master's degree to 1 (2.2%) African American; and 3 doctorates (8.5%) to African Americans. Of 51 library schools reporting a total of 12,480 students enrolled in ALA-accredited master's programs during fiscal year 1998, only 558, or 4.8 percent of African American students, were enrolled. During the same period, with 48 schools reporting, there were only 35 black library educators in U.S. library schools, or 6.4 percent of a total population of 547 faculty.

The 1999 ALA Congress on Professional Education made one of its six recommendations a call for the recruitment, education, and placement of students from diverse populations as a way of addressing multilingual, multiethnic, and multicultural needs of underserved populations.[43]

REFORMA National Conferences

The first national REFORMA conference, celebrating its 25th anniversary, was held in Austin, Texas, from August 22–25, 1996. Sponsored jointly by ALA's Association for Library Services to Children (ALSC and REFORMA, the first Pura Belpre (1899–1982) Award was awarded to honor the first Puerto Rican librarian to work at the New York Public Library in the 1920s and 1930s. Cultural Partnerships: Linking Missions and Visions, the first national conference, was a celebration of the first quarter-century of REFORMA's existence. The second was held in August 3–6, 2000, in Tucson, Arizona, with the conference theme The Power of Language: Planning for the 21st Century.

Institutes were also funded by National Leadership Grants of the U.S. Department of Education under the HEA Title II-B, which ended in 1998. Two institutes on serving multicultural, multiethnic populations were held that last year and sponsored by the University of Minnesota Libraries and the University of South Florida's School of Library and Information Science.[44]

BCALA

Between 1992 and 1999, the BCALA held four national Culture Keepers conferences around the theme of African American libraries as culture keepers of their communities in Columbus (OH) (1992), Milwaukee (1994), Winston-Salem (1997), and Las Vegas (1999). BCALA has established a literary award, an award for excellence in librarianship, a trailblazer's award for outstanding service, and the E.J. Josey Scholarship.[45]

American Indians and the Tribal Self-Governance Act of 1994

In 1994, Congress passed the Tribal Self-Governance Act, which enabled tribes to negotiate annual agreements to allow them to have greater involvement in planning and setting priorities for themselves, including in some instances, the development of library services. Tribal libraries must compete for scarce funds with roads, utilities, and other basic services on reservations. In a survey of 300 tribes in the lower 48 states in 1994, approximately one-half reported having a library, an improvement over a 1980 survey that documented less than 50 tribes having a tribal library.

Statistical data on ethnic categories for persons awarded degrees by ALA-accredited programs in the United States and Canada are collected annually by the ALISE. The report for 1995–96 showed 19 American Indian or Alaska Native graduates at the master's level; the 1996–97 report listed 26 master's and 2 doctorates. At the master's level, the 1996–97 figures represented only one-half of 1 percent of all graduates for that year.

In 1995, there were three full-time American Indian faculty in all schools of library and information studies, a number that represented less than 0.5 percent of total library and information science educators.

In 1999, the National Telecommunications Information Administration (NTIA) reported that only 18.9 percent of Native Americans had Internet access at home as compared to the national average of 26.2 percent. The study also indicated that Native Americans were more likely to access the Internet at schools and libraries than any other minority group. This lack of home telecommunication services among American Indians presented a formidable barrier to the elimination of the information technology gap.[46]

Transborder Library Forum (Foro Transfronterizo de Bibliotecas)

The Transborder Library Forum (Foro Transfronterizo de Bibliotecas) began in 1989, when librarians from Arizona and Sonora identified the need for better communication between libraries in Mexico and the United States in the so-called borderlands region, which extends nearly 2,000 miles across the states of Texas, New Mexico, Arizona, and California in the United States, and the states of Nuevo Leon, Coahuila, Tamaulipas, Chihuahua, Sonora, and Baja California Norte in Mexico.

In 1990, Arizona and Sonoran librarians invited their counterparts from Sonora, Mexico, to participate in organizing Foro I, to be held in Rio Rico, Arizona, in 1991. In 1992, librarians in Hermosillo, Sonora, hosted the group. Between 1993 and 2000, conferences were held in El Paso, Texas (1993); Monterrey, Nuevo Leon (1994); Mexico City (1995); Tucson, Arizona (1996); Ciudad Juarez, Chihuahua (1997); Riverside, California (1998); Mexicali, Baja California (1999); and Albuquerque, New Mexico (2000). The February 1994 conference held in Monterrey, Nuevo Leon, Mexico, became the Trinational Library Forum, as Canadian librarians were invited to explore issues related to NAFTA and other topics of interest to librarians throughout North America.[47]

Traditionally, multiculturalism has focused on a country's internal minorities, who often have been the disadvantaged, refugees, or immigrants. The focus of multiculturalism should be expanded to include not only minorities within a nation, but also ethnocultural groups within a global society and economy. In a global society, we are all members of minority groups, interacting and developing as human beings in a multicultural context. Information technology has reduced the impact of geography and of national borders. People are now able to communicate regularly and with ease on a global scale.[48]

As virtual communities are being created, libraries must be vigilant that minority groups do not get lost in the technological push. The struggle for equality is no longer a national or even international issue but rather a pervasive global issue. As the new millennium unfolds, public libraries are still struggling for equality in library service with minorities within a context of globalization.

NOTES

1. U.S. Census Bureau, "No. 10: Resident Population—Selected Characteristics, 1950 to 2000, and Projections, 2025 and 2050," in *Statistical Abstract of the United States: 2001,* 121st ed. (Washington, DC: U.S. G.P.O., 2001), 13; Marcia J. Nauratil, *Public Libraries and Nontraditional Clienteles: The Politics of Special Services* (Westport, CT: Greenwood Press, 1985), 102–3; Alice Robbin, "We the People: One Nation, a Multicultural Society," *Library Trends* 49 (Summer 2000): 6–48; Harlow G. Unger, ed., "Hispanic Americans," in *Encyclopedia of American Education,* 2nd ed. (New York: Facts on File, c2001, 1996), 527–28; Harlow G. Unger, ed., "Mexican Americans," in *Encyclopedia of American Education,* 668; Julie Tao Su, "Library Services in an Asian American Context," in *Diversity and Multiculturalism in Libraries,* ed. Katherine Hoover Hill (Greenwich, CT: JAI Press, 1994), 121–22; Rudolph J. Vecoli, "Immigration," in *Oxford Companion to United States History,* ed. Paul S. Boyer and Melvyn Dubofsky (New York: Oxford University Press, 2001), 364; Otis L. Graham Jr., *Unguarded Gates: A History of America's Immigration Crisis* (Lanham, MD: Rowman & Littlefield Publishers, 2004), 158.

2. U.S. Immigration and Naturalization Service, "Appendix 1: Immigration and Naturalization Legislation," in *Statistical Yearbook of the Immigration and Naturalization Service, 1997* (Washington, DC: U.S. G.P.O., 1999), A.1–20, A. 1–21; M.A. Jones, *American Immigration,* 289–90; Hans P. Johnson, "Immigrants in California: Findings from the 1990 Census," *California State Library Foundation Bulletin,* no. 45 (Oct. 1993): 7–11; E. Willard Miller and Ruby M. Miller, *United States Immigration: A Reference Handbook* (Santa Barbara, CA: ABC-CLIO, 1996), 103–7; Thomas J. Archdeacon, "Immigration Law," in *Oxford Companion to United States History,* 366.

3. U.S. Immigration and Naturalization Service, "Appendix 1: Immigration and Naturalization Legislation," A.1–21; Graham, *Unguarded Gates,* xiv, 155–56.

4. U.S. Immigration and Naturalization Service, "Appendix 1: Immigration and Naturalization Legislation," A.1–22.

5. Ibid., A.1–22, A.1–23

6. U.S. Immigration and Naturalization Service, "Appendix 1: Immigration and Naturalization Legislation," A.1–23, A.1–24; Michael LeMay and Elliott

Robert Barkan, eds., *U.S. Immigration and Naturalization Laws and Issues: A Documentary History* (Westport, CT: Greenwood Press, 1999), 301–10; Graham, *Unguarded Gates,* xiv, 123, 156–58.

7. U.S. Immigration and Naturalization Service, "Appendix 1: Immigration and Naturalization Legislation," A.1–24, A.1–25; LeMay and Barkan, *U.S. Immigration and Naturalization Laws and Issues,* 310–11.

8. U.S. Immigration and Naturalization Service, "Appendix 1: Immigration and Naturalization Legislation," A.1–23, A.1–24; LeMay and Barkan, *U.S. Immigration and Naturalization Laws and Issues,* 301–10.

9. U.S. Immigration and Naturalization Service, "Appendix 1: Immigration and Naturalization Legislation," A.1–25.

10. J. Ingrid Lesley, "Library Services for Special Groups: 1991 Trends and Selected Innovative Services for Immigrants, the Homeless, Children After School, the Disabled, and the Unemployed," in *Bowker Annual 1992: Library and Book Trade Almanac,* 37th ed. (New Providence, NJ: R.R. Bowker, 1992), 29; Su, "Library Services in an Asian American Context," 139; Ray M. Fry, "U.S. Department of Education Library Programs, 1992," in *Bowker Annual 1993: Library and Book Trade Almanac,* 38th ed. (New Providence, NJ: R.R. Bowker, 1993), 266–78, 291–95, 298–305; Ray M. Fry, "U.S. Department of Education Library Programs, 1995," in *Bowker Annual 1995: Library and Book Trade Almanac,* 40th ed. (New Providence, NJ: R.R. Bowker, 1995), 297–303, 306–9, 311–12, 332–337; Diane Frankel, "Institute of Museum and Library Services Library Programs," in *Bowker Annual 1998: Library and Book Trade Almanac,* 43rd ed. (New Providence, NJ: R.R. Bowker, 1998), 302–27; Christina Dunn, "U.S. Department of Education Discretionary Library Programs, Fiscal Year 1997," in *Bowker Annual 1998: Library and Book Trade Almanac,* 307–14; Beverly Sheppard, "Institute of Museum and Library Services Library Programs," in *Bowker Annual 2001: Library and Book Trade Almanac,* 46th ed. (New Providence, NJ: R.R. Bowker, 2001), 286–98.

11. R. Kathleen Molz, *The Federal Roles in Support of Public Library Services: An Overview,* prepared for the Federal Roles in Support of Public Library Services Project (Chicago: ALA, 1990), 23; Kathleen de la Pena McCook and Paul Geist, preps., *Toward a Just and Productive Society: An Analysis of the Recommendations of the White House Conference on Library and Information Services* (Washington, DC: NCLIS, 1993 [i.e., 1994]), 1, 4–6, 11–13, 17, 19–20, 22–27, 29–34; R. Taylor Walsh, prep., *National Information Infrastructure and the Recommendations of the 1991 White House Conference on Library and Information Services* (Washington, DC: NCLIS, 1994), 1–6, 24.

12. Rhonda Rios Kravitz, Rhonda Rios, Adelia Lines, and Vivian Sykes, "Serving the Emerging Majority: Documenting Their Voices," *Library Administration & Management* 5 (Fall 1991): 184–86; David B. Carlson, Arabella Martinez, Sarah A. Curtis, Janet Coles, and Nicholas A. Valenzuela, *Adrift in a Sea of Change: California's Public Libraries Struggle to Meet the Information Needs of Multicultural Communities,* Partnerships for Change Series, no. 2 (Sacramento:

California State Library, Center for Policy Development, 1990), iii–x, 38–56, 65–78, 103–12; Cheryl Metoyer-Duran, *Gatekeepers in Ethnolinguistic Communities* (Norwood, NJ: Ablex Publishing, 1993), 19; Su, "Library Services in an Asian American Context," 139; Xiwen Zhang, "The Anti-Affirmative Action Movement in California: Implications for Public Library Services to Asian Immigrants," in *Library Services to Latinos: An Anthology,* ed. Salvador Guerena (Jefferson, NC: McFarland, 2000), 118.

13. Kravitz et al., "Serving the Emerging Majority," 187–88; Lesley, "Library Services for Special Groups," 28; Katharine T. A. Scarborough, ed., *Developing Library Collections for California's Emerging Majority: A Manual of Resources for Ethnic Collection Development,* produced in conjunction with the conference Developing Library Collections for California's Emerging Majority, September 22–23, 1990, San Francisco, California (Berkeley: Bay Area Library and Information System; University Extension, University of California; School of Library and Information Studies, University of California, 1990); Vivian Sykes, "Advocacy for Ethnic Collection Development," in *Developing Library Collections for California's Emerging Majority,* 8–13; Luis Herrera and Albert J. Milo, "Managing Administrative Change for Ethnic Collection Development," in *Developing Library Collections for California's Emerging Majority,* 14–21; Rita Torres, "Assessment of Community Needs," in *Developing Library Collections for California's Emerging Majority,* 47–52; Edith Maureen Fisher, "Identification of Multiethnic Resources," in *Developing Library Collections for California's Emerging Majority,* 53–60; Suzanne Lo and Susan Ma, "Resources for Asian/ Southeast Asian Collection Development," in *Developing Library Collections for California's Emerging Majority,* 172–74; Salvador Guerena and Elissa Miller, "Resources for Chicano/Latino Collection Development," in *Developing Library Collections for California's Emerging Majority,* 215–16; Mary Ellen Quinn, "Hispanic Collections in the Public Library: The Chicago Public Library Experience," in *Multicultural Acquisitions,* ed. Karen Parrish and Bill Katz (New York: Haworth Press, 1993), 222; Metoyer-Duran, *Gatekeepers in Ethnolinguistic Communities,* 13–16.

14. Amado M. Padilla, *Public Library Services for Immigrant Populations in California: A Report to the State Librarian of California* (Sacramento: California State Library Foundation, 1991), 5–14, 23–31, 37, 40–46; James McShane, "Confronting Diversity in a Homogeneous Environment," in *Venture into Cultures: A Resource Book of Multicultural Materials and Programs,* ed. Olga R. Kuharets for the Ethnic and Multicultural Information Exchange Round Table, 2nd ed. (Chicago: ALA, 2001), vii–ix; Carla Hayden, *Venture into Cultures: A Resource Book of Multicultural Materials and Programs,* 1st ed. (Chicago: ALA, 1992); Hans P. Johnson, "Immigrants in California: Findings from the 1990 Census," *California State Library Foundation Bulletin,* no. 45 (Oct. 1993): 7–11; Ben Ocon, "Effective Outreach Strategies to the Latino Community: A Paradigm for Public Libraries," in *Library Services to Latinos,* 183–93.

15. Robert A. Seal, "Mexican and U.S. Library Relations," in *Advances in Librarianship,* ed. Irene Godden, vol. 20 (New York: Academic Press, 1974), 69–121, 88, 96; Salvador Guerena and Edward Erazo, "Latinos and Librarianship," *Library Trends* 49 (Summer 2000): 160.

16. Seal, "Mexican and U.S. Library Relations," 93; Gitinet Belay, "Conceptual Strategies for Operationalizing Multicultural Curricula," *Journal of Education for Library and Information Science* 4 (Fall 1992): 295–306; David Cohen, "Narrative Evaluation Report on the Institute for Ethnicity and Librarianship: Based on Proceedings of the Institute for Ethnicity and Librarianship, Queens College, CUNY, New York, July 7–25, 1975," ED 120 312 ([Washington, DC]: ERIC, 1975); David Cohen and Laurence Sherrill, "Model and Course of Study for Library School Ethnic Curricula," *Ethnic Forum* 2 (Spring 1982): 51–58; Clara Chu, "Education for Multicultural Librarianship," in *Multiculturalism in Libraries,* by Rosemary Ruhig DuMont, Lois Buttlar, and William Caynon (Westport, CT: Greenwood Press, 1994), 142–45; ALA, Ethnic and Multicultural Information Exchange Round Table, Library Education Task Force, "Ethnic and Minority Concerns in Library Education," *EMIE Bulletin* 6 (Summer 1989): 6–10; Donna L. Gilton, "A World of Difference: Preparing for Information Literacy Instruction for Diverse Groups," *MultiCultural Review* 3 (Sept. 1994): 54–62; Oralia Garza de Cortes, Amy Kellman, Patricia M. Wong, Peter Sis, Kyoko Mori, and George Ancona, "A Nation of Immigrants: Are We Us or Them?" *Journal of Youth Services in Libraries* 9 (Winter 1996): 129–42; Hayden, *Venture into Cultures.*

17. Seal, "Mexican and U.S. Library Relations," 101–2.

18. Camila Alire and Orlando Archibeque, *Service to Latino Communities: A How-To-Do-It Manual for Librarians* (New York: Neal-Schuman Publishers, 1998), 244.

19. Barbara Immroth, Kathleen de la Pena McCook, and Catherine Jasper, eds., *Library Services to Youth of Hispanic Heritage* (Jefferson, NC: McFarland, 2000), 10–11; Arnulfo D. Trejo, "Bicultural Americans with a Hispanic Tradition," *Wilson Library Bulletin* 44 (Mar. 1970): 716–23; Arnulfo Trejo, "REFORMITA: A Gang for the New Millennium," in *Library Services to Youth of Hispanic Heritage,* 187–89; Guerena and Erazo, "Latinos and Librarianship," 161.

20. Lesley, "Library Services for Special Groups," 29; Su, "Library Services in an Asian American Context," 139; Fry, "U.S. Department of Education Library Programs, 1992," 266–78, 291–95, 298–305; Fry, "U.S. Department of Education Library Programs, 1995," 297–303, 306–9, 311–12, 332–337; Frankel, "Institute of Museum and Library Services Library Programs," 302–27; Dunn, "U.S. Department of Education Discretionary Library Programs, Fiscal Year 1997," 307–14; Sheppard, "Institute of Museum and Library Services Library Programs," 286–98.

21. Renee Tjoumas, "Giving New Americans a Green Light in Life: A Paradigm for Serving Immigrant Communities," *Public Libraries* 26 (Fall 1987): 103–8; Renee Tjoumas, "Opening Doorways to New Immigrants: Queens Bor-

ough Public Library's Coping Skills Component," *Public Library Quarterly* 14, no. 4 (1995): 5–19; Su, "Library Services in an Asian American Context," 126–28, 132; Monica Scheliga Carnesi and Maria A. Fiol, "Queens Library's New Americans Program: 23 Years of Services to Immigrants," in *Library Services to Latinos,* 133–42; Patricia Beilke and Frank J. Sciara, *Selecting Materials for and about Hispanic and East Asian Children and Young People* (Hamden, CT: Library Professional Publications, 1986), 10–11; State Library of New South Wales, "Multicultural Library Services in New South Wales Public Libraries 2001, Part 8: International Case Studies," www.sl.nsw.gov.au/multicultural/services/case5. cfm, 8.1.1 "Queens Borough Public Library Multilingual Information System and Services—World LinQ."

22. Annette Salo, "Ethnic Diversity in a Northern Climate," in *Multicultural Acquisitions,* 267–71.

23. Lesley, "Library Services for Special Groups," 31; State Library of New South Wales, "Multicultural Library Services in New South Wales Public Libraries 2001, Part 8," 8.3.3 "Illinois: Rolling Meadows Library and the Biblioteca del Centro."

24. State Library of New South Wales, "Multicultural Library Services in New South Wales Public Libraries 2001, Part 8," 8.3.2 "New Jersey: Newark Public Library."

25. Stephanie Asch, "Urban Libraries Confront Linguistic Minorities: Programs That Work," in *Literacy, Access, and Libraries Among the Language Minority Population,* ed. Rebecca Constantino (Lanham, MD: Scarecrow Press, 1998), 74; Lucia M. Gonzalez, "Developing Culturally Integrated Children's Programs," in *Library Services to Youth of Hispanic Heritage,* 21–23.

26. Lesley, "Library Services for Special Groups," 29.

27. Judy Fuller, "Citizenship Class a First in Longview!" *ALKI: The Washington Library Association Journal* 11 (Dec. 1995): 28.

28. Asch, "Urban Libraries Confront Linguistic Minorities," 74.

29. State Library of New South Wales, "Multicultural Library Services in New South Wales Public Libraries 2001, Part 8," 8.3.4 "California: San Francisco Public Library International Centre."

30. Frances H. Flythe, "Identification of the Information Needs of Newly Arrived Hispanic/Latino Immigrants in Durham County, North Carolina, and How the Public Library May Address Those Needs," (Master's thesis, University of North Carolina at Chapel Hill, 2001), 39–42; Jon Sundell, "Library Service to Hispanic Immigrants of Forsyth County, North Carolina: A Community Collaboration," in *Library Services to Latinos,* 143–68; Guerena and Erazo, "Latinos and Librarianship," 168. For similar work on a statewide level with Hispanics in Nebraska, see Mary Nash, "Public Library Service to Hispanic Immigrants: An Anecdotal Survey," *Nebraska Library Association Quarterly* 29 (Spring 1998): 17–25.

31. Kathleen de la Pena McCook, *A Place at the Table: Participating in Community Building* (Chicago: ALA, 2000), 59–61.

32. Alire and Archibeque, *Service to Latino Communities*, 173.

33. Lowell A. Martin, *Enrichment: A History of the Public Library in the United States in the Twentieth Century* (Lanham, MD: Scarecrow Press, 1998), 144–45, 171; Guerena and Erazo, "Latinos and Librarianship," 164–65; Fry, "U.S. Department of Education Library Programs, 1992," 266–78, 291–95, 298–305; Fry, "U.S. Department of Education Library Programs, 1995," 297–303, 306–9, 311–12, 332–337; Frankel, "Institute of Museum and Library Services Library Programs," 302–6; Dunn, "U.S. Department of Education Discretionary Library Programs, Fiscal Year 1997," 307–14; Beverly Sheppard "Institute of Museum and Library Services Library Programs," 286–98.

34. Plummer Alston Jones Jr. "Cultural Oasis or Ethnic Ghetto?: The North Carolina Foreign Language Center and Statewide Multilingual Public Library Service," *North Carolina Libraries* 50 (Summer 1992): 100-5; P.A. Jones Jr., "Serving the Silent: We Are Still a Nation of Immigrants," *North Carolina Libraries* 56 (Fall 1998): 118.

35. Martin, *Enrichment*, 144–45, 171; Guerena and Erazo, "Latinos and Librarianship," 164–65; Fry, "U.S. Department of Education Library Programs, 1992," 266–78, 291–95, 298–305; Fry, "U.S. Department of Education Library Programs, 1995," 297–303, 306–9, 311–12, 332–337; Frankel, "Institute of Museum and Library Services Library Programs," 302–6; Dunn, "U.S. Department of Education Discretionary Library Programs, Fiscal Year 1997," 307–14; Sheppard, "Institute of Museum and Library Services Library Programs," 286–98.

36. Harlow G. Unger, ed., "Bilingual Instruction," in *Encyclopedia of American Education*, 138–39; Harlow G. Unger, ed., "Minority Education," in *Encyclopedia of American Education*, 679–81; JoAnn K. Aguirre, "Passport to Promise: Public Libraries as Intellectual Spaces for Immigrant Students," in *Library Services to Latinos*, 74–75; Zhang, "The Anti-Affirmative Action Movement in California," 102–24; Evelyn Escatiola, "Anti-Immigrant Literature: A Selected Bibliography," in *Library Services to Latinos*, 161–81.

37. Harlow G. Unger, ed., "Illiteracy," in *Encyclopedia of American Education*, 546–48.

38. Unger, "Hispanic Americans," 527–28.

39. U.S. National Commission on Libraries and Information Science, *Pathways to Excellence: A Report on Improving Library and Information Services for Native American Peoples* (Washington, DC: NCLIS, 1992); Lotsee Patterson, "Historical Overview of Tribal Libraries in the Lower Forty-Eight States," in *Libraries to the People: Histories of Outreach*, ed. Robert S. Freeman and David M. Hovde, foreword by Kathleen de la Pena McCook (Jefferson, NC: McFarland & Company, 2003), 159, 161; Fry, "U.S. Department of Education Library Programs, 1992," 266–69.

40. Reynaldo Ayala and Marta Stiefel Ayala, *Report Card on Public Library Services to the Latino Community* (Calexico, CA: REFORMA, 1994); Marta Stiefel

Ayala, "How One Library-less Librarian Got the Word Out," *Wilson Library Bulletin* 53 (Nov. 1978): 255–57; Oralia Garza de Cortes, "Give Them What They Need," in *Library Services to Youth of Hispanic Heritage,* 93–94; Susan J. Freiband, "Developing Collections for the Spanish Speaking," *RQ* 35 (Spring 1996): 330–42.

41. Martin, *Enrichment,* 170–73.

42. Guerena and Erazo, "Latinos and Librarianship," 169–70; Zhang, "The Anti-Affirmative Action Movement in California," 123.

43. Guerena and Erazo, "Latinos and Librarianship," 172; Fry, "U.S. Department of Education Library Programs, 1995," 297–303, 306–9, 311–12, 332–337.

44. Oralia Garza de Cortes, "Celebracion [presentation of the Pura Belpre Award for Latino Authors and Illustrators at the Annual Conference, American Library Association, June 28, 1998, Washington, D.C.]," *MultiCultural Review* 50 (June 1999): 49–50; Oralia Garza de Cortes, "Developing the Spanish Children's Collection," in *Library Services to Latinos,* 75–90; Garza de Cortes, "Give Them What They Need," 89–97; Oralia Garza de Cortes, "Justice in the Publishing Field: A Look at Multicultural Awards for Children's Literature," *MultiCultural Review* 8 (June 1999): 42–48; Garza de Cortes et al., "A Nation of Immigrants: Are We Us or Them?," 129–42; Guerena and Erazo, "Latinos and Librarianship," 169; REFORMA: National Association to Promote Library and Information Services to Latinos and the Spanish-speaking, http://www.reforma.org.

45. Black Caucus of the American Library Association, http://www.bcala.org/history;about.htm.

46. American Indian Library Association, http://www.nativeculture.com/lisamitten/aila.html; National Indian Education Association, www.niea.org/index.html; Loriene Roy, "To Support and Model Native American Library Services," http://www.txla.org/pubs/tlj76_1/native.html; National Telecommunications Information Administration, "Fact Sheet: Native Americans Lacking Information Resources: Falling Through the Net: Defining the Digital Divide, July 1999," http://www.ntia.doc.gov/ntiahome/digitaldivide/factsheets/native-americans.htm.

47. Seal, "Mexican and U.S. Library Relations," 94, 102; Theresa Salazar and Maria Segura Hoopes, "U.S./Mexican Borderlands Acquisition: Defining and Pursuing the Materials," in *Multicultural Acquisitions,* 233; Guerena and Erazo, "Latinos and Librarianship," 159.

48. Lucy Tse, "Seeing Themselves through Borrowed Eyes: Asian Americans in Ethnic Ambivalence/Evasion," *MultiCultural Review* 7 (June 1998): 28–34; Stan Skrzeszewski and Maureen Cubberley, "The INTERNET and a Vision for the Future: Multicultural Library Services," *MultiCultural Review* 7 (Dec. 1998): 34–38.

AFTERWORD

Public opinion polls since large-scale immigration resumed in the 1960s have reported pluralities or majorities in all ethnic groups in favor of reducing immigration. In 2000, the Brookings Institution gathered a panel of historians and political scientists to reflect on the U.S. government's greatest achievements and failures since World War II. The panel ranked controlling immigration as second among the top five failures.

New Americans are now selected by a system placing primary emphasis on kinship, that is family ties to recent immigrants, rather than on national needs. The radical shift in immigrants' countries of origin from Europe to Latin America, especially Mexico, the Middle East, and Asia, causes many politicians, economists, and even historians to question once again the nation's capacity for assimilation.

At the beginning of the twenty-first century, after four decades characterized by historian Otis L. Graham Jr. as the Second Great Wave of primarily Asian and Western Hemisphere immigration, legal and illegal, the U.S. government's performance in the immigration arena has been a mixed bag. In 2001, the United States contained more foreign-born residents than ever before, 10.4 percent of the total population, and one in five Americans was either born abroad or to parents born abroad. Estimates of the illegal population ranged between 7 and 11 million.[1]

Legal and Judicial Decisions Affecting Minorities

During the 2000 presidential election campaign, talk of immigration reform was avoided in view of the dynamic growth of the Spanish-speaking population in the United States and the potential hostility of that voting block toward enforcement of immigration law. Neither Texas governor George W. Bush nor Vice President Al Gore had anything to say on immigration, and neither was pressed on the issue.

After the much-disputed election, involving a U.S. Supreme Court decision in *Bush v. Gore*, the newly selected president George W. Bush moved to capitalize on the ebbing of immigration-reform sentiment. He responded to Mexican president Vicente Fox's overtures in the summer of 2001 for some sort of grand bargain between the two countries that would legalize all Mexican illegal immigrants in the United States and provide a new permanent guest-worker program. Democratic Party leaders made no objections to the Fox-Bush plan. As the summer ended, the U.S. media predicted that the two presidents were on their way to an astonishing historic agreement under which Mexicans would be allowed to come to the United States for work and residence without impediment.[2]

Terrorist Attack of September 11, 2001

On September 11, 2001, approximately eight months into the Bush administration, Muslim extremists from the Middle East commandeered four American airliners and crashed two of them into the World Trade Center in New York City, one into the Pentagon, and one, supposedly intended for the Capitol, into a field in Pennsylvania. All of the terrorists had resided and trained in the comparatively wide-open U.S. society under various mixtures of legal and illegal entry and extended illegal residency for months before the attacks.

USA PATRIOT Act

The awkwardly titled Uniting and Strengthening America by Providing Appropriate Tools Required to Intercept and Obstruct Terrorism (USA PATRIOT) Act was one of several legislative proposals in response to the terrorist attacks of September 11, 2001. President Bush signed the final bill into law on October 26, 2001. Though the act made significant amendments to over 15 important statutes, it was introduced with great haste. It was passed with little debate and without a House, Senate, or conference report.

The USA PATRIOT Act was a compromised version of the Anti-Terrorism Act (ATA) of 2001. The ATA contained several provisions expanding the authority of law enforcement and intelligence agencies to monitor private communications and access personal information. The USA PATRIOT retains provisions expanding government investigative authority, especially with respect to the Internet—provisions that are complex and involve the revocation of fundamental constitutional protections of individual liberty.[3]

Post–September 11, 2001, Reexamination of the Immigration Process

After the attack of September 11, 2001, the Fox-Bush deal for liberalizing Mexican immigration to the United States slipped into limbo as American immigration policy came under serious scrutiny. Governmental abandonment of virtually all interior-immigration controls had allowed terrorists to move at will into, around, and out of the country, legally and illegally. Many had come as students, tourists, and business visitors and had become lawful permanent residents and even naturalized citizens. Some had reached this status by making fraudulent marriages or applying for asylum. Some 1,200 aliens suspected of terrorist activities were detained by the Department of Justice for questioning during the months after September 11, 2001.

In the six months following September 11, 2001, the U.S. Department of State's visa-issuance process that had admitted most of the terrorists and over 3 million overstayers showed no signs that anyone had acknowledged the events of that day. In the half-year following the attacks, 50,000 new tourist, business, and student visas were issued to non-Israeli citizens of the Middle East and three times that many from areas of Southern Asia where Al Qaeda had strongholds. The variety of visas available seemed designed to accommodate everyone, whatever their background and intentions. H1-B visas allowed and continue to allow nearly 200,000 temporary workers per year for stays of up to six years, from software engineers to fashion models. The Diversity Visa Lottery program provides 55,000 visas annually.

Michelle Malkin, in her 2002 exposé of the immigration problem titled *Invasion,* calculated that over 7,000 of such visas over the previous five years had gone to applicants from Iraq, Iran, Syria, Libya, Sudan, and Afghanistan. Investment visas can be obtained by creating or significantly underwriting a U.S.-based business. Religious worker visas admit foreigners for up to five years to work for religious organizations in any capacity, as preacher, teacher, or even janitor.

Student or F-1 visas were used by several of the September 11 terrorists for initial entry into the United States, as well as to obtain flight training.

In 1999, it was estimated that 565,000 foreign students and their relatives had entered and stayed in the country for extended periods. If all other visa programs were unavailable, Malkin found that the Transit Without a Visa Program existed for people traveling through the United States on their way somewhere else, and the Visa Waiver Program allowed 17 million people in 2001 to travel to the United States from 28 specified countries, where only a passport from one of those countries is sufficient to enter for 90 days. Once in the country, immigrants had many legal ways to convert from visitor to immigrant status without going home to get a visa. Asylum claims while in the country and marriage to a U.S. citizen were well-known loopholes.[4]

Profiling of Immigrants from Muslim Countries

The practice of profiling, treating Muslim immigrants differently from other immigrants, became the norm. An August 2002 report by the Center for Immigration Studies reported that Middle Easterners (defined as people from Pakistan, Bangladesh, Afghanistan, Turkey, the Levant, the Arabian Peninsula, and Arab North Africa) were one of the fastest-growing immigrant groups in the United States. Their total size had increased by more than sevenfold since 1970 to about 1.5 million, of whom 150,000 were illegal. As of 2000, it was estimated that 75 percent of the Middle Eastern population was Muslim.

Public support for a ban on further immigration from Muslim countries was high. A 2002 Chicago Council on Foreign Relations poll found 79 percent of the U.S. population in agreement with such a policy.

The U.S. government took more limited action. The INS decided to fingerprint, photograph, and track all visitors from Iran, Iraq, Sudan, and Libya and all males aged 16 to 45 from several other Muslim countries. In late 2002, the INS began a special registration program for noncitizens from 25 Arab and Muslim countries. Of the 82,000 men who came forward to register, 13,000 were found to be in the United States illegally. The INS officials claimed that the screening of incoming visitors or immigrants, as well as registering those already in the United States, led to the arrest of more than 800 deportable criminal aliens.

A General Accounting Office official reported to a Congressional panel in 2003 that the State Department had recently revoked the visas of 240 foreigners because of terrorist connections, but because of gaps in communication between the investigators and FBI and border agents, 30 of these entered the United States and were still at large.[5]

Illegal immigration should be reduced through a system of identification and tracking of immigrants and other visa holders. A national identification system for Americans should enhance travel and identity security. Convictions on illegal entry should include a bar against future U.S. citizenship.

Enhanced Border Security and Visa Entry Reform Act of 2002

In the area of homeland security, the Enhanced Border Security and Visa Entry Reform Act of 2002 was signed by President Bush on May 14, 2002. In late 2002, the Border Patrol reported that the slowdown of immigration pressures at the Mexican border had ended and that apprehensions of illegal immigrants were back at the level they had been before September 11. The INS estimated in 2002 that there were 8 million to 9 million illegal immigrants in residence in the United States. California had attracted 30 percent of the total, but even in the 1990s, North Carolina's illegal immigrant population increased 692 percent, Colorado's 364 percent, and Georgia's 570 percent.

Another irony occurred in the fall of 2002, when John Lee Malvo, an illegal immigrant from Jamaica in the company of an American passport forger John Allen Muhammad, terrorized the Washington, D.C., area with a series of sniper attacks killing 14 people. The tragedies of September 11, 2001, seemed to have made no difference in the volume of immigration or in public officials' thinking about the linkage between legal and illegal immigration and national security.[6]

Homeland Security Act of 2002

On November 25, 2002, President Bush signed the Homeland Security Act of 2002 into law. This act transferred INS functions to the new U.S. Department of Homeland Security. Immigration enforcement functions were placed within the Directorate of Border and Transportation Security, and the immigration service functions were placed into a separate U.S. Citizenship and Immigration Services. The INS would then cease to exist on the date the last of its functions have been transferred to other agencies.

U.S. Department of Homeland Security Established in 2003

On January 30, 2003, U.S. Department of Homeland Security Secretary Tom Ridge announced the creation of two new bureaus within the Border and Transportation Security Directorate. The Bureau of U.S. Customs and Border Protection would include the Border Patrol, as well as INS, Customs, and Agricultural Quarantine inspectors. The Bureau of U.S. Immigration and Customs Enforcement would include the enforcement and investigation components of INS, Customs, and the Federal Protective Services. On March 1, 2003, President Bush formally abolished the INS, transferring most of its functions to the new U.S. Department of Homeland Security.[7]

Recommendations for Further Immigration Reform

Immigration historian Otis L. Graham Jr. has recommended that illegal immigration should be reduced through a system of identification and tracking of immigrants and other visa holders. A national identification system for Americans should enhance travel and identity security. Convictions on illegal entry should include a bar against future U.S. citizenship. The numbers of legal immigrants arriving annually should be reduced as well, with numbers tailored to national population goals and real ceilings enforced. A policy shift toward a skills-based system should be initiated and the preference allowed for citizens to bring in brothers and sisters should be repealed.

Graham's recommendations have been based partially on the four-pronged approach to controlling the immigration process promulgated by the nongovernmental think tank, the Center for Immigration Studies. The center has recommended (1) improved visa application processing overseas; (2) control of the border and ports of entry with a tripling of Border Patrol personnel; (3) interior enforcement made more effective through a tracking system for foreign students and workers based a national computerized system allowing employers to submit data on new hires and more workplace inspections; and (4) reducing the overall level of immigration in the student, exchange, temporary worker visa categories. Both Graham's and the center's recommendations have been reminiscent of the 1997 recommendations of the 1995 U.S. Commission on Immigration Reform chaired by Barbara Jordan.[8]

LIBRARY SERVICES WITH MINORITIES

ALA Resolution on Intellectual Freedom

At the January 2002 ALA midwinter meeting in New Orleans, the ALA Council responded to legislation passed by Congress in the wake of the September 11, 2001, terrorist attacks, by unanimously approving a resolution affirming the principal of intellectual freedom. Author and radio commentator Andrei Codrescu delivered the third annual Arthur Curley memorial lecture on censorship and repression under totalitarian regimes.[9]

Black Caucus of the ALA

At the opening general session of the 2002 ALA annual conference in Atlanta, E.J. Josey, librarian, educator, and cofounder of the Black Caucus, of the ALA, was awarded ALA's highest honor, an honorary membership. More than 900 librarians and library supporters attended the BCALA "Culture Keepers V: Access" conference, held in August 2002 in Fort Lauderdale, Florida. Hugh B. Price, president of the National Urban League and a member of President Bush's Education Transition Team, presented the John C. Tyson memorial lecture.[10]

ALA Publications

In 2002, *Booklist* celebrated its 97th year of consecutive publication. *Booklist*'s bibliographies of foreign-language books have guided school and public library collection development. *Booklist* also has sponsored two important book awards for young adults, both administered by YALSA: the Michael L. Printz Award and the Alex Award.

During 2002, ALA introduced a bilingual Read Please/Lea Por Favor! clothing line for babies and toddlers; a multilingual poster, a bookmark, and notecards featuring more than 20 languages; and a number of gifts and incentives that promoted libraries, literacy, and reading.[11]

Association of Library Services to Children

In 2002, the ALSC received a $50,000 grant from the W.K. Kellogg Foundation to produce and distribute a brochure for parents featuring a list of recommended books by and about Latinos. ALSC collaborated with REFORMA in this effort. Free copies of the brochure were mailed to ALSC, REFORMA, and National Association of Bilingual Education members. The brochures also included tips for parents on how, when, and why to read to very young children, and ideas for encouraging reading in older children.[12]

Public Library Association

The Public Library Association board voted during the 2002 ALA annual conference in Atlanta to contribute $100,000 to the ALA Spectrum Scholarship Endowment to award scholarships to minority students. In honor of ALA's retiring executive director, the William R. Gordon Scholarship to benefit the Spectrum Initiative was established.[13]

ALA Office for Diversity

The ALA Office for Diversity began sponsorship in 2002 of an Annual Diversity Research Grant program to address critical gaps in the knowledge of diversity issues within library and information science. The winning research proposals for $5,000 grants were "Integrating Diversity into Library School Curriculum," submitted by Lorna Peterson, library school professor at the State University of New York at Buffalo; "Strategies for Promoting Mentoring Among Minorities," submitted by Ashley E. Bonnette, bibliographic instruction/distance learning librarian at the University of Louisiana at Lafayette; and "From the Inside Out: Collaborating for Recruitment, Outreach, and Diversity Through the Promotion of Literacy," submitted by Rosi Andrade, research associate with the Community Outreach Project on AIDS in Southern Arizona of the Southwest Institute for Research on Women, University of Arizona, and Cheryl Knott Malone, library school professor at the School of Information Resources and Library Science, University of Arizona.[14]

ALA Council Committee on Diversity

In June 2002, the ALA Council Committee on Minority Concerns and Cultural Diversity changed its name to the Council Committee on Diversity (COD). More than 160 librarians participated in the fifth year of the ALA-FIL Free Pass Program to the Guadalajara Book Fair, which provided participants an opportunity to review and purchase the latest in Spanish-language materials from around the world at discounted rates. It is estimated that ALA-FIL Free Pass participants have and continue to purchase approximately $1 million for Spanish-language materials at the fair.[15]

ALA Office of Intellectual Freedom

After the September 11, 2001, attacks, the ALA Office of Intellectual Freedom (OIF) addressed heightened concerns about library-patron confidentiality and access to information. The OIF developed a document Confidentiality and Coping with Law Enforcement Inquiries: Guidelines for the Library and Its Staff. World Wide Web resources addressing the FBI in Your Library, the Terrorism Information and Prevention System (TIPS), and the USA PATRIOT Act were made available to interested parties via the Internet.

The ALA OIF completed its Interpretation of the ALA Library Bill of Rights on privacy. The interpretation was adopted by the ALA Council on June 19, 2002.

ALA Resolution on the USA PATRIOT Act

On January 29, 2003, at the ALA midwinter meeting in Philadelphia, the ALA Council passed a Resolution on the USA PATRIOT Act and Related Measures that Infringe on the Rights of Library Users. The resolution was forwarded to President Bush and Attorney General John Ashcroft.

The ALA specifically opposed measures of the act that would suppress a citizen's right to free and open access to knowledge and information or to intimidate individuals in the exercise of free inquiry and free expression of opinion. The ALA and the thousands of librarians and library personnel it represented were appalled at the fact that they would be expected to reveal records of patrons' use of library materials, including the Internet.[16]

IMLS and LSTA Funds

Approximately $207.5 million in LSTA funds were made available through the IMLS for library programs in fiscal year 2001 and just over $197.5 million in fiscal year 2002. One of the five major purposes of the LSTA is to promote targeted library service to people of diverse geographic, cultural, and socioeconomic backgrounds, to individuals with disabilities, and to people with limited functional literacy or information skills.

Within the IMLS, the Office of Library Services is responsible for the administration of LSTA funds. The office is composed of the Division of State Programs, which administers the Grants to States Program, and the Division of Discretionary Programs, which administers the National Leadership Grant Program, the Native American Library Services Program, and the Native Hawaiian Library Services Program. Approximately 90 percent of the annual appropriation under LSTA is distributed through the Grants to State Program to the state library administrative agencies, usually the state libraries of the various states, according to a population-based formula. The formula consists of a minimum amount set by law of $340,000 for the states and $40,000 for the Pacific territories, plus an additional amount based on population. State agencies may use the appropriation for statewide initiatives and services. States are expected to match every $2 in federal funds with $1 in state funds.[17]

IMLS National Leadership Grants

In 2001, IMLS awarded 49 grants totaling approximately $11 million for National Leadership Grants in the areas of education and training, research and demonstration, preservation or digitization of library materials, and library and museum collaborations. Of direct interest to minorities, IMLS funds projects to attract individuals from diverse cultural backgrounds to the field of librarianship and information science, as well as projects that conduct research and/or demonstrations that will assist in the evaluation of library services, including economic, social, and cultural implications of services and other contributions to a community.

The University of Arizona School of Information Resources and Library Science (SIRLS) in Tucson was awarded approximately $500,000 for a two-year project to create the Knowledge River Institute, a master's degree program to attract Native Americans and Hispanics to the field of library and information science. The Enoch Pratt Free Library of Baltimore was granted $84,000 for a two-year project to produce 20 multimedia storytelling performances of multicultural stories to be featured on the library's Web site and distributed to area schools, Maryland library systems, and other institutions. The WGBH Educational Foundation Archives of Boston received just over $165,000 for a one-year Ten O'Clock News project to digitize and make available on the Web a video archive of the history and culture of Boston's African American community from 1974 to 1991 and to create a Web guide to the videos. The Cherokee National Historical Society of Tahlequah, Oklahoma, received just under $250,000 for a project to bring together the Cherokee Heritage Center and the Eastern Oklahoma District Library System to create eight traveling exhibits on the Cherokee tribe, along with programming packages that rotate to each of the 14 participating libraries throughout a two-year time frame.

In 2002, IMLS awarded 46 National Leadership Grants totaling just over $12 million. The University of California, Los Angeles received a grant of just over $196,000 to train eight professional librarians of diverse backgrounds in research, information technology, and policy to prepare them for future doctoral studies. Drexel University College of Information Science and Technology of Philadelphia received just over $233,000 to collaborate with the Free Library of Philadelphia in a three-year research project, Everyday Information-Seeking Behavior of Urban Young Adults, to develop and test tools for improving library and information service to young adults. The John M. Echols Collection on Southeast Asia of the Cornell University Library of Ithaca, New York, received a grant of approximately $281,500 for the Images of Southeast Asia project to digitize text and illustrations taken from early Western travel narratives and first-person accounts of life in Southeast Asia before 1927.[18]

IMLS Native American Library Services Enhancement Grants

In 2001, IMLS Native American Library Services Program awarded 13 Enhancement Grants averaging over $100,000. Tribes benefiting from the grants included the Central Council Tlingit and Haida Indian Tribes and the Sealaska Corporation, both of Juneau, Alaska; the Chilkoot Indian Association of Haines, Alaska; the Confederated Salish and Kootenai Tribes of the Flathead Reservation of Pablo, Montana; the Eastern Band of Cherokee Indians of Cherokee, North Carolina; the Fort Peck Assiniboine and Sioux Tribes of Poplar, Montana; the Igiugig Village in Igiugig, Alaska; the Iowa Tribe of Oklahoma of Perkins, Okalahoma; the Lac Courte Oreilles Band of the Lake Superior Chippewa of Hayward, Wisconsin; the Miami Tribe of Oklahoma in Miami, Oklahoma; the Saginaw Chippewa Indian Tribe of Michigan of Mount Pleasant, Michigan; the Washoe Tribe of Nevada and California of Gardnerville, Nevada; and the Yurok Tribe of Klamath, California.

In 2002, IMLS received 38 applications and awarded 12 Enhancement Grants totaling just over $1.5 million. Native Americans from Alaska, Montana, California, Michigan, Minnesota, South Dakota, and New Mexico benefited from grants for innovative service projects, staff and training, collections, furniture, shelving, equipment, and digitization.[19]

2002 White House Conference on School Libraries

During fiscal year 2002, the budget for the NCLIS was reduced from $1.5 million to $1 million. Ironically, NCLIS officials attended the first-ever First Lady Laura Bush White House Conference on School Libraries on June 4, 2002, the first White House Conference not under its sponsorship but under the sponsorship of the newly created IMLS. The conference spotlighted research that tied academic achievement directly to strong school-library media programs, at the same time that funding for educational projects were underfunded.[20]

ALA Presidential Initiatives for Minorities

At the 2003 ALA annual conference in Toronto, then President Maurice J. Freedman set in motion an initiative called the ALA Campaign for America's Librarians: Advocating for Better Salaries and Pay Equity for All Library Workers. Freedman's presidency also saw the launching in 2002 of the ALA Campaign to Save America's Libraries, a public-awareness effort focused on the impact of library funding cuts nationwide. Freedman commented that "these cuts are deeper than those sustained even in the Great Depression, and they are affecting library services in schools, college and university campuses, and communities everywhere." Freedman pledged to use his presidency to fight for programs and funding to ensure the recruitment, education, and retention of a diverse library workforce, including active support of the ALA Spectrum Scholarship Fund. The ALA Campaign to Save America's Libraries, trademarked "@ your library," took place in libraries nationwide in 2002 with the message that libraries are dynamic places of opportunity that present the world to their patrons. The campaign's global presence increased with 13 countries—Armenia, Australia, Azerbaijan, Bulgaria, Canada, Georgia, Iceland, Italy, Japan, Kazakhstan, Mexico, South Korea, and Turkey— joining the campaign.

During National Library Week in 2002, ALA launched the Rediscover America @ Your Library initiative as a response to the terrorist attacks of September 11, 2001. The message was that libraries are a resource for community dialogue on topics of national importance affecting all Americans. ALA also received a major cash sponsorship from Wells Fargo Home Mortgage for The Path to Homeownership Begins @ Your Library project, which was unveiled in July 2002 at the Mount Pleasant branch of the District of Columbia Public Library. U.S. Secretary of Housing and Urban Development Mel Martinez, and Derek Parra, program spokesperson and first Mexican American to win a medal in the Olympics, presided. The program was designed to promote home ownership among low- to moderate-income families and minorities. The program has been administered by ALA's Reference and Users Services Association (RUSA), which has provided new online reference materials and free home-ownership workshops in 10 U.S. cities.[21]

Future of Library Services with Minorities

The future of library services with minorities is inexplicably tied to the continuance of federal funding through LSTA and perhaps the establishment of other library funding initiatives at the federal level. As the United States has become more entangled in the global war on terror, library services have already suffered from substantial cuts. The latest cut in the budget of the NCLIS, from $1.5 to $1 million, is tantamount to the death knell for this organization. The very fact that LSCA funds were distributed by the Department of Education and the LSTA funds by the newly created IMLS, both circumventing NCLIS involvement, further accentuates the reality that NCLIS's influence is waning rapidly.

When federal funding is cut, the first library services to suffer are those geared toward minority and special population groups—immigrants, Native Americans, Hispanic Americans, and the disabled. Federal funding of libraries is relatively new, lasting for 50 years as of 2006. The levels of funding, however, are decreasing, and federal grant funds are not increasing to match higher levels of immigration alone. Federal funding for libraries in times of concerns for homeland security and the global war on terrorism has begun the downward slope.

Will the struggle for equality for all U.S. citizens, regardless of race or national origins, move forward? The answer is complex and unclear. What is clear is that federal funding for libraries is no longer the priority it was 50 years ago.

NOTES

1. Otis L. Graham Jr., *Unguarded Gates: A History of America's Immigration Crisis* (Lanham, MD: Rowman & Littlefield Publishers, 2004), xiii–xv, 158.

2. Ibid., 164.

3. Electronic Privacy Information Center, "The USA Patriot Act," http://www.epic.org/privacy/terrorism/usapatriot/.

4. Graham, *Unguarded Gates*, 165–69.

5. Ibid., 174–76.

6. Ibid., 173–77.

7. Ibid., 173.

8. Ibid., 172, 193; Center for Immigration Studies, http://www.cis.org/aboutcis.html.

9. Maurice J. Freedman, "American Library Association," in *Bowker Annual 2003: Library and Book Trade Almanac*, 48th ed. (Medford, NJ: Information Today, 2003), 137–38; Emily Sheketoff and Mary R. Costabile, "Legislation and Regula-

tions Affecting Libraries in 2001," in *Bowker Annual 2002: Library and Book Trade Almanac,* 47th ed. (Medford, NJ: Information Today, 2002), 306–10.

10. Freedman, "American Library Association," 138–39.

11. Ibid., 139–41.

12. Ibid., 142.

13. Ibid., 142–43.

14. Ibid., 144.

15. Ibid., 144–45.

16. Ibid., 133; ALA Resolution on the USA PATRIOT Act, http://www. ala.org/ala/washoff/WOissues/civilliberties/theusapatriotact/alaresolution.htm; Sheketoff and Costabile, "Legislation and Regulations Affecting Libraries in 2001," 319–20.

17. Robert S. Martin, "Institute of Museum and Library Services, Library Programs," in *Bowker Annual 2002: Library and Book Trade Almanac,* 47th ed. (Medford, NJ: Information Today, 2002), 343–44; Robert S. Martin, "Institute of Museum and Library Services, Library Programs," in *Bowker Annual 2003: Library and Book Trade Almanac,* 48th ed. (Medford, NJ: Information Today, 2003), 348–49; Sheketoff and Costabile, "Legislation and Regulations Affecting Libraries in 2001," 303; Emily Sheketoff and Mary R. Costabile, "Legislation and Regulations Affecting Libraries in 2002," in *Bowker Annual 2003: Library and Book Trade Almanac,* 48th ed. (Medford, NJ: Information Today, 2003), 306–8.

18. Martin, "Institute of Museum and Library Services, Library Programs," in *Bowker Annual 2002,* 346–53; Martin, "Institute of Museum and Library Services, Library Programs," in *Bowker Annual 2003,* 351–58.

19. Martin, "Institute of Museum and Library Services, Library Programs," in *Bowker Annual 2002,* 354–56; Martin, "Institute of Museum and Library Services, Library Programs," in *Bowker Annual 2003,* 358–60.

20. Robert S. Willard, "National Commission on Libraries and Information Science," in *Bowker Annual 2003: Library and Book Trade Almanac,* 48th ed. (Medford, NJ: Information Today, 2003), 104; Sheketoff and Costabile, "Legislation and Regulations Affecting Libraries in 2001," in *Bowker Annual 2002,* 302–3; Freedman, "American Library Association," 131.

21. Freedman, "American Library Association," 130–32.

SELECTED BIBLIOGRAPHY

BOOKS, PAMPHLETS, AND GOVERNMENT DOCUMENTS

Alire, Camila, and Orlando Archibeque. *Service to Latino Communities: A How-To-Do-It Manual for Librarians.* New York: Neal-Schuman Publishers, 1998.

Allen, Adela Artola, ed. *Library Services for Hispanic Children: A Guide for Public and School Librarians.* Phoenix: Oryx Press, 1987.

Allerton Park Institute, 17th, 1971. *Libraries and Neighborhood Information Centers.* Papers presented at an Institute conducted by the University of Illinois, Graduate School of Library Science, October 25–27, 1971, ed. Carol L. Kronus and Linda Crowe. Urbana: University of Illinois, Graduate School of Library Science, 1972.

Archdeacon, Thomas J. *Becoming American: An Ethnic History.* New York: Free Press, 1983.

Ayala, Reynaldo, and Marta Stiefel Ayala. *Report Card on Public Library Services to the Latino Community.* Calexico, CA: REFORMA, 1994.

Beilke, Patricia, and Frank J. Sciara. *Selecting Materials for and about Hispanic and East Asian Children and Young People.* Hamden, CT: Library Professional Publications, 1986.

Bennett, Marion T. *American Immigration Policies: A History.* Washington, DC: Public Affairs Press, 1963.

Black, Donald V., Herbert R. Seiden, and Ann W. Luke. *Evaluation of LSCA Services to Special Target Groups: Final Report.* Washington, DC: Systems Development Corporation, 1973.

Book Reading and Library Usage; A Study of Habits and Perceptions. Conducted for the American Library Association. Princeton: Gallup Organization, 1978.

Boyer, Paul S., and Melvyn Dubofsky, eds. *Oxford Companion to United States History.* New York: Oxford University Press, 2001.

Brown, Eleanor Frances. *Library Service to the Disadvantaged.* Metuchen, NJ: Scarecrow Press, 1971.

Brown, Mary Elizabeth. *Shapers of the Great Debate on Immigration: A Biographical Dictionary.* Westport, CT: Greenwood Press, 1999.

Bundy, Mary Lee, and Sylvia Goodstein, eds. *The Library's Public Revisited: By Members of the Class in The Public Library in the Political Process.* Student Contribution Series, no. 1. College Park: School of Library and Information Services, University of Maryland, 1967.

California State Library. *Catalog of Local Assistance: Library Services and Construction Act, Titles I, II, III, 1976–1989.* Sacramento: California State Library, 1988.

———. "Special Issue: LSCA in California [LSCA Projects, 1957–1976]." Foreword by Ethel S. Crockett, California State Librarian. Introduction by Ruth Kerstead, State Library Consultant. *News Notes of California Libraries* 71, no. 2 (1976): 1–119.

Carlson, David B., Arabella Martinez, Sarah A. Curtis, Janet Coles, and Nicholas A. Valenzuela. *Adrift in a Sea of Change: California's Public Libraries Struggle to Meet the Information Needs of Multicultural Communities.* Partnerships for Change Series, no. 2. Sacramento: California State Library, Center for Policy Development, 1990.

Chiswick, Barry R., ed. *The Gateway: U.S. Immigration Issues and Policies.* Washington, DC: American Enterprise Institute for Public Policy Research, 1982.

Cohen, David. *Multi-Ethnic Media: Selected Bibliographies in Print.* Chicago: American Library Association, 1975.

Collantes, Lourdes Y., ed. *Asian/Pacific American Librarians: A Cross Cultural Perspective.* Papers of the 1984 Program of the Asian/Pacific American Librarians Association, June 25, 1984, Dallas, Texas. New York: Asian/Pacific American Librarians Association, 1985.

Constantino, Rebecca, ed. *Literacy, Access, and Libraries Among the Language Minority Population.* Lanham, MD: Scarecrow Press, 1998.

Coplan, Kate, and Edwin Castagna, eds. *The Library Reaches Out: Reports on Library Service and Community Relations by Some Leading American Librarians.* Dobbs Ferry, NY: Oceana Publications, 1965.

Cordasco, Francesco ed. *Dictionary of American Immigration History.* Metuchen, NJ: Scarecrow Press, 1990.

Cordasco, Francesco. *The Immigrant Woman in North America: An Annotated Bibliography of Selected References.* Metuchen, NJ: Scarecrow Press, 1985.

Divine, Robert A. *American Immigration Policy, 1924–1952.* New Haven: Yale University Press, 1957.

Dougherty, Richard M., Jane Anne Hannigan, James W. Liesener, Peggy Sullivan, Douglas L. Zweizig, and American Association of School Librarians. *Libraries and the Learning Society: Papers in Response to* A Nation at Risk. Chicago: ALA, 1984.

DuMont, Rosemary Ruhig, Lois Buttlar, and William Caynon. *Multiculturalism in Libraries.* Westport, CT: Greenwood Press, 1994.

Dyer, Esther R., comp. *Cultural Pluralism & Children's Media.* Chicago: ALA, 1978.

Equity at Issue: Library Services to the Nation's Four Major Minority Groups, 1985– 86; Report of the President's Committee on Library Services to Minorities. Chicago: ALA, 1986.

Freeman, Robert S., and David M. Hovde, eds. *Libraries to the People: Histories of Outreach.* Foreword by Kathleen de la Pena McCook. Jefferson, NC: McFarland, 2003.

Glass Schuman, Patricia, comp. and ed. *Social Responsibilities and Libraries: A Library Journal/School Library Journal Selection.* New York: R.R. Bowker, 1976.

Gleason, Eliza Atkins. *The Southern Negro and the Public Library: A Study of the Government and Administration of Public Library Service to Negroes in the South.* With a foreword by Louis R. Wilson. Chicago: University of Chicago Press, 1941.

Graham, Patterson Toby. *A Right to Read: Segregation and Civil Rights in Alabama's Public Libraries, 1900–1965.* Tuscaloosa: University of Alabama Press, 2002.

Guerena, Salvador, ed. *Latino Librarianship: A Handbook for Professionals.* Jefferson, NC: McFarland, 1990.

———. *Library Services to Latinos: An Anthology.* Jefferson, NC: McFarland, 2000.

Haar, Charles M. *Between the Idea and the Reality: A Study in the Origin, Fate, and Legacy of the Model Cities Program.* Boston: Little, Brown, 1975.

Haro, Robert P. *Developing Library and Information Services for Americans of Hispanic Origin.* Metuchen, NJ: Scarecrow Press, 1981.

Hayden, Carla, ed. *Venture into Cultures: A Resource Book of Multicultural Materials and Programs.* 1st ed. Chicago: ALA, 1992.

Heim, Kathleen M. and Danny P. Wallace, eds. *Adult Services: An Enduring Focus for Public Libraries.* Chicago: ALA, 1990.

Hill, Katherine Hoover, ed. *Diversity and Multiculturalism in Libraries.* Greenwich, CT: JAI Press, 1994.

Hispano Library Services for Arizona, Colorado and New Mexico: A Workshop Held in Santa Fe, New Mexico. Boulder, CO: Western Interstate Commission for Higher Education, 1970.

Holley, Edward G., and Robert F. Schremser. *The Library Services and Construction Act: An Historical Overview from the Viewpoint of Major Participants.* Greenwich, CT: JAI Press, 1983.

Hornsby, Alton. *Chronology of African–American History: Significant Events and People from 1619 to the Present.* Detroit: Gale Research, 1991.

Hoxie, Frederick E., ed. *Encyclopedia of North American Indians.* Boston: Houghton Mifflin, 1996.

Hubach, Charlotte J. "New York's Ottendorfer Branch Library." *Stechert-Hafner Book News* 8 (May 1954): 101–3.

Huff, Delores J. *To Live Heroically: Institutional Racism and American Indian Education.* Albany: State University of New York, 1997.

Hutchinson, Edward Prince. *Legislative History of American Immigration Policy, 1798–1965.* Philadelphia: Published for the Balch Institute for Ethnic Studies, by the University of Pennsylvania Press, 1981.

Immroth, Barbara, Kathleen de la Pena McCook, assisted by Catherine Jasper, eds. *Library Services to Youth of Hispanic Heritage.* Jefferson, NC: McFarland, 2000.

International Research Associates, prep. *Access to Public Libraries: A Research Project.* Prepared for the Library Administration Division, American Library Association. Chicago: ALA, 1963.

Jiobu, Robert M. *Ethnicity and Assimilation.* Albany: State University New York Press, 1988.

Jones, Maldwyn Allen. *American Immigration.* 2nd ed. Chicago: University of Chicago Press, 1992.

Jones, Plummer Alston, Jr. *Libraries, Immigrants, and the American Experience.* Westport, CT: Greenwood Press, 1999.

Josey, E. J., and Marva L. DeLoach, eds. *Ethnic Collections in Libraries.* New York: Neal-Schuman Publishers, 1983.

Josey, E. J., and Ann Allen Shockley, comps and eds. *Handbook of Black Librarianship.* Littleton, CO: Libraries Unlimited, 1977.

Josey, E. J., ed. *Libraries in the Political Process.* Phoenix: Oryx Press, 1980.

Josey, E. J., and Kenneth E. Peeples Jr., eds. *Opportunities for Minorities in Librarianship.* Metuchen, NJ: Scarecrow Press, 1977.

Kahn, Alfred J., Lawrence Grossman, Jean Bandler, Felicia Clark, Florence Galkin, and Kent Greenawatt. *Neighborhood Information Centers: A Study and Some Proposals.* New York: Columbia University School of Social Work, 1966.

Kent, Allen, and Harold Lancour, eds. *Encyclopedia of Library and Information Science.* New York: Marcel Dekker, 1968– .

Knight, Douglas M., and E. Shepley Nourse, eds. *Libraries at Large: Tradition, Innovation, and the National Interest.* New York: R. R. Bowker, 1969.

Kobayashi, Vivian, and Irene Yeh, coords. *Asian Languages Library Materials: Chinese, Phillipino, Vietnamese Bibliographies.* Sacramento: California Ethnic Services Task Force, California State Library, 1979.

Kuharets, Olga R., ed. *Venture into Cultures: A Resource Book of Multicultural Materials and Programs.* For the Ethnic and Multicultural Information Exchange Round Table. 2nd ed. Chicago: ALA, 2001.

Ladenson, Alex. *Library Law and Legislation in the United States.* Metuchen, NJ: Scarecrow Press, 1982.

Lee, Robert Ellis. *Continuing Education for Adults through the American Public Library, 1833–1964.* Chicago: ALA, 1966.

LeMay, Michael C. *From Open Door to Dutch Door: An Analysis of U.S. Immigration Policy Since 1820.* New York: Praeger, 1987.

Liu, Grace F. *Promoting Library Awareness in Ethnic Communities: Based on the Experiences of the South Bay Cooperative Library System, 1984–1985.* Sacramento: Underserved Community Library Awareness Project, California State Library, 1985.

Lollock, Lisa. *The Foreign Born Population in the United States: March 2000.* Current Population Reports, P20–534. Washington, DC: U.S. Census Bureau, 2000.

MacCann, Donnarae, ed. *Social Responsibility in Librarianship: Essays on Equality.* Jefferson, NC: McFarland, 1989.

Martin, Lowell A. *Baltimore Reaches Out: Library Service to the Disadvantaged.* Deiches Fund Studies of Public Library Services, no. 3. Baltimore: Enoch Pratt Free Library, 1967.

———. *Enrichment: A History of the Public Library in the United States in the Twentieth Century.* Lanham, MD: Scarecrow Press, 1998.

———. *Library Response to Urban Change: A Study of the Chicago Public Library.* Chicago: American Library Association, 1969.

Martin, William, ed. *Library Services to the Disadvantaged.* Hamden, CT: Linnet Books, 1975.

Mersel, Jules, Morton H. Friedman, Emory H. Holmes, John F. Knudson, and Eugene R. Streich. *An Overview of the Library Services and Construction Act-Title I.* New York: R.R. Bowker, 1969.

Metoyer-Duran, Cheryl. *Gatekeepers in Ethnolinguistic Communities.* Norwood, NJ: Ablex Publishing, 1993.

Michael, M.E., and L. Encarnacion. *An Evaluation of the El Centro de la Causa library and Information Center: August 1973 through July 1974: Final Report.* ED 107291. Urbana: University of Illinois Library Research Center, 1973.

Miller, E. Willard, and Ruby M. Miller. *United States Immigration: A Reference Handbook.* Santa Barbara, CA: ABC-CLIO, 1996.

Moen, William E., and Kathleen M. Heim, eds. *Librarians for the New Millennium.* Chicago: ALA, Office for Library Personnel Resources, 1988.

Molz, R. Kathleen. *The Federal Roles in Support of Public Library Services: An Overview.* Prepared for the Federal Roles in Support of Public Library Services Project. Chicago: ALA, 1990.

Monroe, Margaret E. *Library Adult Education: The Biography of An Idea.* New York: Scarecrow Press, 1963.

National Citizens Emergency Committee to Save Our Public Libraries. *Continu-ing Education Services: How Public Libraries Can Expand Educational Horizons for All Americans.* In *The Changing Role of Public Libraries: Background Papers from the White House Conference,* comp. Whitney North Seymour Jr. Metuchen, NJ: Scarecrow Press, 1980; copyright 1979, 1980 by the New York Public Library.

————. *Neighborhood Information Service Centers: Public Library "Information and Referral": Provides Significant New Personal Service to the Individual Library User.* In *The Changing Role of Public Libraries: Background Papers from the White House Conference,* comp. Whitney North Seymour Jr. Metuchen, NJ: Scarecrow Press, 1980; copyright 1979, 1980 by the New York Public Library.

————. *Serving Citizens with Special Needs: How Libraries Can Enrich Lives and Fulfill Aspirations for the Elderly and the Handicapped, the Functionally Illiterate, Hispanic Americans, Native Americans, the Homebound and Inmates of Correctional Institutions.* In *The Changing Role of Public Libraries: Background Papers from the White House Conference,* comp. Whitney North Seymour Jr. Metuchen, NJ: Scarecrow Press, 1980; copyright 1979, 1980 by the New York Public Library.

————. *Strengthening the Library Profession: New Approaches Are Needed in the Recruiting and Training of America's Future Librarians.* In *The Changing Role of Public Libraries: Background Papers from the White House Conference,* comp. Whitney North Seymour Jr. Metuchen, NJ: Scarecrow Press, 1980; copyright 1979, 1980 by the New York Public Library.

Nauratil, Marcia J. *Public Libraries and Nontraditional Clienteles: The Politics of Special Services.* Westport, CT: Greenwood Press, 1985.

New York State Education Department, Social Studies Review and Development Committee. *One Nation, Many Peoples: A Declaration of Cultural Independence: The Report of the New York State Social Studies Review and Development Com-mittee.* Albany: New York State Education Dept., 1991.

New York State Education Department, Task Force on Minorities. *"A Curricu-lum of Inclusion": A Report to the Commissioner of Education by the Task Force on Minorities: Equity and Excellence.* Albany: New York State Education Dept., 1989.

Padilla, Amado M. *Public Library Services for Immigrant Populations in Califor-nia: A Report to the State Librarian of California.* Sacramento: California State Library Foundation, 1991.

Parrish, Karen, and Bill Katz, eds. *Multicultural Acquisitions.* New York: Haworth Press, 1993.

Payne, Judith, Martha Samulon, Peter Morrison, Carole Oken, Rick Eden, and Larry Picus. *Public Libraries Face California's Ethnic and Racial Diversity.* Pre-pared for the Stanford University Libraries with a grant from the California State Library. Santa Monica, CA: Rand Corporation, 1988.

Public Library Service to the Disadvantaged. Proceedings of an Institute, December 7th and 8th, 1967. Atlanta: Division of Librarianship, Emory University, 1969.

Samore, Theodore, ed. *Acquisition of Foreign Materials for U.S. Libraries.* Metuchen, NJ: Scarecrow Press, 1973.

———. *Acquisition of Foreign Materials for U.S. Libraries.* 2nd ed. Metuchen, NJ: Scarecrow Press, 1982.

Scarborough, Katharine T. A., ed. *Developing Library Collections for California's Emerging Majority: A Manual of Resources for Ethnic Collection Development.* Produced in conjunction with the conference Developing Library Collections for California's Emerging Majority, September 22–23, 1990, San Francisco, California. Berkeley: Bay Area Library and Information System; University Extension, University of California; School of Library and Information Studies, University of California, 1990.

Seymour, Whitney North, Jr., comp. *The Changing Role of Public Libraries: Background Papers from the White House Conference.* Metuchen, NJ: Scarecrow Press, 1980; copyright 1979, 1980 by the New York Public Library.

Sherrill, Laurence L., ed. *Library Service to the Unserved: Papers Presented at a Library Conference Held at the University of Wisconsin–Milwaukee, School of Library and Information Science, November 16–18, 1967.* Library and Information Science Studies, no. 2. New York: R. R. Bowker, 1970.

Smith, Helen Lyman. *Adult Education Activities in Public Libraries.* Chicago: ALA, 1954.

Smith, Joshua I., ed. *Library and Information Services for Special Groups.* New York: Published in cooperation with the American Society for Information Science and the ERIC Clearinghouse on Library and Information Sciences, by Science Associates/International, 1974.

Stueart, Robert D., ed. *Information Needs of the 80s: Libraries and Information Services Role in "Bringing Information to People" Based on the Deliberations of the White House Conference on Library and Information Services.* Foundations in Library and Information Science, vol. 15. Greenwich, CT: JAI Press, 1982.

Taylor, Theodore W. *The Bureau of Indian Affairs.* Foreword by Phillip Martin. Boulder, CO: Westview Press, 1984.

Thernstrom, Stephan, Ann Orlov, and Oscar Handlin, eds. *Harvard Encyclopedia of American Ethnic Groups.* Cambridge: Belknap Press of Harvard University Press, 1980.

Thomison, Dennis. *A History of the American Library Association, 1876–1972.* Chicago: ALA, 1978.

Turick, Dorothy. *Community Information Services in Libraries.* *LJ* Special Report #5. New York: Library Journal, 1978.

Unger, Harlow G., ed. *Encyclopedia of American Education.* 2nd ed. New York: Facts on File, c2001, 1996.

Urzua, Roberto, Martha P. Cotera, and Emma Gonzalez Stupp, eds. *Library Services to Mexican Americans: Policies, Practices and Prospects.* Prepared by Project Staff, University of Texas, Nettie Lee Benson Latin American Collection,

Mexican American Library Project. Las Cruces, NM: New Mexico State University for Educational Resources Information Center Clearinghouse on Rural Education and Small Schools, 1978.

U.S. Census Bureau. *Statistical Abstract of the United States: 2001.* 121st ed. Washington, DC: Government Printing Office, 2001.

U.S. Immigration and Naturalization Service. "Appendix 1: Immigration and Naturalization Legislation." In *Statistical Yearbook of the Immigration and Naturalization Service, 1997.* Washington, DC: U.S.G.P.O, 1999.

U.S. National Commission on Libraries and Information Science. *Library and Information Services Needs of the Nation: Proceedings of a Conference on the Needs of Occupational, Ethnic, and Other Groups in the United States.* Washington, DC: U.S. G.P.O., 1974.

———. Task Force on Library and Information Services to Cultural Minorities. *Report of the Task Force on Library and Information Services to Cultural Minorities.* Washington, DC: NCLIS, 1983.

U.S. Office of Education. *Public Libraries in the United States: Their History, Condition, and Management.* Washington, DC: U.S. G.P.O., 1976.

Walsh, R. Taylor, prep. *National Information Infrastructure and the Recommendations of the 1991 White House Conference on Library and Information Services.* Washington, DC: NCLIS, 1994.

Wasserman, Paul, and Alice E. Kennington, eds. *Ethnic Information Sources of the United States: A Guide to Organizations, Agencies, Foundations, Institutions, Media, Commercial and Trade Bodies, Government Programs, Research Institutes, Libraries and Museums, Religious Organizations, Banking Firms, Festivals and Fairs, Travel and Tourist Offices, Airlines and Ship Lines, Book Dealers and Publishers' Representatives, and Books, Pamphlets, and Audiovisuals on Specific Ethnic Groups.* 2nd ed. Detroit: Gale Research, 1983.

Weibel, Kathleen. *Interagency Cooperation in Expanding Library Services to Disadvantaged Adults.* Appalachian Adult Education Center, Morehead State University, Public Library Training Institutes, Library Service Guide, no. 25. Chicago: ALA, 1977.

Wetterau, Bruce. *The New York Public Library Book of Chronologies.* New York: Stonesong Press of Prentice Hall Press, 1990.

Wiegand, Wayne A. *"An Active Instrument for Propaganda": The American Public Library during World War I.* Foreword by Edward G. Holley. Beta Phi Mu Monograph, no. 1. Westport, CT: Greenwood Press, 1989.

Wiegand, Wayne A., and Davis, Donald G. Jr., eds. *Encyclopedia of Library History.* New York: Garland Publishing, 1994.

World Encyclopedia of Library and Information Services. 3rd ed. Chicago: ALA, 1993.

Wynar, Lubomyr R., Lois Buttlar, and Anna T. Wynar, eds. *Encyclopedic Directory of Ethnic Organizations in the United States.* Littleton, CO: Libraries Unlimited, 1975.

Yin, Robert K., Brigitte L. Kenney, and Karen B. Possner. *Neighborhood Communications Centers: Planning Information and Referral Services in the Urban Library.* Prepared under a grant from the John and Mary R. Markle Foundation. Santa Monica, CA: RAND Corporation, 1974.

ARTICLES, CHAPTERS, AND ESSAYS

Abdullahi, Ismail. "Library Services to Multicultural Populations." In *Encyclopedia of Library and Information Science*, ed. Allen Kent. Vol. 48. New York: Marcel Dekker, 1976.

Aguirre, JoAnn K. "Passport to Promise: Public Libraries as Intellectual Spaces for Immigrant Students." In *Library Services to Latinos: An Anthology*, ed. Salvador Guerena. Jefferson, NC: McFarland, 2000.

"Alabama Civil Rights Campaigners Start with Public Library." *Library Journal* 90 (July 1965): 2992.

Allen, Ardela Artola. "Library Services for Hispanic Young Adults." *Library Trends* 37 (Summer 1988): 80–105.

Alloway, David Nelson. "Asia Pacific Triangle." In *Dictionary of American Immigration History*, ed. Francesco Cordasco. Metuchen, NJ: Scarecrow Press, 1990.

American Library Association. Ethnic and Multicultural Information Exchange Round Table. Library Education Task Force. "Ethnic and Minority Concerns in Library Education." *EMIE Bulletin* 6 (Summer 1989): 6–10.

American Library Association. Reference and Adult Services Division. Committee on Library Services to the Spanish Speaking "Guidelines for Library Services to Hispanics." *RQ* 27 (Summer 1988): 491–93. Also published in *Journal of Multicultural Librarianship* 2 (Mar. 1988): 57–60.

Archdeacon, Thomas J. "Immigration Law." In *Oxford Companion to United States History*, ed. Paul S. Boyer and Melvyn Dubofsky. New York: Oxford University Press, 2001.

Ardito-Kirkland, Stephanie. "Chicago: Suburban Libraries and the Spanish Speaking." *Wilson Library Bulletin* 53 (Nov. 1978): 239–42.

Asch, Stephanie. "Urban Libraries Confront Linguistic Minorities: Programs That Work." In *Literacy, Access, and Libraries Among the Language Minority Population*, ed. Constantino, Rebecca. Lanham, MD: Scarecrow Press, 1998.

Aversa, Alfred, Jr. "Ethnic Studies." In *Dictionary of American Immigration History*, ed. Francesco Cordasco. Metuchen, NJ: Scarecrow Press, 1990.

Axam, John A. "Philadelphia: The Reader Development Program." *Wilson Library Bulletin* 43 (May 1969): 894–97.

Ayala, John L. "REFORMA." In *ALA Yearbook 1976: A Review of Library Events, 1975.* Chicago: American Library Association, 1976.

Ayala, Marta Stiefel. "Daniel Flores Duran [Interview]." *Wilson Library Bulletin* 53 (Nov. 1978): 235.

———. "Laura Gutierrez-Witt [Interview]." *Wilson Library Bulletin* 53 (Nov. 1978): 238.

———. "Laurita Moore [Interview]." *Wilson Library Bulletin* 53 (Nov. 1978): 258.

———. "Lilian [i.e., Lillian] Lopez [Interview]." *Wilson Library Bulletin* 53 (Nov. 1978): 249.

———. "Luis Chaparro [Interview]." *Wilson Library Bulletin* 53 (Nov. 1978): 267.

———. "Martha Cotera [Interview]." *Wilson Library Bulletin* 53 (Nov. 1978): 254.

———. "Martha Tome [Interview]." *Wilson Library Bulletin* 53 (Nov. 1978): 243.

———. "How One Library-less Librarian Got the Word Out." *Wilson Library Bulletin* 53 (Nov. 1978): 255–57.

Baeza, Gilda. "The Evolution of Educational and Public Library Services to Spanish-Speaking Children." In *Library Services for Hispanic Children: A Guide for Public and School Librarians,* ed. Adela Artola Allen. Phoenix: Oryx Press, 1987.

Barber, Philip W. "Relocation Centers: Heart Mountain, Wyoming." *Library Journal* 68 (15 Feb. 1943): 174–75.

Belay, Gitinet. "Conceptual Strategies for Operationalizing Multicultural Curricula." *Journal of Education for Library and Information Science* 4 (Fall 1992): 295–306.

Bell, Bernice Lloyd. "Public Library Integration in Thirteen Southern States." *Library Journal* 88 (15 Dec. 1963): 4713–15.

Benavides, Alfredo H. "Social Responsibility: A Bilingual/Multicultural Perspective." In *Social Responsibility in Librarianship: Essays on Equality,* ed. Donnarae MacCann. Jefferson, NC: McFarland, 1989.

Bennette, Guy. "San Francisco: Down These Meaningful Streets." *Wilson Library Bulletin* 43 (May 1969): 872–75.

Benson, Nancy Dollahite. "Welcome to America From the Library." *Public Libraries* 22 (Summer 1983): 54–56.

"Bergenfield Public Teaches English." *Wilson Library Bulletin* 55 (Dec. 1980): 253.

Bernard, William S. "Immigration: History of U.S. Policy." In *Harvard Encyclopedia of American Ethnic Groups,* ed. Stephan Thernstrom, Ann Orlov, and Oscar Handlin. Cambridge: Belknap Press of Harvard University Press, 1980.

Berry, John. "A TIP from Detroit." *Library Journal* 100 (July 1975): 1287–90.

Betancourt, Ingrid. "REFORMA." In *ALA Yearbook of Library and Information Services, 1989: A Review of Library Events, 1988.* Chicago: American Library Association, 1989.

Bezugloff, Natalia B. "Library Services to Non-English-Language Ethnic Minorities in the United States." *Library Trends* 29 (Fall 1980): 259–74.

"Bilingual Program at Newark Public Library Wins Approval of the Florence & John Schumann Foundation & the Victoria Foundation." *New Jersey Libraries* 12 (Feb. 1979): 28.

Biro, Ruth Ghering. "Multicultural Resources for Libraries." *Catholic Library World* 51 (Mar. 1980): 331–35.

Black, Donald V. "Library Needs of the Disadvantaged." In National Commission on Libraries and Information Science, *Library and Information Services Needs of the Nation: Proceedings of a Conference on the Needs of Occupational, Ethnic, and Other Groups in the United States.* Washington, DC: U.S. G.P.O., 1974.

Boles, Suzanne. "Helping Vietnamese Refugees." *The Unabashed Librarian* No. 16 (Summer 1975): 5.

Bolino, August C. "Ellis Island." In *Dictionary of American Immigration History,* ed. Francesco Cordasco. Metuchen, NJ: Scarecrow Press, 1990.

Borman, Leonard D. "Melting Pots, Vanishing Americans, and Other Myths." *Library Trends* 20 (Oct. 1971): 210–22.

Boyvey, Mary. "Library Services to Mexican Americans." *Texas Libraries* 32 (Fall 1970): 136–37.

Brady, Kathy. "Letters from Home: Love and Friendship in Times of War: With Books and Moral Support, a Children's Librarian [Clara Estelle Breed] Helped Young Japanese Americans Endure Internment During World War II." *American Libraries* 33 (May 2002): 73–74.

Braverman, Miriam. "In Touch: Connecting the Library's Resources to the Ghetto." *Wilson Library Bulletin* 43 (May 1969): 854–57.

Breed, Clara E. "All But Blind." *Library Journal* 68 (1 Feb. 1943): 119–21.

Britto, Kay. "What Language Do You Speak?" *Voice of Youth Advocates* 10 (Apr. 1987): 19–20.

Brown, Mary Elizabeth. "Alan K. Simpson (1931–): "There Can Be No Perfect Immigrant Reform Bill." In *Shapers of the Great Debate on Immigration: A Biographical Dictionary.* Westport, CT: Greenwood Press, 1999.

———. "Edward M. Kennedy (1932–): Immigration as a Solution to Other Problems." In *Shapers of the Great Debate on Immigration: A Biographical Dictionary.* Westport, CT: Greenwood Press, 1999.

———. "Patrick Anthony McCarran (1876–1954): Cold War Immigration." In *Shapers of the Great Debate on Immigration: A Biographical Dictionary.* Westport, CT: Greenwood Press, 1999.

Bruno, Frank Alan, and Patricia F. Beilke. "Filipinos and Filipino Americans: Helping K-8 School Librarians and Educators Understand Their History, Culture, and Literature." *MultiCultural Review* 9 (June 2000): 30–37, 53–54.

Bucy, Frances A. "Denver, Colorado: El Numero Cinco." *Wilson Library Bulletin* 44 (March 1970): 765–66.

Caballero, Cesar. "El Paso: The Movement Is Forward." *Wilson Library Bulletin* 53 (Nov. 1978): 232–34.

———. "REFORMA." In *ALA Yearbook 1981: A Review of Library Events, 1980.* Chicago: ALA, 1981.

Cabello-Argandona, Roberto. "Academic Librarianship and the Chicano." In *Opportunities for Minorities in Librarianship,* ed, E.J. Josey and Kenneth E. Peeples Jr. Metuchen, NJ: Scarecrow Press, 1977.

————. "Recruiting Spanish-Speaking Library Students." In *Social Responsibilities and Libraries: A Library Journal/School Library Journal Selection,* comp. and ed. Patricia Glass Schuman. New York: R. R. Bowker, 1976.

————, and Eleanor Ross Crary. "The California Spanish Language Data Base: Development of Bilingual Access to Collections." *Catholic Library World* 52 (Apr. 1981): 372–75.

————, and Eleanor Ross Crary. "California Spanish Language Data Base: Bilingual Access to Collections." In *Latin American Economic Issues: Information Needs and Sources: Papers of the Twenty-Sixth Seminar on the Acquisition of Latin American Library Materials, Tulane University, New Orleans, Louisiana, April 1–4, 1981.* [Madison]: SALALM Secretariat, University of Wisconsin–Madison; [Los Angeles]: UCLA Latin American Center Publications, University of California, Los Angeles, 1984.

————, and Roberto P. Haro. "Library Services for the Spanish Speaking: A Systematic Review and Analysis." In *Library Services to Mexican Americans: Policies, Practices and Prospects,* ed. Roberto Urzua, Martha P. Cotera, and Emma Gonzalez Stupp. Prepared by Project Staff, University of Texas, Nettie Lee Benson Latin American Collection, Mexican American Library Project. Las Cruces, NM: New Mexico State University for Educational Resources Information Center Clearinghouse on Rural Education and Small Schools, 1978.

Cain, Charlene. "Public Library Service to Minorities." In *Adult Services: An Enduring Focus for Public Libraries,* ed. Kathleen M. Heim and Danny P. Wallace. Chicago: ALA, 1990.

Carnesi, Monica Scheliga, and Maria A. Fiol. "Queens Library's New Americans Program: 23 Years of Services to Immigrants." In *Library Services to Latinos: An Anthology,* ed. Salvador Guerena. Jefferson, NC: McFarland, 2000.

Casey, Genevieve M. "Library Service to the Handicapped and Institutionalized." *Library Trends* 20 (Oct. 1971): 350–66.

Castagna, Edwin. "A Troubled Mixture: Our Attitudes Toward the Unserved as Librarians in a Professional Capacity." In *Library Service to the Unserved: Papers Presented at a Library Conference Held at the University of Wisconsin–Milwaukee, School of Library and Information Science, November 16–18, 1967,* ed. Laurence L. Sherrill. Library and Information Science Studies, no. 2. New York: R. R. Bowker, 1970.

Celnik, Max, and Aronovitch, David. "Ethnic Groups, Library Service to: Jewish Americans." In *ALA Yearbook 1978: A Review of Library Events, 1977.* Chicago: ALA, 1978.

————. "Jewish Americans." In *ALA Yearbook 1977: A Review of Library Events, 1976.* Chicago: ALA, 1977.

Chabran, Richard. "U.S. Hispanic Data Bases: Contemporary Building Blocks for Future Information Systems." In *Latin American Economic Issues: Information Needs and Sources: Papers of the Twenty-Sixth Seminar on the Acquisition of Latin American Library Materials, Tulane University, New Orleans, Louisiana, April*

1–4, 1981. [Madison]: SALALM Secretariat, University of Wisconsin–Madison; [Los Angeles]: UCLA Latin American Center Publications, University of California, Los Angeles, 1984.

Chan, Sucheng. "Asians in California: A Selected Bibliography on Chinese, Japanese, Korean, Filipino, Asian Indian, and Vietnamese Immigrants and Their Descendants." *Immigration History Newsletter* 18 (Nov. 1986): 2–12.

———. "Selected Bibliography on the Chinese in the United States, 1850–1920." *Immigration History Newsletter* 16 (Nov. 1984): 7–15.

Chang, Henry C. "Asian/Pacific American Librarians: A Profile." In *Asian/Pacific American Librarians: A Cross Cultural Perspective*, ed. Lourdes Y. Collantes. Papers of the 1984 Program of the Asian/Pacific American Librarians Association, June 25, 1984, Dallas, Texas. New York: Asian/Pacific American Librarians Association, 1985.

———, and Suzine Har-Nicolescu. "Needs Assessment of Library Information Service for Asian American Community Members in the United States." In National Commission on Libraries and Information Science, Task Force on Library and Information Services to Cultural Minorities, *Report of the Task Force on Library and Information Services to Cultural Minorities*. Washington, DC: NCLIS, 1983.

Chapin, Helen G. "Hawaii, Ethnic Caucasians in Hawaii." In *Dictionary of American Immigration History*, ed. Francesco Cordasco. Metuchen, NJ: Scarecrow Press, 1990.

———. "Hawaiians." In *Dictionary of American Immigration History*, ed. Francesco Cordasco. Metuchen, NJ: Scarecrow Press, 1990.

Childers, Thomas. "The Neighborhood Information Center Project." *Library Quarterly* 46 (July 1976): 271–89.

Chiu, Norine. "Library Service to the Chinese-American Community." *Journal and Library & Information Science* 5 (Apr. 1979): 16–42.

Chu, Clara. "Education for Multicultural Librarianship." In *Multiculturalism in Libraries*, by Rosemary Ruhig DuMont, Lois Buttlar, and William Caynon. Westport, CT: Greenwood Press, 1994.

Clack, Doris Hargrett. "Segregation and the Library." In *Encyclopedia of Library and Information Science*, ed. Allen Kent, Harold Lancour, and Jay E. Daily. Vol. 27. New York: Marcel Dekker, 1979.

Coats, Reed. "Santa Clara: The Land of YAP." *Wilson Library Bulletin* 43 (May 1969): 901–903.

Cohen, David. "Ethnicity in Librarianship: A Rationale for Multiethnic Library Services in a Heterogeneous Society." *Library Trends* 29 (Fall 1980): 179–90.

———. "Ethnicity in Librarianship: Imperatives of Library Training Programs for Minority Groups." *Catholic Library World* 51 (Mar. 1980): 342–46.

———. "Narrative Evaluation Report on the Institute for Ethnicity and Librarianship: Based on Proceedings of the Institute for Ethnicity and Librarianship,

Queens College, CUNY, New York, July 7–25, 1975." ED 120 312. [Washington, DC]: ERIC, 1975.

———, and Laurence Sherrill. "Model and Course of Study for Library School Ethnic Curricula." *Ethnic Forum* 2 (Spring 1982): 51–58.

Cohen, Philip S. "The U.S. Immigration and Naturalization Service." In *Dictionary of American Immigration History*, ed. Francesco Cordasco. Metuchen, NJ: Scarecrow Press, 1990.

Colson, John C. "The United States: An Historical Critique." In *Library Services to the Disadvantaged*, ed. William Martin. Hamden, CT: Linnet Books, 1975.

"Coming from the Americas: A Profile of the Nation's Latin American Foreign Born." Census Brief. Washington, DC: U.S. Census Bureau, 2000.

"Coming to America: A Profile of the Nation's Foreign Born." Census Brief. Washington, DC: U.S. Census Bureau, 2000.

Conant, Ralph W. "Black Power in Urban American." *Library Journal* 93 (15 May 1968): 1963.

Conaway, Mary Christine. "Reaching the Unreached 'No Place' People." *Catholic Library World* 43 (Dec. 1971): 187–92.

Connor, Jean L. "The Ripple Effect: Patterns of Library Service to the Unserved as Seen from the State Level." In *Library Service to the Unserved: Papers Presented at a Library Conference Held at the University of Wisconsin–Milwaukee, School of Library and Information Science, November 16–18, 1967*, ed. Laurence L. Sherrill. Library and Information Science Studies, no. 2. New York: R. R. Bowker, 1970.

Constantino, Rebecca. " 'It's Like a Lot of Things in America': Linguistic Minority Parents' Use of Libraries." *School Library Media Quarterly* 22 (Winter 1994): 87–89.

Cooke, Eileen D. "Legislation to Assist Libraries to Serve the Unserved." In *Library Service to the Unserved: Papers Presented at a Library Conference Held at the University of Wisconsin–Milwaukee, School of Library and Information Science, November 16–18, 1967*, ed. Laurence L. Sherrill. Library and Information Science Studies, no. 2. New York: R. R. Bowker, 1970.

Coombs, Norman. "Afro-Americans." In *Dictionary of American Immigration History*, ed. Francesco Cordasco. Metuchen, NJ: Scarecrow Press, 1990.

Cordasco, Francesco. "Bilingual Education." In *Dictionary of American Immigration History*, ed. Francesco Cordasco. Metuchen, NJ: Scarecrow Press, 1990.

———. "Bilingual Education in American Schools: A Bibliographical Essay." *Immigration History Newsletter* 14 (May 1982): 1–8.

———. "Bracero Program." In *Dictionary of American Immigration History*, ed. Francesco Cordasco. Metuchen, NJ: Scarecrow Press, 1990.

———. "Brain Drain." In *Dictionary of American Immigration History*, ed. Francesco Cordasco. Metuchen, NJ: Scarecrow Press, 1990.

———. "Ethnic Studies Heritage Act." In *Dictionary of American Immigration History*, ed. Francesco Cordasco. Metuchen, NJ: Scarecrow Press, 1990.

———. "Hispanics, Changing the Face of America." In *Dictionary of American Immigration History*, ed. Francesco Cordasco. Metuchen, NJ: Scarecrow Press, 1990.

———. "Immigration Act of 1965." In *Dictionary of American Immigration History*, ed. Francesco Cordasco. Metuchen, NJ: Scarecrow Press, 1990.

———. "Immigration and Nationality Act of 1981." In *Dictionary of American Immigration History*, ed. Francesco Cordasco. Metuchen, NJ: Scarecrow Press, 1990.

———. "Immigration Law of 1965, Effects." In *Dictionary of American Immigration History*, ed. Francesco Cordasco. Metuchen, NJ: Scarecrow Press, 1990.

———. "Immigration Reform and Control Act of 1986." In *Dictionary of American Immigration History*, ed. Francesco Cordasco. Metuchen, NJ: Scarecrow Press, 1990.

———. "Immigration Restriction." In *Dictionary of American Immigration History*, ed. Francesco Cordasco. Metuchen, NJ: Scarecrow Press, 1990.

———. *"Lau v. Nichols."* In *Dictionary of American Immigration History*, ed. Francesco Cordasco. Metuchen, NJ: Scarecrow Press, 1990.

———. "McCarran-Walter Act of 1952." In *Dictionary of American Immigration History*, ed. Francesco Cordasco. Metuchen, NJ: Scarecrow Press, 1990.

———. "Mexicans, Migration and Rural Development." In *Dictionary of American Immigration History*, ed. Francesco Cordasco. Metuchen, NJ: Scarecrow Press, 1990.

———. "Operation Wetback." In *Dictionary of American Immigration History*, ed. Francesco Cordasco. Metuchen, NJ: Scarecrow Press, 1990.

———. "Statue of Liberty." In *Dictionary of American Immigration History*, ed. Francesco Cordasco. Metuchen, NJ: Scarecrow Press, 1990.

Corrigan, Nancy W. "The Urban Negro and the Library." In *The Library's Public Revisited: By Members of the Class in The Public Library in the Political Process*, ed. Mary Lee Bundy and Sylvia Goodstein. Student Contribution Series, no. 1. College Park: School of Library and Information Services, University of Maryland, 1967.

Cortes, Carlos E. "Mexicans." In *Dictionary of American Immigration History*, ed. Francesco Cordasco. Metuchen, NJ: Scarecrow Press, 1990.

Cory, John Mackenzie. "The New York Public Library." In *Encyclopedia of Library and Information Science*, ed. Allen Kent, Harold Lancour, and Jay E. Daily. Vol. 19. New York: Marcel Dekker, 1976.

Coyne, Joanne. " 'Los Amigos' for the Spanish-Speaking Mother." *Library Journal* 91 (15 Jan. 1966): 329–31.

Cragin, Shelah-Bell. "Mexican-Americans: A Part of the Reading Public." *Texas Libraries* 32 (Fall 1970): 139–44.

Crosby, Charles W. "Providence: A Community Relations Program." *Wilson Library Bulletin* 43 (May 1969): 892–93.

Cuesta, Yolanda J. "Ethnic Groups, Library Service to: Hispanic Americans." In *ALA Yearbook 1978: A Review of Library Events, 1977.* Chicago: ALA, 1978.

———. "From Survival to Sophistication—Hispanic Library Needs." *Library Journal* 115 (15 May 1990): 26–28.

———, and Patricia Tarin. "Guidelines for Library Services to the Spanish Speaking." *Library Journal* 103 (July 1978): 1354–55.

Cunningham, William D. "The Changing Environment and Changing Institution: Indian Project of the Northeast Kansas Library System." *Library Trends* 20 (Oct. 1971): 376–81.

Curley, Arthur. "Montclair Free Public Library." In *Encyclopedia of Library and Information Science,* ed. Allen Kent, Harold Lancour, and Jay E. Daily. Vol. 18. New York: Marcel Dekker, 1976.

———. "Social Responsibility and Libraries." In *Advances in Librarianship,* ed. Melvin J. Voigt. New York: Academic Press, 1974.

Daly, Lillie K. "Progress Is Noted in Negro Libraries." *Library Journal* 75 (1 Feb. 1950): 147–49.

Dawood, Rosemary Smith. "An Informal Information Service at the Chicago Public Library's Bezazian Branch." In Allerton Park Institute, *Libraries and Neighborhood Information Centers,* ed. Carol L. Kronus and Linda Crowe. Papers presented at an Institute conducted by the University of Illinois, Graduate School of Library Science, October 25–27, 17th ser., 1971. Urbana: University of Illinois, Graduate School of Library Science, 1972.

Dawson, Patrick Jose. "The History and Role of REFORMA." In *Latino Librarianship: A Handbook for Professionals,* ed. Salvador Guerena. Jefferson, NC: McFarland, 1990.

DeLoach, Marva L., and Glenderlyn Johnson. "Afro-American Collections." In *Ethnic Collections in Libraries,* ed. E. J. Josey and Marva L. DeLoach. New York: Neal-Schuman Publishers, 1983.

Diodati, Carmine Michael, Jr. "Ethnic Groups, Library Service to: Italian Americans." In *ALA Yearbook 1978: A Review of Library Events, 1977.* Chicago: ALA, 1978.

———. "Identifying Ethnic Communities." *Catholic Library World* 51 (Mar. 1980): 347–49.

———. "Italian-Americans." In *ALA Yearbook 1977: A Review of Library Events, 1976.* Chicago: ALA, 1977.

———. "Italian Americans." In *ALA Yearbook 1979: A Review of Library Events, 1978.* Chicago: ALA, 1979.

———. "Italian Americans." In *ALA Yearbook 1980: A Review of Library Events, 1979.* Chicago: ALA, 1980.

———. "Italian-Americans and Libraries." In *ALA Yearbook 1976: A Review of Library Events, 1975.* Chicago: ALA, 1976.

———. "Italian Americans and Libraries." In *ALA Yearbook 1981: A Review of Library Events, 1980.* Chicago: ALA, 1981.

———. "Italian Americans and Libraries." In *ALA Yearbook 1982: A Review of Library Events, 1981*. Chicago: ALA, 1982.

———. "Italian Americans and Libraries." In *ALA Yearbook 1983: A Review of Library Events, 1982*. Chicago: ALA, 1983.

———. "Italian Americans and Libraries." In *ALA Yearbook of Library and Information Services, 1984: A Review of Library Events, 1983*. Chicago: ALA, 1984.

———. "Italian Americans and Libraries." In *ALA Yearbook of Library and Information Services, 1985: A Review of Library Events, 1984*. Chicago: ALA, 1985.

Downs, Robert B. "The Significance of Foreign Materials for U.S. Collections: Problems of Acquisitions." In *Acquisition of Foreign Materials for U.S. Libraries*, ed. Theodore Samore. Metuchen, NJ: Scarecrow Press, 1973.

———, and Norman B. Brown. "The Significance of Foreign Materials for U.S. Collections: Problems of Acquisitions. In *Acquisition of Foreign Materials for U.S. Libraries*, ed. Theodore Samore. 2nd ed. Metuchen, NJ: Scarecrow Press, 1982.

Drennan, Henry. "Libraries and Literacy Education." *Catholic Library World* 52 (Apr. 1981): 376–85.

Dunn, Christina. "U.S. Department of Education Discretionary Library Programs, Fiscal Year 1997." In *Bowker Annual 1998: Library and Book Trade Almanac*. 43rd ed. New Providence, NJ: R.R. Bowker, 1999.

Duran, Daniel Flores. "Non-English Speaking, Library Service to the." In *ALA Yearbook 1976: A Review of Library Events, 1975*. Chicago: ALA, 1976.

Duran, F. "The Chicano School Library Media Specialist." In *Opportunities for Minorities in Librarianship*, ed. E.J. Josey and Kenneth E. Peeples Jr. Metuchen, NJ: Scarecrow Press, 1977.

———. "REFORMA." In *ALA Yearbook 1979: A Review of Library Events, 1978*. Chicago: ALA, 1979.

———. "REFORMA." In *ALA Yearbook 1980: A Review of Library Events, 1979*. Chicago: ALA, 1980.

Dyer, Esther R. "Children's Media for a Culturally Pluralistic Society." In *Cultural Pluralism & Children's Media*, comp. Esther R. Dyer. Chicago: ALA, 1978.

Eason, Helga H. "Miami, Florida." *Wilson Library Bulletin* 44 (March 1970): 760–62.

———. "More Than Money." *Wilson Library Bulletin* 36 (June 1962): 825–28.

Eastlick, John T., and Theodore A. Schmidt. "The Impact of Serving the Unserved on Public Library Budgets." *Library Trends* 23 (Apr. 1975): 603–15.

Ellison, John W., and Clara DiFelice. "Libraries and Multi-Cultural Understanding." *Public Library Quarterly* 3 (Fall 1982): 23–32.

Escatiola, Evelyn. "Anti-Immigrant Literature: A Selected Bibliography." In *Library Services to Latinos: An Anthology*, ed. Salvador Gucrena. Jefferson, NC: McFarland, 2000.

Estrada, Eugene. "Changing Latino Demographics and American Libraries." In *Latino Librarianship: A Handbook for Professionals*, ed. Salvador Guerena. Jefferson, NC: McFarland, 1990.

Evans, G. Edward. "Library Resources on Native Americans." In *Ethnic Collections in Libraries*, ed. E.J. Josey and Marva L. DeLoach. New York: Neal-Schuman Publishers, 1983.

Farrington, William H. "Library Services to Mexican-Americans." In *Library and Information Services for Special Groups*, ed. Joshua Smith. New York: Published in cooperation with the American Society for Information Science and the ERIC Clearinghouse on Library and Information Sciences, by Science Associates/International, 1974.

———. "Statewide Outreach: Desert Booktrails to the Indians." *Wilson Library Bulletin* 43 (May 1969): 864–71.

Feinberg, Renee. "Jewish Caucus, ALA." In *ALA Yearbook 1976: A Review of Library Events, 1975*. Chicago: ALA, 1976.

Fernandez, Nelly. "Outreach Program for Chicanos." *California Librarian* 34 (Jan. 1973): 14–17.

Figueredo, Danilo H. "Love's Labour's Not Lost: Latino Publishing." *MultiCultural Review* 7 (Sept. 1998): 24–33.

Fisher, Edith Maureen. "Ethnic Materials and Information Exchange Round Table." In *ALA Yearbook of Library and Information Services, 1988: A Review of Library Events, 1987*. Chicago: ALA, 1988.

———. "Ethnic Materials Information Exchange Round Table." In *ALA Yearbook of Library and Information Services, 1987: A Review of Library Events, 1986*. Chicago: ALA, 1987.

———. "Identification of Multiethnic Resources." In *Developing Library Collections for California's Emerging Majority: A Manual of Resources for Ethnic Collection Development*, ed. Katharine T.A. Scarborough. Produced in conjunction with the conference Developing Library Collections for California's Emerging Majority, September 22–23, 1990, San Francisco, California. Berkeley: Bay Area Library and Information System; University Extension, University of California; School of Library and Information Studies, University of California, 1990.

Fogel, Walter. "Twentieth-Century Migration to the United States." In *The Gateway: U.S. Immigration Issues and Policies*, ed. Barry R. Chiswick. Washington, DC: American Enterprise Institute for Public Policy Research, 1982.

Frankel, Diane. "Institute of Museum and Library Services Library Programs." In *Bowker Annual: Library and Book Trade Almanac*, ed. Dave Bogart. 43rd ed. New Providence, NJ: R.R. Bowker, 1998.

Frary, Mildred P. "School Library Service to the Disadvantaged Student." *Library Trends* 20 (Oct. 1971): 405–15.

Freedman, Maurice J. "American Library Association." In *Bowker Annual 2003: Library and Book Trade Almanac*. 48th ed. Medford, NJ: Information Today, 2003.

Freiband, Susan J. "Developing Collections for the Spanish Speaking." *RQ* 35 (Spring 1996): 330–42.

———. "Ethnic Materials Information Exchange Round Table." In *ALA Yearbook of Library and Information Services, 1986: A Review of Library Events, 1985.* Chicago: ALA, 1986.

———. "Multicultural Issues and Concerns in Library Education." *Journal of Education for Library and Information Science* 4 (Fall 1992): 287–94.

Fry, Ray M. "U.S. Department of Education Library Programs, 1984." In *Bowker Annual of Library & Book Trade Information 1985.* 30th ed. New York: R.R. Bowker, 1985.

———. "U.S. Department of Education Library Programs, 1985." In *Bowker Annual of Library & Book Trade Information 1986.* 31st ed. New York: R.R. Bowker, 1986.

———. "U.S. Department of Education Library Programs, 1992." In *Bowker Annual 1993: Library and Book Trade Almanac.* 38th ed. New Providence, NJ: R.R. Bowker, 1993.

———. "U.S. Department of Education Library Programs, 1995." In *Bowker Annual 1994: Library and Book Trade Almanac.* 40th ed. New Providence, NJ: R.R. Bowker, 1995.

Fuller, Judy. "Citizenship Class a First in Longview!" *ALKI: The Washington Library Association Journal* 11 (Dec. 1995): 28.

Gabaccia, Donna R. "Immigrant Labor." In *Oxford Companion to United States History,* ed. Paul S. Boyer and Melvyn Dubofsky. New York: Oxford University Press, 2001.

Gala, Victoria M. "Ethnic Groups, Library Service to: Polish Americans." In *ALA Yearbook 1978: A Review of Library Events, 1977.* Chicago: ALA, 1978.

———. "Polish Americans." In *ALA Yearbook 1977: A Review of Library Events, 1976.* Chicago: ALA, 1977.

———. "Polish Americans." In *ALA Yearbook 1979: A Review of Library Events, 1978.* Chicago: ALA, 1979.

Galvin, Hoyt. "Mecklenburg County [NC]: Reaching for the Unreached." *Wilson Library Bulletin* 43 (May 1969): 899–900.

Garza de Cortes, Oralia. "Celebracion [presentation of the Pura Belpre Award for Latino Authors and Illustrators at the Annual Conference, American Library Association, June 28, 1998, Washington, D.C.]." *MultiCultural Review* 50 (June 1999): 49–50.

———. "Developing the Spanish Children's Collection." In *Library Services to Latinos: An Anthology,* ed. Salvador Guerena. Jefferson, NC: McFarland, 2000.

———. "Give Them What They Need." In *Library Services to Youth of Hispanic Heritage,* ed. Barbara Immroth and Kathleen de la Pena McCook; assisted by Catherine Jasper. Jefferson, NC: McFarland, 2000.

———. "Justice in the Publishing Field: A Look at Multicultural Awards for Children's Literature." *MultiCultural Review* 8 (June 1999): 42–48.

————, Amy Kellman, Patricia M. Wong, Peter Sis, Kyoto Mori, and George Ancona. "A Nation of Immigrants: Are We Us or Them?" *Journal of Youth Services in Libraries* 9 (Winter 1996): 129–42.

Gilton, Donna L. "A World of Difference: Preparing for Information Literacy Instruction for Diverse Groups." *MultiCultural Review* 3 (Sept. 1994): 54–62.

Gleason, Philip. "American Identity and Americanization." In *Harvard Encyclopedia of American Ethnic Groups*, ed. Stephan Thernstrom, Ann Orlov, and Oscar Handlin. Cambridge: Belknap Press of Harvard University Press, 1980.

Godoy, Alicia. "Miami: Two Decades of Latin Accent." *Wilson Library Bulletin* 53 (Nov. 1978): 236–37.

Gonzalez, Lena. "Public Libraries Reach Out to New North Carolinians: Meeting the Information Needs of Immigrants and Refugees." *North Carolina Libraries* 57 (Spring 1999): 4–7.

Gonzalez, Lucia M. "Developing Culturally Integrated Children's Programs." In *Library Services to Youth of Hispanic Heritage*, ed. Barbara Immroth and Kathleen de la Pena McCook; assisted by Catherine Jasper. Jefferson, NC: McFarland, 2000.

Gonzalez, Michael, Bill Greeley, and Stephen Whitney. "Assessing the Library Needs of the Spanish-Speaking." *Library Journal* 105 (1 Apr. 1980): 786–89.

Gordon, Milton M. "Assimilation in America: Theory and Reality." In *The Shaping of Twentieth-Century America: Interpretive Essays*. Selected and with commentary by Richard M. Abrams and Lawrence W. Levine. 2nd ed. Boston: Little, Brown, 1971.

Goren, Ruth. "Milwaukee Public Library." In *Encyclopedia of Library and Information Science*, ed. Allen Kent, Harold Lancour, and Jay E. Daily. Vol. 18. New York: Marcel Dekker, 1976.

Greer, Natalia. "Which Came First—The Chicken or the Egg?" *Colorado Libraries* 8 (Sept. 1982): 22–24.

Guerena, Salvador, ed. "The English-Only Movement: A Selected Bibliography." In *Latino Librarianship: A Handbook for Professionals*, ed. Salvador Guerena. Jefferson, NC: McFarland, 1990.

————. "Latinos and Librarianship." *Library Trends* 49 (Summer 2000): 138–81.

————. "REFORMA." In *ALA Yearbook of Library and Information Services, 1985: A Review of Library Events, 1984*. Chicago: ALA, 1985.

————, and Edward Erazo, "Latinos and Librarianship," *Library Trends* 49 (Summer 2000): 155–72.

————, Edward Erazo, and Elissa Miller. "Resources for Chicano/Latino Collection Development." In *Developing Library Collections for California's Emerging Majority: A Manual of Resources for Ethnic Collection Development*, ed. Katharine T. A. Scarborough. Produced in conjunction with the conference Developing Library Collections for California's Emerging Majority, September 22–23, 1990, San Francisco, California. Berkeley: Bay Area Library and Information

System; University Extension, University of California; School of Library and Information Studies, University of California, 1990.

Haines, David W. "Refugees." In *Dictionary of American Immigration History,* ed. Francesco Cordasco. Metuchen, NJ: Scarecrow Press, 1990.

Halpin, Keum Chu. "The Hinomoto Library of Los Angeles." *California Librarian* 33 (Oct. 1972): 216–19.

Haro, Robert P. "Bicultural and Bilingual Americans: A Need for Understanding." *Library Trends* 20 (Oct. 1971): 256–70.

———. "How Mexican-Americans View Libraries: One-Man Survey." *Wilson Library Bulletin* 44 (March 1970): 736–42.

———. "Libraries on the Border." *California Librarian* 34 (Jan. 1973): 10.

———. "Viva la Evolucion: Libraries Reach Out, But Changes Come Too Slowly for America's Fastest-Growing Minority." *American Libraries* 10 (June 1979): 355.

———, and Elizabeth Martinez Smith, eds. "Si Se Puede! Yes, It Can Be Done: Service to the Spanish Speaking, 1978." *Wilson Library Bulletin* 53 (Nov. 1978): 228–67.

Harvell, Tony A. "Miami and the Cuban Revolution: Ties Across the Straits of Florida." In *SALALM and the Area Studies Community: Papers of the Thirty-Seventh Annual Meeting of the Seminar on the Acquisition of Latin American Library Materials, Nettie Lee Benson Latin American Collection, University of Texas at Austin, Austin, Texas, May 30-June 4, 1992,* ed. David Block. [Albuquerque]: SALALM Secretariat, General Library, University of New Mexico, 1992.

Heim, Kathleen M. "Adult Services: An Enduring Focus." In *Adult Services: An Enduring Focus for Public Libraries,* ed. Kathleen M. Heim and Danny P. Wallace. Chicago: ALA, 1990.

———. "Librarians for the New Millennium." In *Librarians for the New Millennium,* ed. William E. Moen and Kathleen M. Heim. Chicago: ALA, Office for Library Personnel Resources, 1988.

Heinze, Frederick W. "The Freedom Libraries: A Wedge in the Closed Society." *Library Journal* 90 (15 Apr. 1965): 1991.

Hellwig, David J. "Afro-American Views of Immigrants, 1830–1930: A Historiographical-Bibliographical Essay." *The Immigration History Newsletter* 13 (Nov. 1981): 1–5.

Hengen, Jamie Lynn. "Service to the Disadvantaged." *Mississippi Libraries* 43 (Autumn 1979): 155–56.

Hennessy, Mildred L. "The Operation Head Start Project at the Queens Borough Public Library." In *Public Library Services to the Disadvantaged,* Proceedings of an Institute, December 7th and 8th, 1967. Atlanta: Division of Librarianship, Emory University, 1969.

Herrera, Luis. "REFORMA." In *ALA Yearbook 1982: A Review of Library Events, 1981.* Chicago: ALA, 1982.

———. "SALALM and the Public Library." In *Latin American Studies into the Twenty-First Century: New Focus, New Formats, New Challenges: Papers of the Thirty-Sixth Annual Meeting of the Seminar on the Acquisition of Latin American Library Materials, University of California, San Diego, and San Diego State University, San Diego, California, June 1–6, 1991* ed. Deborah L. Jakubs. [Albuquerque, NM]: SALALM Secretariat, General Library, University of New Mexico, 1993.

———, and Albert J. Milo. "Managing Administrative Change for Ethnic Collection Development." In *Developing Library Collections for California's Emerging Majority: A Manual of Resources for Ethnic Collection Development*, ed. Katharine T. A. Scarborough. Produced in conjunction with the conference Developing Library Collections for California's Emerging Majority, September 22–23, 1990, San Francisco, California. Berkeley: Bay Area Library and Information System; University Extension, University of California; School of Library and Information Studies, University of California, 1990.

Hodgman, Suzanne. "SALALM Membership, 1956–1990: A Brief Overview." In *Latin American Studies into the Twenty-First Century: New Focus, New Formats, New Challenges: Papers of the Thirty-Sixth Annual Meeting of the Seminar on the Acquisition of Latin American Library Materials, University of California, San Diego, and San Diego State University, San Diego, California, June 1–6, 1991*, ed. Deborah L. Jakubs. [Albuquerque]: SALALM Secretariat, General Library, University of New Mexico, 1993.

Hoffman, Luther T. "Relocation Centers: Rivers, Arizona." *Library Journal* 68 (15 Apr. 1943): 335.

Holt, Thomas C. "Afro-Americans." In *Harvard Encyclopedia of American Ethnic Groups,* ed. Stephan Thernstrom, Ann Orlov, and Oscar Handlin. Cambridge: Belknap Press of Harvard University Press, 1980.

Hoover, Austin. "Workshop on Library Services and Materials for Mexican-Americans." *Texas Library Journal* 46 (Winter 1970): 206–8.

Horton, Marion. "Library Work with the Japanese." *LJ* 47 (15 Feb. 1922): 157–60.

Howard, Edward N. "Terre Haute: No One Has Asked." *Wilson Library Bulletin* 43 (May 1969): 888–92.

Hoxie, Frederick E., ed. "Education." In *Encyclopedia of North American Indians.* Boston: Houghton Mifflin, 1996.

Ichioka, Yuji. "Recent Japanese Scholarship on the Origins and Causes of Japanese Immigration. *Immigration History Newsletter* 15 (Nov. 1983): 2–7.

Johnson, Hans P. "Immigrants in California: Findings from the 1990 Census." *California State Library Foundation Bulletin,* no. 45 (Oct. 1993): 7–11.

Johnson, Mary Frances. "A Guide to Spanish-Language Books for Children." *Wilson Library Bulletin* 53 (Nov. 1978): 244–48.

Jones, Plummer Alston, Jr. "The ALA Committee on Work with the Foreign Born and the Movement to Americanize the Immigrant." In *Libraries to the*

People, ed. Robert S. Freeman and David M. Hovde. Foreword by Kathleen de la Pena McCook. Jefferson, NC: McFarland & Company, 2003.

————. "Cultural Oasis or Ethnic Ghetto?: The North Carolina Foreign Language Center and Statewide Multilingual Public Library Service," *North Carolina Libraries* 50 (Summer 1992): 100-105.

————. "The Odyssey of the Immigrant in American History: From the Changed to the Changer; A Bibliographic Essay." *Immigrants and Minorities* 7 (Nov. 1988): 314–23.

————. "Serving the Silent: We Are Still a Nation of Immigrants." *North Carolina Libraries* 56 (Fall 1998): 118.

Jordan, Casper Leroy. "Library Service to Black Americans." *Library Trends* 20 (Oct. 1971): 271–79.

Josey, E.J. "Libraries, Reading, and the Liberation of Black People." *Library Scene* 1 (Winter 1972): 4–8.

————. "Minority Groups, Library Service for." In *Encyclopedia of Library and Information Science* ed. Allen Kent, Harold Lancour, and Jay E. Daily. Vol. 18. New York: Marcel Dekker, 1976.

————. "A Mouthful of Civil Rights and an Empty Stomach." *Library Journal* 90 (15 Jan. 1965): 202–5.

Kamm, Marlene S., and Tracey Heskett. " 'So Juan Can't Speak English': The Library's Role in a Multicultural and Multilingual Society." *Illinois Libraries* 62 (Dec. 1980): 886–90.

Knox, Kenneth M. "Santa Ana Public Library Staff Perceptions of Immigrant Language Usage." In *Library Services to Latinos: An Anthology,* ed., Salvador Guerena. Jefferson, NC: McFarland, 2000.

Kobayashi, Vivian. "Ethnic Groups, Library Service to: Asian Americans." In *ALA Yearbook 1978: A Review of Library Events, 1977.* Chicago: ALA, 1978.

Kobrak, Fred. "Fairs Around the World: A User's Guide." In *Bowker Annual 1993: Library and Book Trade Almanac.* 38th ed. New Providence, NJ: R.R. Bowker, 1993.

Kopan, Andrew T. "Multicultural Education." In *Dictionary of American Immigration History,* ed. Francesco Cordasco. Metuchen, NJ: Scarecrow Press, 1990.

Kravitz, Rhonda Rios. "REFORMA." In *ALA Yearbook of Library and Information Services, 1990: A Review of Library Events, 1989.* Chicago: ALA, 1990.

————, Adelia Lines, and Vivian Sykes. "Serving the Emerging Majority: Documenting Their Voices." *Library Administration & Management* 5 (Fall 1991): 184–88.

Kreissman, Bernard. "Asian/Pacific American Librarians: An American Perspective." In *Asian/Pacific American Librarians: A Cross Cultural Perspective,* ed. Lourdes Y. Collantes. Papers of the 1984 Program of the Asian/Pacific American Librarians Association, June 25, 1984, Dallas, Texas. New York: Asian/Pacific American Librarians Association, 1985.

Krettek, Germaine. "Library Legislation, Federal." In *Encyclopedia of Library and Information Science,* ed. Allen Kent, Harold Lancour, and Jay E. Daily. Vol. 15. New York: Marcel Dekker, 1975.

Lacy, Dan. "Social Change and the Library: 1945–1980." In *Libraries at Large: Tradition, Innovation, and the National Interest,* ed. Douglas M. Knight and E. Shepley Nourse. New York: R. R. Bowker, 1969.

Ladenson, Alex. "Chicago: The Public Library Reaches Out." *Wilson Library Bulletin* 43 (May 1969): 875–81.

Lai, John Yung-Hsiang. "Chinese American Librarians Association." In *ALA Yearbook 1983: A Review of Library Events, 1982.* Chicago: ALA. 1983.

———. "Chinese-American Librarians Association." In *ALA Yearbook of Library and Information Services, 1984: A Review of Library Events, 1983.* Chicago: ALA, 1984.

Lam, R. Errol. "The Reference Interview: Some Intercultural Considerations." *RQ* (Spring 1988): 390–95.

Lapham, Susan J., Patricia Montgomery, and Debra Niner, preps. "We the American ... Foreign Born." Washington, DC: U.S. Bureau of the Census, 1993.

Lee, Minja P. "An Assessment of Asian/Pacific American Librarians' Status and Achievement." In *Asian/Pacific American Librarians: A Cross Cultural Perspective,* ed. Lourdes Y. Collantes. Papers of the 1984 Program of the Asian/Pacific American Librarians Association, June 25, 1984, Dallas, Texas. New York: Asian/Pacific American Librarians Association, 1985.

Lee, Mollie Huston. "Development of Negro Libraries in North Carolina." *North Carolina Libraries* 3 (May 1944): 3.

Leonard, Gillian D. "Multiculturalism and Library Services." In *Multicultural Acquisitions,* ed. Karen Parrish and Bill Katz. New York: Haworth Press, 1993. Published simultaneously in *Acquisitions Librarian,* no. 9/10 (1993): 3–19.

Lerman, Linda P. "Association of Jewish Libraries (AJL)." In *ALA Yearbook of Library and Information Services, 1989: A Review of Library Events, 1988.* Chicago: ALA, 1989.

Lesley, J. Ingrid. "Library Services for Special Groups: 1991 Trends and Selected Innovative Services for Immigrants, the Homeless, Children After School, the Disabled, and the Unemployed." In *Bowker Annual, 1992: Library and Book Trade Almanac.* 37th ed. New Providence, NJ: R.R. Bowker, 1992.

Li, Tze-Chung. "Chinese American Librarians Association." In *ALA Yearbook 1978: A Review of Library Events, 1977.* Chicago: ALA, 1978.

———. "Chinese American Librarians Association." In *ALA Yearbook 1979: A Review of Library Events, 1978.* Chicago: ALA, 1979.

———. "Chinese American Librarians Association." In *ALA Yearbook 1980: A Review of Library Events, 1979.* Chicago: ALA, 1980.

———. "Chinese American Librarians Association." In *ALA Yearbook 1981: A Review of Library Events, 1980.* Chicago: ALA, 1981.

————. "Chinese American Librarians Association." In *ALA Yearbook 1982: A Review of Library Events, 1981.* Chicago: ALA, 1982.

Light, Jerome T. "Relocation Centers: Hunt, Idaho." *Library Journal* 68 (1 Apr. 1943): 281–82.

Lindley, James G. "Relocation Centers: Amache, Colorado." *Library Journal* 68 (15 Feb. 1943): 174.

Liu, Mengxiong. "The History and Status of Chinese Americans in Librarianship." *Library Trends* 49 (Summer 2000): 109–37.

Lo, Suzanne, and Susan Ma. "Resources for Asian/Southeast Asian Collection Development." In *Developing Library Collections for California's Emerging Majority: A Manual of Resources for Ethnic Collection Development*, ed. Katharine T. A. Scarborough. Produced in conjunction with the conference Developing Library Collections for California's Emerging Majority, September 22–23, 1990, San Francisco, California. Berkeley: Bay Area Library and Information System; University Extension, University of California; School of Library and Information Studies, University of California, 1990.

Long, Fern. "New Citizens in the Library." *ALA Bulletin* 51 (Jan. 1957): 27–28.

Lopez, Lillian. "The South Bronx Project." *Wilson Library Bulletin* 44 (Mar. 1970): 757–59.

Lubetski, Edith. "Association of Jewish Libraries." In *ALA Yearbook of Library and Information Services, 1986: A Review of Library Events, 1985.* Chicago: ALA, 1986.

Luevano, Susan C. "REFORMA." In *ALA Yearbook of Library and Information Services, 1986: A Review of Library Events, 1985.* Chicago: ALA, 1986.

Luevano-Molina, Susan. "Ethnographic Perspectives on Trans-National Mexican Immigrant Library Users." In *Library Services to Latinos: An Anthology*, ed. Salvador Guerena. Jefferson, NC: McFarland, 2000.

————. "Introduction: New Immigrants, Neo-Nativism, and the Public Library." In *Library Services to Latinos: An Anthology*, ed. Salvador Guerena. Jefferson, NC: McFarland, 2000.

————. "Mexican/Latino Immigrants and the Santa Ana Public Library: An Urban Ethnography." In *Library Services to Latinos: An Anthology*, ed. Salvador Guerena. Jefferson, NC: McFarland, 2000.

Lyman, Helen Huguenor. "Reading Materials for Adults with Limited Reading Experience." *Library Trends* 20 (Oct. 1971): 326–49.

Lyman, Helen Huguenor, ed. "Library Programs and Services to the Disadvantaged." Helen *Library Trends* 20 (Oct. 1971): 187–471.

MacCann, Donnarae. "Libraries for Immigrants and 'Minorities': A Study in Contrasts." In *Social Responsibility in Librarianship: Essays on Equality*, ed. Donnarae MacCann. Jefferson, NC: McFarland, 1989.

Macias, Ysidro Ramon. "The Chicano Movement." *Wilson Library Bulletin* 44 (March 1970): 731–35.

Malus, Susan. "El Centro Hispano de Information: A Unique Service of the Brooklyn Public Library." *Catholic Library World* 52 (Apr. 1981): 368–70.

Manoogian, Sylva N. "The Importance of Ethnic Collections in Libraries." In *Ethnic Collections in Libraries*, ed. E.J. Josey and Marva L. DeLoach. New York: Neal-Schuman Publishers, 1983.

Manthorne, Jane. "Provisions and Programs for Disadvantaged Young People." *Library Trends* 20 (Oct. 1971): 416–31.

Marcum, Deanna B., and Elizabeth W. Stone. "Literacy: The Library Legacy." *American Libraries* 22 (Mar. 1991): 202–5.

Marino, Hector. "Considerations for the Development of Spanish Language Collections in School Libraries." In *Library Services to Latinos: An Anthology*, ed. Salvador Guerena. Jefferson, NC: McFarland, 2000.

Marshall, A.P. "Service to Afro-Americans." In *A Century of Service: Librarianship in the United States and Canada*, ed. Sidney L. Jackson, Eleanor B. Herling, and E.J. Josey. Chicago: ALA, 1976.

Martin, Robert S. "Institute of Museum and Library Services, Library Programs." In *Bowker Annual 2002: Library and Book Trade Almanac*. 47th ed. Medford, NJ: Information Today, 2002.

———. "Institute of Museum and Library Services, Library Programs." In *Bowker Annual 2003: Library and Book Trade Almanac*. 48th ed. Medford, NJ: Information Today, 2003.

Masling, Charles. "Information Services for Cultural Minorities." *Catholic Library World* 55 (May-June 1984): 445–49.

McAllister, Dorothy. "Library Service in Mississippi." *Library Journal* 80 (1 Feb. 1950): 536–39.

McCook, Kathleen de la Pena. "Concepts of Culture: The Role of the Trejo Foster Foundation." In *Library Services to Youth of Hispanic Heritage*, ed. Barbara Immroth and Kathleen de la Pena McCook; assisted by Catherine Jasper. Jefferson, NC: McFarland, 2000.

———. *A Place at the Table: Participating in Community Building*. Chicago: ALA, 2000.

McCook, Kathleen de la Pena, with the assistance of Paul Geist, preps. *Toward a Just and Productive Society: An Analysis of the Recommendations of the White House Conference on Library and Information Services*. Washington, DC: NCLIS, 1993 [i.e., 1994].

McCormick, Regina. "Ethnic Studies Materials for School Libraries: How to Choose and Use Them." *Catholic Library World* 51 (Mar. 1980): 339–41.

McMullen, Haynes. "Services to Ethnic Minorities Other than Afro-Americans and American Indians." In *A Century of Service: Librarianship in the United States and Canada*, ed. Sidney L. Jackson, Eleanor B. Herling, and E.J. Josey. Chicago: ALA, 1976.

McNiff, Philip J. "Cooperation in the Acquisition of Foreign Materials." In *Acquisition of Foreign Materials for U.S. Libraries,* ed. Theodore Samore. Metuchen, NJ: Scarecrow Press, 1973.

McShane, James. "Confronting Diversity in a Homogeneous Environment." In *Venture into Cultures: A Resource Book of Multicultural Materials and Programs,* ed. Olga R. Kuharets for the Ethnic and Multicultural Information Exchange Round Table. 2nd ed. Chicago: ALA, 2001.

Miah, Abdul J. "Asian/Pacific American Librarians Association." In *ALA Yearbook of Library and Information Services, 1990: A Review of Library Events, 1989.* Chicago: ALA, 1990.

Miller, Liz Rodriguez. "REFORMA." In *ALA Yearbook of Library and Information Services, 1988: A Review of Library Events, 1987.* Chicago: ALA, 1988.

Miller, Stuart Creighton. "Cultural Pluralism." In *Dictionary of American Immigration History,* ed. Francesco Cordasco. Metuchen, NJ: Scarecrow Press, 1990.

Milo, Albert J. "Reference Service to the Spanish-Speaking." In *Latino Librarianship: A Handbook for Professionals,* ed. Salvador Guerena. Jefferson, NC: McFarland, 1990.

———. "REFORMA." In *ALA Yearbook 1983: A Review of Library Events, 1982.* Chicago: ALA, 1983.

———. "REFORMA." In *ALA Yearbook of Library and Information Services, 1984: A Review of Library Events, 1983.* Chicago: ALA, 1984.

Moen, William E. "Library and Information Science Student Attitudes, Demographics and Aspirations Survey: Who We Are and Why We Are Here." In *Librarians for the New Millennium,* ed. William E. Moen and Kathleen M. Heim. Chicago: ALA, Office for Library Personnel Resources, 1988.

Mohl, Raymond A. "Cubans." In *Dictionary of American Immigration History,* ed. Francesco Cordasco. Metuchen, NJ: Scarecrow Press, 1990.

———. "Cubans in Miami; A Preliminary Bibliography." *The Immigration History Newsletter* 16 (May 1984): 1–10.

———. "Haitians." In *Dictionary of American Immigration History,* ed. Francesco Cordasco. Metuchen, NJ: Scarecrow Press, 1990.

———. "The New Haitian Immigration; A Preliminary Bibliography." *Immigration History Newsletter* 17 (May 1985): 1–8.

Molz, Kathleen. "People Call Their Crying Rain." *Wilson Library Bulletin* 43 (May 1969): 860–63.

Monroe, Margaret E. "The Adult and the Public Library." *Minnesota Libraries* 21 (Sept. 1965): 191–97.

———. "The Cultural Role of the Public Library." In *Advances in Librarianship,* ed. Michael H. Harris. Vol. 11. New York: Academic Press, 1981.

———. "Education in Librarianship for Serving the Disadvantaged." *Library Trends* 20 (Oct. 1971): 445–62.

————. "Reader Services to the Disadvantaged in Inner Cities." In *Advances in Librarianship*, ed. Melvin J. Voigt. Vol. 2. New York: Academic Press, 1971.

Moses, Richard. "Hindsight on High John." In *Social Responsibilities and Libraries: A Library Journal/School Library Journal Selection*, comp. and ed. Patricia Glass Schuman. New York: R.R. Bowker, 1976.

————. "The Training of Librarians to Service the Unserved: The "High John" Project." In *Library Service to the Unserved: Papers Presented at a Library Conference Held at the University of Wisconsin–Milwaukee, School of Library and Information Science, November 16–18, 1967*, ed. Laurence L. Sherrill. Library and Information Science Studies, no. 2. New York: R.R. Bowker, 1970.

Murphey, John A., Jr. "Corpus Christi, Texas." *Wilson Library Bulletin* 44 (March 1970): 763–65.

Nakaji, Chizuri. "Relocation Centers: Manzanar, California." *Library Journal* 68 (1 Mar. 1943): 204.

Nash, Mary. "Public Library Service to Hispanic Immigrants: An Anecdotal Survey." *Nebraska Library Association Quarterly* 29 (Spring 1998): 17–25.

"National Commission on Libraries and Information Science Establishes Cultural Minorities Task Force." *School Media Quarterly* 9 (Spring 1981): 139–40.

Naumer, Janet N. "Library Services to American Indians." In *Library and Information Services for Special Groups*, ed. Joshua I. Smith. New York: Published in cooperation with the American Society for Information Science and the ERIC Clearinghouse on Library and Information Sciences, by Science Associates/International, 1974.

"NCLIS Appoints Minority Task Force." *Wilson Library Bulletin* 55 (May 1981): 650.

New Jersey Library Association. Committee on Service to the Disadvantaged. "Service to Migrant Workers." *New Jersey Libraries* 7 (February 1974): 4.

Nicolescu, Suzine Har. "Asian/Pacific American Librarians Association." In *ALA Yearbook of Library and Information Services, 1987: A Review of Library Events, 1986*. Chicago: ALA, 1987.

Ocon, Ben. "Effective Outreach Strategies to the Latino Community: A Paradigm for Public Libraries." In *Library Services to Latinos: An Anthology*, ed. Salvador Guerena. Jefferson, NC: McFarland, 2000.

Ogi, Mary. "The Tanforan Assembly Center Library." *Library Journal* 68 (1 May 1943): 352–54.

Okim, Victor. "Asian/Pacific American Librarians Association." In *ALA Yearbook of Library and Information Services, 1986: A Review of Library Events, 1985*. Chicago: ALA, 1986.

Olvera, Joseph B., Jr., Evelyn Escatiola, Margaret Mercado, Benjamin Ocon, and Albert Tovar. "Chicano Collections of Library Resources." In *Ethnic Collections in Libraries*, ed. E.J. Josey and Marva L. DeLoach. New York: Neal-Schuman Publishers, 1983.

Orange, Satia. "ALA's OLOS: Reaching Out to Library Outreach Programs." *North Carolina Libraries* 57 (Spring 1999): 20–21.

Parker, Thomas F. "Can We Afford to Ignore the Negro?" *Library Journal* 88 (15 Dec. 1963): 4716–17.

Patterson, Lotsee. "Historical Overview of Tribal Libraries in the Lower Forty-Eight States." In *Libraries to the People: Histories of Outreach*, ed. Robert S. Freeman and David M. Hovde. Foreword by Kathleen de la Pena McCook. Jefferson, NC: McFarland & Company, 2003.

Pearson, Lois R., ed. "In the News [column]: From Mt. St. Helens to Miami, Librarians Face Unique Challenges of Summer, 1980." *American Libraries* 11 (Sept. 1980): 463–64.

Petty, J.B. "Reflections on the Role of EMIERT in the Past and in the Future: A Message from the Chair." *EMIE Bulletin: Ethnic and Multicultural Information Exchange Round Table* 17 (Spring 2001): 1, 3, 13.

Pillsbury, Penelope, and Mary Van Buren. "French Canadians in Vermont Focus of Northwest Libraries Section Meeting." *Vermont Libraries* 4 (Nov. 1975): 116–17.

"Pilot Project Offers Expanded Services to NYC Spanish Community." *NYLA Bulletin* 15 (Sept. 1967): 152.

Pineda, Conchita J. "Asian/Pacific American Librarians Association." In *ALA Yearbook of Library and Information Services, 1989: A Review of Library Events, 1988.* Chicago: ALA, 1989.

Pisano, Vivian H., and Margaret Skidmore. "Community Survey—Why Not Take an Eclectic Approach?" *Wilson Library Bulletin* 53 (Nov. 1978): 250–53.

Plotnik, Art. "Summing Up After Three Years: The Success of Information and Referral Services in the Five-City Neighborhood Information Center Project." *American Libraries* 6 (July-Aug. 1975): 412–13.

Poitras, Guy E. "Issues in Immigration Policy for the 1980s." In *Latin American Economic Issues: Information Needs and Sources: Papers of the Twenty-Sixth Seminar on the Acquisition of Latin American Library Materials, Tulane University, New Orleans, Louisiana, April 1–4, 1981.* [Madison]: SALALM Secretariat, University of Wisconsin–Madison; [Los Angeles]: UCLA Latin American Center Publications, University of California, Los Angeles, 1984.

Poon, Wei Chi. "Asian American Collections." In *Ethnic Collections in Libraries,* ed. E.J. Josey and Marva L. DeLoach. New York: Neal-Schuman Publishers, 1983.

Queens Borough (NY) Public Library. " 'Say Si' Manual." In *Latino Librarianship: A Handbook for Professionals,* ed. Salvador Guerena. Jefferson, NC: McFarland, 1990.

Quimby, Harriet, and Margaret Dennehy. "Creative Connection: School Library Resources for the E.S.L. Child." *Catholic Library World* 52 (Apr. 1981): 387–91.

Quinn, Mary Ellen. "Hispanic Collections in the Public Library: The Chicago Public Library Experience." In *Multicultural Acquisitions,* ed. Karen Parrish and Bill Katz. New York: Haworth Press, 1993. Published simultaneously in *Acquisitions Librarian,* no. 9/10 (1993): 221–32.

Ramirez, William L. "Libraries and the Spanish-Speaking." *Wilson Library Bulletin* 44 (March 1970): 714–15.

Randall, Ann Knight. "Library Service to Minorities." In *Bowker Annual of Library & Book Trade Information.* 32nd ed. New York: R. R. Bowker, 1987.

———. "Minority Recruitment in Librarianship." In *Librarians for the New Millennium,* ed. William E. Moen and Kathleen M. Heim. Chicago: ALA, Office for Library Personnel Resources, 1988.

Ratliff, Debra D. "The Refugees in Our Midst." *Colorado Libraries* 16 (Sept. 1990): 18–19.

Rebenack, John H. "Public Libraries, International: Contemporary Libraries in the United States." In *Encyclopedia of Library and Information Science,* ed. Allen Kent, Harold Lancour, and Jay E. Daily. Vol. 24. New York: Marcel Dekker, 1978.

Reimers, David M. "Immigration Legislation." In *Dictionary of American Immigration History,* ed. Francesco Cordasco. Metuchen, NJ: Scarecrow Press, 1990.

———. "Recent Immigration Policy: An Analysis." In *The Gateway: U.S. Immigration Issues and Policies,* ed. Barry R. Chiswick. Washington, DC: American Enterprise Institute for Public Policy Research, 1982.

Reynolds, Mary B. "San Joaquin Valley, California: La Biblioteca Ambulante." *Wilson Library Bulletin* 44 (March 1970): 767.

Robbin, Alice. "We the People: One Nation, a Multicultural Society." *Library Trends* 49 (Summer 2000): 6–48.

Robinson, H. Alan, Florence Korn, and Shirley N. Winters. "The Library and the Disadvantaged Reader." *Library Trends* 20 (Oct. 1971): 308–25.

Rodriguez, Armando. "The Necessity of Bilingual Education." *Wilson Library Bulletin* 44 (Mar. 1970): 724–30.

Rosenthal, Joseph A. "Special Services for the Spanish-Speaking Public Served by the Branch Libraries of the New York Public Library." In *Twelfth Seminar on the Acquisition of Latin American Library Materials, Los Angeles, California, June 22–24, 1967.* Sponsored by the University of California at Los Angeles and the Pan American Union. Peter J. de la Garza, Rapporteur General. Vol. I. Working Paper, no. 11. Washington, DC: Pan American Union, General Secretariat, Organization of American States, 1968.

Rountree, Elizabeth. "Users and Nonusers Disclose Their Needs: New Orleans Public Library Survey." *American Libraries* 10 (Sept. 1979): 486–87.

Ryan, Kathryn E. "Libraries, Prejudice, and the Portuguese." *Current Studies in Librarianship* [Graduate Library School, University of Rhode Island] (Spring/Fall 1985): 59–64.

Salazar, Theresa, and Maria Segura Hoopes. "U.S./Mexican Borderlands Acquisition: Defining and Pursuing the Materials." In *Multicultural Acquisitions,* ed. Karen Parrish and Bill Katz. New York: Haworth Press, 1993. Published simultaneously in *Acquisitions Librarian,* no.9/10 (1993): 233–46.

Salinas, Romelia. "CLNet: Redefining Latino Library Services in the Digital Era." In *Library Services to Latinos: An Anthology,* ed. Salvador Guerena. Jefferson, NC: McFarland, 2000.

Salo, Annette. "Ethnic Diversity in a Northern Climate." In *Multicultural Acquisitions,* ed. Karen Parrish and Bill Katz. New York: Haworth Press, 1993. Published simultaneously in *Acquisitions Librarian,* no. 9/10 (1993): 267–74.

Sandler, Jerrold. "Washington, D.C.: Reading Is Fun-damental." *Wilson Library Bulletin* 43 (May 1969): 881–85.

Sanudo, Karen. "A Case for Bilingual Librarianship in New Jersey." *New Jersey Libraries* 12 (Feb. 1979): 3–9.

Schenk, Gretchen Knief. "Our Libraries Can Keep Last 50 Years' Promises." *Library Journal* 75 (Jan. 1950): 7–9.

Seal, Robert A. "Mexican and U.S. Library Relations." In *Advances in Librarianship,* ed. Irene Godden. Vol. 20. New York: Academic Press, 1996.

Seavey, Charles A. "Public Libraries." In *Encyclopedia of Library History,* ed. Wayne Wiegand and Donald G. Davis Jr. New York: Garland Publishing, 1994.

Sessa, Frank B. "Public Libraries, International: History of the Public Library." In *Encyclopedia of Library and Information Science,* ed. Allen Kent, Harold Lancour, and Jay E. Daily. Vol. 24. New York: Marcel Dekker, 1976.

Sexton, Irwin. "San Antonio: Books by Phone." *Wilson Library Bulletin* 43 (May 1969): 885–87.

Sharma, R.N. "Library Services to Indian-Americans in the United States." *MultiCultural Review* 3 (Mar. 1994): 44–51.

Sheketoff, Emily, and Mary R. Costabile. "Legislation and Regulations Affecting Libraries in 2001." In *Bowker Annual: Library and Book Trade Almanac,* ed. Dave Bogart. 47th ed. Medford, NJ: Information Today, 2002.

———. "Legislation and Regulations Affecting Libraries in 2002." In *Bowker Annual: Library and Book Trade Almanac,* ed. Dave Bogart. 48th ed. Medford, NJ: Information Today, 2003.

Shepard, Marietta Daniels. "Reading Resources and Project LEER." *Wilson Library Bulletin* 44 (Mar. 1970): 743–50.

Sheppard, Beverly. "Institute of Museum and Library Services Library Programs." In *Bowker Annual: Library and Book Trade Almanac,* ed. Dave Bogart. 46th ed. New Providence, NJ: R.R. Bowker, 2001.

Sherman, Jake. "Library Programs for Ethnic Americans." *The Library Scene* 4 (Dec. 1975/Mar. 1976): 11–13.

Shields, Gerald R. "Federal Legislation and Libraries." In *Libraries in the Political Process,* ed. E.J. Josey. Phoenix: Oryx Press, 1980.

Shores, Louis. "Public Library Service to Negroes." *Library Journal* 55 (Feb. 1930): 150–54.

Sinclair, Dorothy. "Materials to Meet Special Needs." *Library Trends* 17 (July 1968): 36–47.

Skrzeszewski, Stan, and Maureen Cubberley. "The INTERNET and a Vision for the Future: Multicultural Library Services." *MultiCultural Review* 7 (Dec. 1998): 34–38.

Smith, Eleanor T. "Public Library Service to the Economically and Culturally Deprived: A Profile of the Brooklyn Public Library." In *The Library Reaches Out: Reports on Library Service and Community Relations by Some Leading American Librarians,* comp. and ed. Kate Coplan and Edwin Castagna. Dobbs Ferry, NY: Oceana Publications, 1965.

Smith, Jesse Carney. "Ethnic Groups, Library Service to." In *ALA Yearbook 1977: A Review of Library Events, 1976.* Chicago: ALA, 1977.

Smith, June Smeck. "Library Service to American Indians." *Library Trends* 20 (Oct. 1971): 223–38.

Sontag, Iliana L. "Ethnic Groups, Library Service to: REFORMA." In *ALA Yearbook 1978: A Review of Library Events, 1977.* Chicago: ALA, 1978.

"South Bronx Library Reopens." *The Bookmark* 28 (Mar. 1969): 200.

Spicer, Edward H. "American Indians, Federal Policy Toward." In *Harvard Encyclopedia of American Ethnic Groups,* ed. Stephan Thernstrom, Ann Orlov, and Oscar Handlin. Cambridge: Belknap Press of Harvard University Press, 1980.

Springman, Mary Adele. "Cleveland: Books/Jobs and the Manpower Crisis." *Wilson Library Bulletin* 43 (May 1969): 897–99.

Stansfield, D. Bryan. "Serving Hispanic Persons: The Cross-Cultural Border Library Experience at Fabens." *RQ* 27 (Summer 1988): 547–61.

Stern, Stephen. "Ethnic Libraries and Librarianship in the United States: Models and Prospects." In *Advances in Librarianship,* ed. Irene P. Godden. Vol. 15. New York: Academic Press, 1991.

Stevens, Charles H. "National Commission on Libraries and Information Science." In *Encyclopedia of Library and Information Science,* ed. Allen Kent, Harold Lancour, and Jay E. Daily. Vol. 19. New York: Marcel Dekker, 1976.

Su, Julie Tao. "Library Services in an Asian American Context." In *Diversity and Multiculturalism in Libraries,* ed. Katherine Hoover Hill. Greenwich, CT: JAI Press, 1994.

Su, Sherry Shiuan, and Charles William Conaway. "Information and a Forgotten Minority: Elderly Chinese Immigrants." *Library and Information Science Research* 17, no. 1 (1995): 69–86.

Sundell, Jon. "Library Service to Hispanic Immigrants of Forsyth County, North Carolina: A Community Collaboration." In *Library Services to Latinos: An Anthology,* ed. Salvador Guerena. Jefferson, NC: McFarland, 2000.

Sykes, Vivian. "Advocacy for Ethnic Collection Development." In *Developing Library Collections for California's Emerging Majority: A Manual of Resources for Ethnic Collection Development,* ed. Katharine T. A. Scarborough. Produced in conjunction with the conference Developing Library Collections for California's Emerging Majority, September 22–23, 1990, San Francisco, California. Berkeley: Bay Area Library and Information System; University Extension, University of California; School of Library and Information Studies, University of California, 1990.

Szasz, Margaret Connell. "Education." In *Encyclopedia of North American Indians*, ed. Frederick E. Hoxie. Boston: Houghton Mifflin, 1996.

Tate, Binnie L. "The Role of the Children's Librarian in Serving the Disadvantaged." *Library Trends* 20 (Oct. 1971): 392–404.

Taylor, Gail Singleton, Jvotsna Sreenivasan, and Arun N. Toke. "Children's Books on India and the Indian-American Experience." *MultiCultural Review* 7 (Dec. 1998): 39–50.

Taylor, J.G. "The Profession and Services to the Spanish-speaking: Library Reform Sought by Bilingual Group (REFORMA)." In *Library Services to Mexican Americans: Policies, Practices and Prospects*, ed. Roberto Urzua, Martha P. Cotera, and Emma Gonzalez Stupp. Prepared by Project Staff, University of Texas, Nettie Lee Benson Latin American Collection, Mexican American Library Project. Las Cruces, NM: New Mexico State University for Educational Resources Information Center Clearinghouse on Rural Education and Small Schools, 1978.

Taylor, Jose. "REFORMA." In *ALA Yearbook 1977: A Review of Library Events, 1976*. Chicago: ALA, 1977.

Taylor, Zada. "War Children on the Pacific: A Symposium Article." *Library Journal* 67 (15 June 1942): 558–62.

Thernstrom, Abigail M. "Language: Issues and Legislation." In *Harvard Encyclopedia of American Ethnic Groups*, ed. Stephan Thernstrom, Ann Orlov, and Oscar Handlin. Cambridge: Belknap Press of Harvard University Press, 1980.

Thomas, Ruth Anne. "The Role of Media Centers in Bilingual Education." In *Cultural Pluralism & Children's Media*, comp. Esther R. Dyer. Chicago: ALA, 1978.

Thompson, Daphne. "Curious George in the Tomato Field: Regional Library Service to Migrant Children." *Top of the News* 30 (June 1974): 420–24.

Tjoumas, Renee. "Giving New Americans a Green Light in Life: A Paradigm for Serving Immigrant Communities." *Public Libraries* 26 (Fall 1987): 103–108.

———. "Opening Doorways to New Immigrants: Queens Borough Public Library's Coping Skills Component." *Public Library Quarterly* 14, no. 4 (1995): 5–19.

Torres, Rita. "Assessment of Community Needs." In *Developing Library Collections for California's Emerging Majority: A Manual of Resources for Ethnic Collection Development*, ed. Katharine T. A. Scarborough. Produced in conjunction with the conference Developing Library Collections for California's Emerging Majority, September 22–23, 1990, San Francisco, California. Berkeley: Bay Area Library and Information System; University Extension, University of California; School of Library and Information Studies, University of California, 1990.

Trejo, Arnulfo D. "Bicultural Americans with a Hispanic Tradition." *Wilson Library Bulletin* 44 (March 1970): 716–23.

———. "REFORMITA: A Gang for the New Millennium." In *Library Services to Youth of Hispanic Heritage,* ed. Barbara Immroth and Kathleen de la Pena McCook; assisted by Catherine Jasper. Jefferson, NC: McFarland, 2000.

———, and Kathleen L. Lodwick. "Needed: Hispanic Librarians—A Survey of Library Policies." *Wilson Library Bulletin* 53 (Nov. 1978): 259–66.

Trejo, Tamiye Fujibayashi, and Mary Kaye. "The Library as a Port of Entry: Library Professionals Get Professional Advice on Helping New Citizens Discover U.S.-Style Service." *American Libraries* 19 (Nov. 1988): 890–92.

Trujillo, Roberto G., and Yolanda J. Cuesta. "Service to Diverse Populations." In *ALA Yearbook of Library and Information Services, 1989: A Review of Library Events, 1988.* Chicago: ALA, 1989.

Tsai, Betty L. "Asian Pacific American Librarians Association." In *ALA Yearbook of Library and Information Services, 1988: A Review of Library Events, 1987.* Chicago: ALA, 1988.

Tscherny, Elena. "REFORMA." In *ALA Yearbook of Library and Information Services, 1987: A Review of Library Events, 1986.* Chicago: ALA, 1987.

Tse, Lucy. "Seeing Themselves Through Borrowed Eyes: Asian Americans in Ethnic Ambivalence/Evasion." *MultiCultural Review* 7 (June 1998): 28–34.

Turick, Dorothy Ann, ed. "The Neighborhood Information Center." *RQ (Readers Quarterly)* 12 (Summer 1973): 341–63.

Ueda, Reed. "Naturalization and Citizenship." In *Harvard Encyclopedia of American Ethnic Groups,* ed. Stephan Thernstrom, Ann Orlov, and Oscar Handlin. Cambridge: Belknap Press of Harvard University Press, 1980.

Unger, Harlow G., ed. "Adult Basic Education (ABE)." In *Encyclopedia of American Education.* 2nd ed. New York: Facts on File, c2001, 1996.

———. "Adult Education." In *Encyclopedia of American Education.* 2nd ed. New York: Facts on File, c2001, 1996.

———. "African Americans." In *Encyclopedia of American Education.* 2nd ed. New York: Facts on File, c2001, 1996.

———. "American Indian." In *Encyclopedia of American Education.* 2nd ed. New York: Facts on File, c2001, 1996.

———. "Americanization." In *Encyclopedia of American Education.* 2nd ed. New York: Facts on File, c2001, 1996.

———. "At-risk Students." In *Encyclopedia of American Education.* 2nd ed. New York: Facts on File, c2001, 1996.

———. "Bilingual/Bicultural Education." In *Encyclopedia of American Education.* 2nd ed. New York: Facts on File, c2001, 1996.

———. "Bilingual Instruction." In *Encyclopedia of American Education.* 2nd ed. New York: Facts on File, c2001, 1996.

———. "Disadvantaged Students." In *Encyclopedia of American Education.* 2nd ed. New York: Facts on File, c2001, 1996.

———. "Economic Opportunity Act (1964)." In *Encyclopedia of American Education*. 2nd ed. New York: Facts on File, c2001, 1996.

———. "Elementary and Secondary Education Act of 1965 (ESEA)." In *Encyclopedia of American Education*. 2nd ed. New York: Facts on File, c2001, 1996.

———. "English as a Second Language (ESL)." In *Encyclopedia of American Education*. 2nd ed. New York: Facts on File, c2001, 1996.

———. "Ethnic Heritage Program." In *Encyclopedia of American Education*. 2nd ed. New York: Facts on File, c2001, 1996.

———. "Higher Education Act of 1965." In *Encyclopedia of American Education*. 2nd ed. New York: Facts on File, c2001, 1996.

———. "Hispanic Americans." In *Encyclopedia of American Education*. 2nd ed. New York: Facts on File, c2001, 1996.

———. "Illiteracy." In *Encyclopedia of American Education*. 2nd ed. New York: Facts on File, c2001, 1996.

———. "Mexican Americans." In *Encyclopedia of American Education*. 2nd ed. New York: Facts on File, c2001, 1996.

———. "Minority Education." In *Encyclopedia of American Education*. 2nd ed. New York: Facts on File, c2001, 1996.

———. "President's Commission on Foreign Language and International Studies." In *Encyclopedia of American Education*. 2nd ed. New York: Facts on File, c2001, 1996.

———. "War on Poverty." In *Encyclopedia of American Education*. 2nd ed. New York: Facts on File, c2001, 1996.

Vale, Michelle R. "Trends in Federal Library Training Programs for Service to the Disadvantaged." *Library Trends* 20 (Oct. 1971): 463–71.

Valentine, Patrick M. "Minority Language Selection: Helping Ourselves to Help Others." *Wilson Library Bulletin* 60 (Jan. 1986): 26–29.

———. "Multilingual Library Services: Why Bother?" *Public Library Quarterly* 4 (Winter 1983): 61–63.

———. "The North Carolina Foreign Language Center: A Public Library Service." *Public Library Quarterly* 5 (Winter 1984): 47–61.

———. "The North Carolina Foreign Language Center: What It Does, and Why." *The Unabashed Librarian*, no. 47 (1983): 19–20.

Van Fleet, Connie. "Lifelong Learning Theory and the Provision of Adult Services." In *Adult Services: An Enduring Focus for Public Libraries*, ed. Kathleen M. Heim and Danny P. Wallace. Chicago: ALA, 1990.

———, and Douglas Raber. "The Public Library as a Social/Cultural Institution: Alternative Perspectives and Changing Contexts." In *Adult Services: An Enduring Focus for Public Libraries*, ed. Kathleen M. Heim and Danny P. Wallace. Chicago: ALA, 1990.

Vasquez, Richard. "Libraries Lure Barrio Youth." *California Librarian* 31 (July 1970): 200–203.

Vecoli, Rudolph J. "Immigration." In *Oxford Companion to United States History,* ed. Paul S. Boyer and Melvyn Dubofsky. New York: Oxford University Press, 2001.

Vega Garcia, Susan A. "Latino Resources on the Web." In *Library Services to Latinos: An Anthology,* ed. Salvador Guerena. Jefferson, NC: McFarland, 2000.

Velez, Manuel E. "Library and Information Needs of the Mexican-American Community." In National Commission on Libraries and Information Science, *Library and Information Services Needs of the Nation: Proceedings of a Conference on the Needs of Occupational, Ethnic, and Other Groups in the United States.* Washington, DC: U.S. G.P.O., 1974.

Verges, Bruni. "Developing Collections on Puerto Rican Heritage." In *Ethnic Collections in Libraries,* ed. E.J. Josey and Marva L. DeLoach. New York: Neal-Schuman Publishers, 1983.

Waldrop, Sondra. "Library Service to Vietnamese Refugees." *Arkansas Libraries* 33, no. 1 (1976): 14–15.

Wallace, Danny P. "The Character of Adult Services in the Eighties: Overview and Analysis of the ASE Questionnaire Data." In *Adult Services: An Enduring Focus for Public Libraries,* ed. Kathleen M. Heim and Danny P. Wallace. Chicago: ALA, 1990.

Wallace, Judi Lawson. "North Carolina's Well-Kept Secret: The North Carolina Foreign Language Center." *Foreign Language Annals* 17 (Feb. 1984): 55–57.

Wertheimer, Leonard. "Language Studies in Public Libraries." *American Library Association Bulletin* 62 (Sept. 1968): 985–92.

———, ed. "Library Services to Ethnocultural Minorities." *Library Trends* 29 (Fall 1980): 175–368.

———. "Library Services to Ethnocultural Minorities: Philosophical and Social Bases and Professional Implications." *Public Libraries* 26 (Fall 1987): 98–102.

———. "Multicultural Populations, Services to." In *World Encyclopedia of Library and Information Services.* 3rd ed. Chicago: ALA, 1993.

Wertheimer, Ruth Jacobs, and Kathleen M. Foy. "Children of Immigrants and Multiethnic Heritage: Australia, Canada, the United Kingdom, and the United States." *Library Trends* 29 (Fall 1980): 335–51.

Wertsman, Vladimir F. "Ethnic American Groups in Four Specialized Encyclopedia Works: A Comparative and Critical Analysis." *MultiCultural Review* 8 (Dec. 1999): 48–53.

Wetterau, Bruce. "Education." In *The New York Public Library Book of Chronologies.* New York: Stonesong Press of Prentice Hall Press, 1990.

Wheeler, Maurice, and Debbie Johnson-Houston. "A Brief History of Library Service to African Americans." *American Libraries* 35 (Feb. 2004): 42–45.

White, Mary Lou. "Ethnic Literature for Children: A View from the Heartland." *Catholic Library World* 51 (Mar. 1980): 326–29.

Wiley, Norbert. "Overview of the American City." In Allerton Park Institute, 17th, 1971. *Libraries and Neighborhood Information Centers,* ed. Carol L. Kronus and Linda Crowe. Papers presented at an Institute conducted by the University of Illinois, Graduate School of Library Science, October 25–27, 1971. Urbana: University of Illinois, Graduate School of Library Science, 1972.

Willard, Robert S. "National Commission on Libraries and Information Science." In *Bowker Annual 2003: Library and Book Trade Almanac.* 48th ed. Medford, NJ: Information Today, 2003.

Williams, Martha Powers. "Doing It: Migrant Workers Library." In *Revolting Librarians,* ed. Celeste West and Elizabeth Katz. San Francisco: Booklegger Press, 1972.

———. "The Migrants: 'Library Project for Migrant Workers.'" *New Jersey Libraries* 7 (Feb. 1974): 1–4.

Wilson, Amy Seetoo. "Chinese-American Librarians Association." In *ALA Yearbook of Library and Information Services, 1985: A Review of Library Events, 1984.* Chicago: ALA, 1985.

———. "Chinese-American Librarians Association." In *ALA Yearbook of Library and Information Services, 1986: A Review of Library Events, 1985.* Chicago: ALA, 1986.

———. "Chinese-American Librarians Association." In *ALA Yearbook of Library and Information Services, 1988: A Review of Library Events, 1987.* Chicago: ALA, 1988.

———. "Chinese-American Librarians Association." In *ALA Yearbook of Library and Information Services, 1987: A Review of Library Events, 1986.* Chicago: ALA, 1987.

———. "Chinese-American Librarians Association (CALA)." In *ALA Yearbook of Library and Information Services, 1989: A Review of Library Events, 1988.* Chicago: ALA, 1989.

Winnick, Pauline. "The Role of the Public Library." In *Public Library Service to the Disadvantaged.* Proceedings of an Institute, December 7th and 8th, 1967. Atlanta: Division of Librarianship, Emory University, 1969.

Wisdom, Donald F. "The First Two Decades of SALALM: A Personal Account." In *SALALM and the Area Studies Community: Papers of the Thirty-Seventh Annual Meeting of the Seminar on the Acquisition of Latin American Library Materials, Nettie Lee Benson Latin American Collection, University of Texas at Austin, Austin, Texas, May 30-June 4, 1992,* ed. David Block. [Albuquerque]: SALALM Secretariat, General Library, University of New Mexico, 1992.

"Work with Negroes Roundtable." *ALA Bulletin* 16 (July 1922): 361–66.

Wratcher, Marcia A. "Integrating Ethnic Studies into the Curriculum." *Catholic Library World* 51 (Mar. 1980): 336–41.

Wynar, Lubomyr R. "Center for the Study of Ethnic Publications in the United States." In *Dictionary of American Immigration History,* ed. Francesco Cordasco. Metuchen, NJ: Scarecrow Press, 1990.

———. "Ethnic Forum: Journal of Ethnic Studies and Ethnic Bibliography." In *Dictionary of American Immigration History*, ed. Francesco Cordasco. Metuchen, NJ: Scarecrow Press, 1990.

———. "Library Services to Ethnic Communities." *Catholic Library World* 49 (Nov. 1977): 156–61.

Wynn, Barbara L. "Oakland, California: La Biblioteca Latino Americana." *Wilson Library Bulletin* 44 (Mar. 1970): 751–56.

Yamashita, Kenneth A. "Asian/Pacific American Librarians Association—A History of APALA and Its Founders." *Library Trends* 49 (Summer 2000): 88–109.

Yang, Eveline L. "Chinese-American Librarians Association (CALA). In *ALA Yearbook of Library and Information Services, 1990: A Review of Library Events, 1989*. Chicago: ALA, 1990.

Yoshiwara, Florence Makita, and Vivian Kobayashi. "The Asian American: Divergent Element of Cultural Pluralism." In *Cultural Pluralism & Children's Media*, comp. Esther R. Dyer. Chicago: ALA, 1978.

Young, Arthur P. "Aftermath of a Crusade: World War I and the Enlarged Program of the American Library Association." *Library Quarterly* 50 (Apr. 1980): 191–207.

Yung, Judy. "Asian Community Library." *Special Libraries* 69 (Mar. 1978): 115–17.

Zhang, Xiwen. "The Anti-Affirmative Action Movement in California: Implications for Public Library Services to Asian Immigrants." In *Library Services to Latinos: An Anthology*, ed. Salvador Guerena. Jefferson, NC: McFarland, 2000.

———. "The Practice and Politics of Public Library Services to Asian Immigrants." In *Library Services to Latinos: An Anthology*, ed. Salvador Guerena. Jefferson, NC: McFarland, 2000.

Zielinska, Marie. "Ethnic Materials Information Exchange Round Table." In *ALA Yearbook of Library and Information Services, 1989: A Review of Library Events, 1988*. Chicago: ALA, 1989.

———. "Ethnic Materials Information Exchange Round Table." In *ALA Yearbook of Library and Information Services, 1990: A Review of Library Events, 1989*. Chicago: ALA, 1990.

———. "Multiculturalism and Library Services to Ethnic Communities." *UNESCO Bulletin for Libraries* 32 (Fan. 1978): 15–22.

———, and Irena Bell. "Selection and Acquisition of Library Materials in Languages Other than English: Some Guidelines for Public Libraries." *Collection Building* 2, no. 1 (1980): 7–28.

Zweig, Douglas L. "Public Libraries and Excellence: The Public Library Response to *A Nation at Risk.*" *Libraries and the Learning Society: Papers in Response to A Nation at Risk* by Richard M. Dougherty, Jane Anne Hannigan, James W. Liesener, Peggy Sullivan, Douglas L. Zweizig, and American Association of School Librarians. Chicago: ALA, 1984.

Zwick, Louise Yarian, and Oralia Garza de Cortes. "Library Programs for Hispanic Children." *Texas Libraries* 50 (Spring 1989): 12–16.

DISSERTATIONS AND THESES

Alvarado, T. I. "Aguilar Branch; A Branch of the New York Public Library Serving a Spanish-Speaking Community." Master's thesis, Drexel Institute of Technology, 1955.

Butrick, May Wendellene. "History of the Foreign Literature Department of Cleveland Public Library, 1925–72." Master's thesis, Kent State University, 1974.

Chow, R. J. "Study of the Chinese Collection and Its Readers at the Chatham Square Branch Library of the New York Public Library." Master's thesis, Pratt Institute Library School, 1951.

Flythe, Frances H. "Identification of the Information Needs of Newly Arrived Hispanic/Latino Immigrants in Durham County, North Carolina, and How the Public Library May Address Those Needs." Master's thesis, University of North Carolina at Chapel Hill, 2001.

Gilmore, E. C. "Survey of Library Services to Puerto Rican Children, with Recommendations for the Public Library of Bridgeport, Connecticut." Master's thesis, Pratt Institute Library School, 1955.

Hanna, P. B. "Public Library Service to the Spanish-speaking in Selected Communities of New York State." Master's thesis, Long Island University, 1975.

Heimanson, Rudolf H. "The Library in the Americanization of the Immigrant." Master's thesis, Pratt Institute, 1953.

Jones, Plummer Alston, Jr. "American Public Library Service to the Immigrant Community, 1876–1948; A Biographical History of the Movement and Its Leaders: Jane Maud Campbell (1869–1947), John Foster Carr (1869–1939), Eleanor (Edwards) Ledbetter (1870–1954), and Edna Phillips (1890–1968)." Ph.D. dissertation, University of North Carolina at Chapel Hill, 1991.

Murray, Mary Elizabeth. "The Branch Library: A Mirror of Its Community, with Case Histories of Several Branches of the Cleveland Public Library." Master's thesis, Western Reserve University, 1951.

Nagy, Mary Catherine. "History and Relationship of the Rice Branch Library to Its Hungarian Patrons." Master's thesis, Western Reserve University, 1952.

Phillips, Virginia S. "Fifty-Six Years of Service to the Foreign-born by the Cleveland Public Library." Master's thesis, Western Reserve University, 1957.

Rodstein, Frances M. "The East 79th Street Branch of the Cleveland Public Library: An Historical Overview 1909–1970." Master's thesis, Kent State University, 1971.

Silver, Robert Alan. "A Description and History of the Foreign Literature Division of the Cleveland Public Library." Master's thesis, Western Reserve University, 1953.

Wong, Rita. "History of the Chatham Square Branch of the New York Public Library." Master's thesis, Pratt Institute, 1955.

Young, Victoria. "From Immigrants to Refugees: American Public Library Service to the Foreign Born from 1920 to 1950." Master's thesis, University of North Carolina at Chapel Hill, 1994.

WORLD WIDE WEB SITES

American Indian Library Association. http://www.nativeculture.com/lisamitten/aila.html.

American Library Association. ALA Resolution on the USA PATRIOT Act. http://www.ala.org/ala/washoff/WOissues/civilliberties/theusapatriotact/alaresolution.htm.

―――. Coretta Scott King Award. http://www.ala.org/ala/srrt/corettascottking/abouttheaward/aboutaward.htm

Asian/Pacific American Librarians Association. http://www.apalaweb.org.

Austin City Connection. Austin Public Library. New Immigrants Project. http://www.ci.austin.tx.us/library/i_about.htm.

Black Caucus of the American Library Association. http://www.bcala.org/history;about.htm.

Bureau of Indian Affairs. http://www.doiu.nbc.gov/orientation/bia2.cfm.

Center for Immigration Studies. Available at: http://www.cis.org/aboutcis.html.

Chinese American Librarians Association. http://www.white-clouds.com/cala/calahead-n.htm.

Colorado River Indian Tribes Public Library/Archive. http://www.critlibrary.com.

Electronic Privacy Information Center. "The USA Patriot Act." http://www.epic.org/privacy/terrorism/usapatriot.

Ethnic and Multicultural Information Exchange Round Table. *EMIE Online.* http://lonestar.utsa.edu/jbarnett/emie.html.

Forsyth County (NC) Public Library. "Hispanic Services." http://www.forsythlibrary.org/pshs.html.

Guadalajara International Book Fair. *FIL: A Cultural Bridge.* http://www.fil.com.mx/ingles/i_que_es/i_que_his.asp.

Institute of Museum and Library Services. www.imls.gov.

LADB: Latin America Data Base. University of New Mexico. http://ladb.unm.edu.

National Indian Education Association. www.niea.org/index.html.

National Telecommunications Information Administration. http://www.ntia.gov/.

Organization of American States. "OAS in Brief." http://www.oas.org/en/pINFO/OAS/oas.htm.

Policy Guidance for Title 1, Part A: Improving Basic Programs Operated by Local Educational Agencies–April 1996. http://www.ed.gov/legislation/ESEA/Title_I/fiscal.html.

Public Library Construction—Grants to State Library Agencies [Archived information]. http://www.ed.gov/pubs/Biennial/603.html.

REFORMA: National Association to Promote Library and Information Services to Latinos and the Spanish-speaking. http://www.reforma.org.

Roy, Loriene. "To Support and Model Native American Library Services." http://www.txla.org/pubs/tlj76_1/native.html.

Seminar on the Acquisition of Latin American Library Materials. "SALALM Organization." http://www.library.cornell.edu/colldev/salalmorganization.html.

Seminole Tribe of Florida. Tribal Library System Services. http://www.seminoletribe.com/services/library.shtml.

Social Responsibilities Round Table of the American Library Association. http://www.libr.org/SRRT.

State Library of New South Wales. "Multicultural Library Services in New South Wales Public Libraries 2001. Part 8: International Case Studies. www.sl.nsw.gov.au/multicultural/services/case5.cfm.

State Library of North Carolina. "Hispanic Services Project: Survey of Library Needs for North Carolina Hispanics." http://statelibrary.dcr.state.nc.us/hispanic/survey.htm.

Trejo Foster Foundation. http://www.tffoundation.org/home.html.

U.S. Citizenship and Immigration Services. "INS Transition to the Department of Homeland Security." http://uscis.gov/graphics/homeland.htm.

U.S. National Commission on Libraries and Information Science. http://nclis.gov/index.cfm.

INDEX

About the Author

PLUMMER ALSTON "AL" JONES JR. is Associate Professor of Library Science, East Carolina University, Greenville, North Carolina. He received the first biennial Phyllis Dain Library History Dissertation Award in 1993 from the ALA Library History Round Table for his dissertation, "American Public Library Services to the Immigrant Community, 1876-1948." His book, *Libraries, Immigrants, and the American Experience*, was published in 1999 by Greenwood Press. For his service as North Carolina Library Association President (1999-2001) and on the State Library Commission (1997-2001), he was made a member of the Order of the Long Leaf Pine by North Carolina Governor Michael F. Easley in 2002. He was presented the 2004 David Cohen/EMIERT Multicultural Award by the ALA Ethnic and Multicultural Information Exchange Round Table for his research and publications on multiculturalism in libraries.

CPSIA information can be obtained at www.ICGtesting.com
Printed in the USA
BVOW01*0432080514

352764BV00008B/25/P